THE PEARSON CUSTOM LIBRARY FOR
GEOGRAPHY & GEOLOGY

Physical Geography Lab Manual
Custom Edition for San Bernardino Valley College
GEOG 111

PEARSON

This special edition published in cooperation with Pearson Learning Solutions.

Please visit our website at *www.pearsonlearningsolutions.com*.

Attention bookstores: For permission to return any unsold stock, contact us at *pe-uscustomreturns@pearson.com*.

Pearson Learning Solutions, 501 Boylston Street, Suite 900, Boston, MA 02116
A Pearson Education Company
www.pearsoned.com

ISBN 10: 1-256-59795-3
ISBN 13: 978-1-256-59795-7

29 2020

Table of Contents

Lab 14b

Geography 111: Physical Geography Lab
Lab One: Measurements and Metric Conversions

During the course of the semester, you will be reading and using various topographic maps. Part of this will require measuring distances on maps. Your answers will ultimately be based on these measurements, so accurately taking measurements is a good technique to master. This lab will allow you to practice this technique prior to the labs which require map measurements. In addition to measuring map distances, you will learn how to convert these map units into real-world units. This is accomplished by understanding and applying the map scale and then converting those units into meaningful distances. As such, we will practice converting units within the English system as well as within the Système International (S.I.) a.k.a. the "metric" system of measurement. You probably recognize the English System, which refers to measurements in miles, pounds, and degrees Fahrenheit (F°). Outside the United States and within the scientific community, the Système International is in use, which refers to measurements in kilometers, kilograms, and degrees Celsius (C°). As a well informed global citizen it is also important that you know how to convert between these two systems of measurement. Finally, it is useful to understand how to record your data using the proper rounding.

Materials:
Ruler & calculator

Objectives:
- To practice measuring items
- To practice converting within a system of measurement
- To practice converting between the English System and Système International (S.I.)
- To practice rounding your answers

Part 1: Measurement

The image below denotes a ruler with centimeters (cm) on top and inches on the bottom.

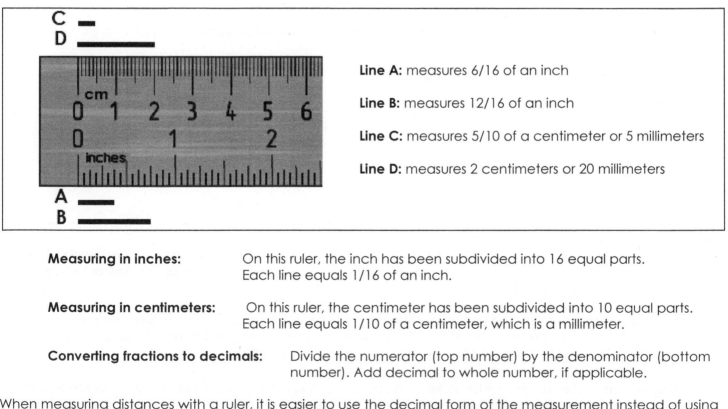

Line A: measures 6/16 of an inch

Line B: measures 12/16 of an inch

Line C: measures 5/10 of a centimeter or 5 millimeters

Line D: measures 2 centimeters or 20 millimeters

Measuring in inches: On this ruler, the inch has been subdivided into 16 equal parts. Each line equals 1/16 of an inch.

Measuring in centimeters: On this ruler, the centimeter has been subdivided into 10 equal parts. Each line equals 1/10 of a centimeter, which is a millimeter.

Converting fractions to decimals: Divide the numerator (top number) by the denominator (bottom number). Add decimal to whole number, if applicable.

When measuring distances with a ruler, it is easier to use the decimal form of the measurement instead of using the fractional form. For example, Line A expressed in decimal form is .375 inches (6 divided by 16), Line B is .75 inches (12 divided by 16), and Line C is .5 centimeters (5 divided by 10). Line D does not need to be converted since it is expressed as a whole number.

Assignment:

Line 1 _____

Line 2 _____

Line 3 _____

1. What is the length of Lines 1, 2, and 3 to the nearest 1/16 of an inch? Express your answer as both a fraction and a decimal.

Line 1 Fraction: _____ inches   Decimal: _____ inches

Line 2 Fraction: _____ inches   Decimal: _____ inches

Line 3 Fraction: _____ inches   Decimal: _____ inches

Line 4 _____

Line 5 _____

Line 6 _____

2. What is the length of Lines 4, 5, and 6 to the nearest 1/10 of a centimeter? Express your answer as a fraction, decimal and the equivalent millimeters.

Line 4 Fraction: _____ centimeters   Decimal: _____ centimeters   Millimeters: _____

Line 5 Fraction: _____ centimeters   Decimal: _____ centimeters   Millimeters: _____

Line 6 Fraction: _____ centimeters   Decimal: _____ centimeters   Millimeters: _____

- -

Part 2: Converting Units of Measurement

Unit conversions involve taking a set of measurements expressed as one set of units (e.g., inches) and putting them into a more useful form (e.g., feet). This can occur within one system (e.g., inches to miles) or between systems (e.g., miles to kilometers).

An easy mistake to make during the unit conversion process is to lose track of your units, which often leads to mathematical errors. Here's a useful method to follow whenever performing unit conversions. Using this method will help you avoid making math errors during your unit conversions.

Conversion Factor: a ratio written in fraction form used to express the same quantity in 2 different units. This fraction will always equal 1.

Example #1: Convert 5 feet into inches.

Step 1 : Decide which conversion factor to use.

Since you a trying to convert feet to inches, you need a ratio that expresses the same quantity in both feet and inches. 1 foot and 12 inches represent the same distance. Therefore, when written as a fraction it is equal to 1.

We can write this fraction as

$$\frac{12 \text{ inches}}{1 \text{ ft}} \qquad \text{or as} \qquad \frac{1 \text{ ft}}{12 \text{ inches}}$$

Step 2: Multiply the original unit of measurement by the conversion factor.

$$5 \text{ ft} * \left[\frac{12 \text{ inches}}{1 \text{ ft}} \right]$$

Notice that when we set things up this way, we are in effect dividing feet by feet, so the units cancel and we are left with inches as the unit of measurement.

$$5 \text{ ft} * \left[\frac{12 \text{ inches}}{1 \text{ ft}} \right] = 60 \text{ inches}$$

Example #2: Convert 25 inches into feet.

Step 1: Decide which conversion factor to use.

Step 2: Multiply the original unit of measurement by the conversion factor.

$$25 \text{ inches} * \left[\frac{1 \text{ ft}}{12 \text{ inches}} \right]$$

Notice how inches cancel each other and you are left with feet as the unit of measurement.

$$25 \text{ inches} * \left[\frac{1 \text{ ft}}{12 \text{ inches}} \right] = 2.1 \text{ feet}$$

Example #3: Convert 500 km into miles.

Step 1: Decide which conversion factor to use.

Since you a trying to convert kilometers to miles, you need a ratio that expresses the same quantity in both kilometers and miles. 1 kilometer and .621 miles represent the same distance. Therefore, when written as a fraction it is equal to 1.

We can write this fraction as

$$\frac{1 \text{ kilometer}}{.621 \text{ miles}} \qquad \text{or as} \qquad \frac{.621 \text{ miles}}{1 \text{ kilometer}}$$

Step 2: Multiply the original unit of measurement by the conversion factor.

$$500 \text{ km} * \left[\frac{.621 \text{ miles}}{1 \text{ km}} \right] = 310.5 \text{ miles}$$

Although this method of unit conversion may seem tedious, it's the best way to avoid making math errors. I highly encourage you to use this method whenever performing unit conversions in this class!!!

One final example, when converting Celsius to Fahrenheit or Fahrenheit to Celsius, insert the given temperature into the equation. If you have Celsius, insert the temperature in place of the C. If you have Fahrenheit, insert the temperature in place of the F. Solve equation.

Example #4: 40° C is what temperature in Fahrenheit?
   Step 1: Rewrite equation inserting the temperature in place of the C.
            (1.8 * **40°**) + 32 ° = ° F

   Step 2: Solve equation
            (72°) + 32° = 104° F   **104° F is your answer**

Example #5: 86° F is what temperature in Celsius?
   Step 1: Rewrite equation inserting the temperature in place of the F.
            (1.8 * C°) + 32 ° = **86** °

   Step 2: Solve equation
            C° = (86° - 32°)   **30° C is your answer**
                     1.8°

Assignment
A. Now you try a few conversions using the following conversion factors. Show your work.

English System	Système International
1 foot = 12 inches (in)	1 meter(m)= 100 centimeters (cm) = 1000 millimeters
1 mile (mi) = 5280 feet = 63360 inches	1 kilometer (km)= 1000 meters
1 gallon (gal) = 4 quarts	1 kilometer = 100,000 cm =1,000,000 mm

3. 28 in * [_____ ft / in] = _____ ft

4. 126720 in * [_____ mi / in] = _____ miles

5. 5000 cm * [_____ m / cm] = _____ meters

6. 6 km * [_____ m / km] = _____ meters

7. 16 quarts = _____ gallons

8. 0 .5 gallons = _____ quarts

9. 0.25 meters = _____ millimeters

10. 500000 centimeters = _____ kilometers

4

B. Practice converting between English System and Système International, using the following conversion factors. Show your work.

Conversion Factors:
1 kilometers (km) = .621 miles(mi)   1 liter = 1.057 quarts
1 kilograms (kg) = 2.205 pounds (lbs) $1 \, °C \leftrightarrow °F = (1.8 * °C)+32° = °F$

11. 80 km * $\left[\dfrac{_____ \, mi}{km} \right]$ = _____ miles

12. 1.5 kg * $\left[\dfrac{_____ \, lbs}{kg} \right]$ = _____ pounds

13. 100 miles * $\left[\dfrac{_____ \, km}{miles} \right]$ = _____ km

14. 0.5 lbs * $\left[\dfrac{_____ \, kg}{lbs} \right]$ = _____ kg

15. 6 liters = _____ quarts

16. 4 quarts = _____ liters

17. 13 °C = _____ °F

18. 20 °C = _____ °F

19. 77 °F = _____ °C

20. 50 °F = _____ °C

Part 3: Rounding

Your answer cannot be more precise than your inputs. When rounding you look 1 digit to the right of the desired precision.

Example # 6: 1.6877 rounded to one decimal place
Step 1: Underline the digit corresponding with the desired precision.
In this case, you are rounding to one decimal place, so underline the 6.

1.<u>6</u>877

Step 2: Look at the digit to the right of the desired precision.
In this example, look at the 8.

Step 3:
If the digit in Step 2 is between 5 – 9 = increase the underlined digit by 1 and drop remaining digits
If the digit in Step 2 is between 0 – 4 = underlined digit remains the same and drop remaining digits

8 is between 5- 9 so, the underlined digit is increased by 1 and the rest of the digits are dropped.

Answer: 1.6877 rounded to one decimal place = 1.7

Assignment
A. Round the following numbers to one decimal place.
21. 1.3556 = _____

22. 21.4333 = _____

23. 10.1879 =_____

24. 5.198 = _____

25. 2. 222 = _____

B. Round the following numbers to two decimal places.
22. 3.546 = _____

23. 24.9312 = _____

24. 19.4829 =_____

25. 51.9874 = _____

26. 28. 6201 = _____

C. Round the following numbers to the nearest whole number.
27. 24.589 = _____

28. 12.158 = _____

29. 7.356 =_____

30. 10.978 = _____

Geography 111: Physical Geography Lab
Lab Two: Map Scale and Map Projections

This lab is designed to introduce you to an important map comprehension skill- the ability to understand the spatial relationships portrayed on maps. Map scale informs the map reader to what degree generalization has occurred on any given map. By making a connection between map distance and real world distance, you can use the map to measure distances, calculate areas and compare regions.

Understanding map projections is another important map comprehension skill. Through the process of converting a 3 dimensional object into a 2 dimensional surface distortion will occur regarding the distance, direction, shape or size of the object portrayed on the map. A basic understanding regarding which property has been distorted or preserved can help you select a map projection suitable for your intended purpose.

Materials:
Ruler & calculator
15 Minute Series Quadrangle

7.5 Minute San Bernardino South Quadrangle
Various Classroom Maps

Objectives:
- Identify types of map scales
- Differentiate between large scale and small scale maps

- Compute distances with map scales
- Identify types of distortion on map projections

Part 1: Identify types of Map Scales
Map scale is the mathematical relationship between distances on the map and the real world. Map scale gives you an idea regarding how much simplification has occurred on the map and can be portrayed in a variety of ways:

Verbal Scale [A] = states in words the relationship between map distance and real world distance

Graphic Scale [B] = uses a line broken into segments. The units on the graphic scale represent real world distances.

Fractional Scale [C] = informs the map reader about the relationship between map distance and real world distance.

The *numerator* (or when expressed as a ratio the number to the left of the colon [:]) refers to the map distance.

The *denominator* (or number to the right of the colon) refers to the real world distance expressed in the same units as the map distance.

In this example, 1 unit on the map equals 5,200,000 of those same units in the real world.

Assignment:

1. Complete the table below using the maps provided in the classroom. Not all scales appear on all maps.

Map	Representative Fraction	Verbal Scale
Wall Map Map of Europe		
15 Minute Series Quadrangle		Not Applicable
Wall Map World Map		

– –

Part 2: Differentiate between large scale and small scale maps

Maps can be drawn at different scales. Some show a large amount of the Earth's surface in very little detail, while others show a small amount of Earth's surface in great detail. The terms small scale and large scale are used to describe the amount of generalization found on a map.

> Small scale map → shows a large portion of the Earth's surface with very little detail
> Large scale map → shows a small portion of Earth's surface with more detail

A quick way to determine if a map is a large or small scale map is to look at the map scale. If the denominator or number to the right of the colon is a large number then a large amount of the Earth's surface is represented on the map and the map is therefore a small scale map.

Small Scale
1: 5,000,000
1in = 80 miles

Large Scale
1:24,000
1 in = .4 miles

Assignment:

2. After completing question 1, list the maps and their corresponding scales in the boxes below, ordering them from the smallest scale to the largest scale.

Map:		Map:		Map:
RF:		RF:		RF:

Small Scale --- Large Scale

Part 3: Map Measurements- Graphic Scale

Let's say we want to measure as accurately as possible the actual, real world distance from A to B on the map below. First, we need to figure out how our map measurement (map distance) relates to the actual distance in real life (real world distance). To do this, we'll use the graphic scale shown in the lower left corner of the map.

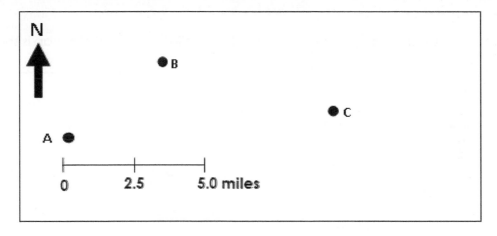

Step 1: Using a ruler, measure the distance from the 0 to the 5.0 mile mark on the scale bar in the lower left corner... This distance is about 1 7/16 inches or 1.44 inches. Now we know that 1.44 inches (map distance) equals 5.0 miles (real world distance).

Step 2: Using a ruler, measure the distance from Point A to Point B (use the center of the dot). When measuring, round to the nearest 1/16 of an inch. You should get a measurement of 1 4/16 inches (1.25 inches).

Step 3 : Now we need to convert map distance to real world distance. The easiest way to do so is to set up a ratio equation:

$$\frac{1.44 \text{ inches —[map distance]}}{5.0 \text{ miles [real world distance]}} = \frac{1.25 \text{ inches- [map distance A to B]}}{X \text{ miles [real world distance]}}$$

Note: We keep the corresponding map and real world distances together as fractions on opposite sides of our equation. Thus 1.44 inches (map dist.) corresponds to 5.0 miles (real world dist.). Likewise, 1.25 inches (map dist. A to B) corresponds to some unknown real world distance. Here, we represent our unknown with the letter, X.

Think of the X in the above equation as the unknown real world distance (in miles) from A to B, which is what we want to know.

Step 4 : To get the real world distance from A to B (that is, to solve for X), cross multiply 1.25 inches x 5.0 miles, then divide the result by 1.44 inches. Here's an easy way to remember this step:

$$\frac{1.44 \text{ in (map dist.)}}{5.0 \text{ miles (real world dist.)}} = \frac{1.25 \text{ inches (map dist. A to B)}}{X \text{ miles (real- world dist.)}} \qquad X = 4.3 \text{ miles}$$

Notice that the units cancel. That is, $\frac{1.25 \text{ inches} \times 5.0 \text{ miles}}{1.44 \text{ inches}} = 4.3 \text{ miles}$

Assignment:

3. What is the distance in **miles** from Point B to C?

4. What is the distance in **miles** from Point A to C?

9

Part 4: Map Measurements- Fractional Scale

Now, let's say we don't have a graphic scale on our map, but instead, the map scale is given as a fractional scale, as in 1:220,000. The great thing about fractional scales is that they don't depend on which units we choose to work with. So...1 inch (map) = 220,000 inches (real world)...and 1 cm (map) = 220,000 cm (real world), etc.

Let's revisit the map we used in part 3, except this time, the fractional scale of the map is shown below the graphic scale:

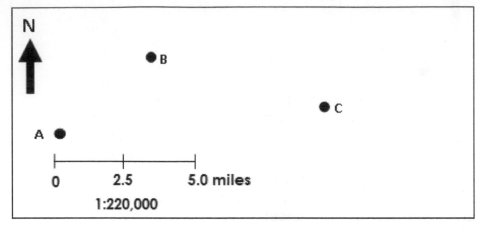

So, based on the fractional scale of the above map, we know that 1 inch on the map equals 220,000 inches in real world.

Let's calculate the real world distance from A to B (in miles) using the fractional scale on the above map.
If the answer will be in miles→ measure in **inches**;
If the answer will be in kilometers → measure in **centimeters**

Step 1 : Measure the distance from A to B in inches : **1.25 inches**

Step 2 : Multiple the Step 1 results (1.25 inches) by 220,000 to convert to real world distance.

Stop: Why do we multiply the Step 1 result by 220,000? Because that's the conversion factor we use to go from map distance to real world distance in this example.

1.25 inches * 220,000 = **275,000 inches** (real world distance)

In other words, if you actually walked from Point A to Point B, you would walk 275,000 inches.

Step 3 : Convert inches to miles:

275,000 inches * $\left[\dfrac{1\ mile}{63,360\ inches}\right]$ = **4.3 miles** (real world distance from Point A to Point B)

Notice that this result (4.3 miles) matches the distance we calculated from A to B using the graphic scale (see Part 3).

Assignment:
5. Using the fractional scale in the map above, calculate the distance in **miles** from Point B to C.

6. Using the fractional scale in the map above, calculate the distance in **kilometers** from Point A to C. (Hint: what is the conversion factor for converting centimeters to kilometers?)

7. On a map with a scale of 1: 50,000, a measured distance of 6.3 inches represents an actual distance of:

_____ miles

8. On a map with a scale of 1: 36,000, a measured distance of 4 cm represents an actual distance of:

_____ kilometers

9. What is the fractional scale on a map with a verbal scale of 1 inch equals 6 miles?

10. Calculate the following distances on the *U.S.G.S.* **7.5** *Minute Series Quadrangle Map* using the fractional scale:
   a.   What is the fractional scale on this map?

   b.   What is the verbal scale expressed in miles?

   1 inch equals _____ **miles**   **Note:** 1 mile = 63360 inches

   c.   What is the verbal scale expressed in kilometers?

   1 centimeter equals _____ **kilometers**   **Note:** 1 kilometer = 100,000 centimeters

   d.   How many **miles** is La Cadena Ave (the portion between 8th St and Mt Vernon)? Measure each segment. Round total measurement to the nearest 1/16". Show your work.

   Map Distance: _____   Real-world Distance: _____

   e.   What is the distance in **kilometers** from the "H" in San Bernardino's City Hall (northeast) and the "V" in Valley College (north central)? Round total measurement to the nearest 1/10 cm. Show your work.

   Map Distance: _____   Real-world Distance: _____

Part 5: Identify types of distortion on map projections

Only a globe can accurately display the properties of shape, size, distance, and direction. Once a 3 dimensional surface has been projected onto a 2 dimensional surface some form of distortion will occur. As a map user, you need to determine what property has been distorted and/or preserved based on the map projection.

Conformal projections → preserve the property of shape
Equivalent (or equal area) projections → preserve the property of size
Compromise projections → seek to minimize overall distortion, but do not preserve any of the properties.

Assignment:

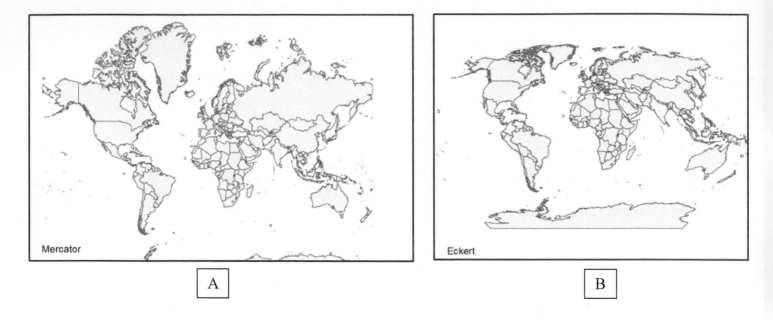

A

B

11. Compare the size of Greenland to Africa on a globe. Which has more land area?

12. Small scale map projections cannot preserve both shape and size. Compare the size of Greenland to Africa on Maps A and B above. Then complete the following table.

Map	Property Preserved (Shape or Size)	Property Distorted (Shape or Size)	Map Projection (Conformal or Equivalent)
A			
B			

13. If I wanted to measure the extent of the Tropical Rainforest in Africa to the extent of the Tropical Rainforest in South America, which projection would I use?

14. If I wanted a general reference world map, which projection would I use?

Geography 111: Physical Geography Lab
Lab Three: Location and Time

This lab is designed to introduce you to the geographic concepts of location and time. The unique location of any point on the Earth's surface may be identified using a series of parallel lines (latitude) and meridians (longitude). Longitude determines the standard time for any given location based on the time zone's controlling meridian.

Materials:
Calculator   Atlas

Objectives:
- Identify locations using latitude/longitude
- Identify grid coordinates of locations
- Convert Degrees, Minutes, and Seconds into Decimal Degrees
- Convert Decimal Degrees into Degrees, Minutes, and Seconds.
- Differentiate between "sun" time and "clock" time
- Calculate time
- Identify date change when crossing the International Date Line (IDL)

Part 1: Location

Locations on Earth's surface can be described using the Geographic Grid. This grid consists of a series of parallel lines called **latitude** and a series of lines which converge at the poles called **longitude**. By knowing a location's specific latitude and longitude you can describe its position on Earth's surface.

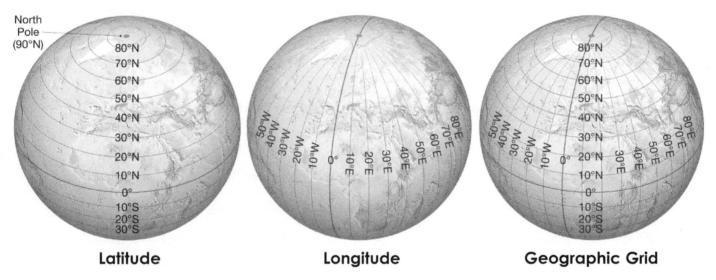

Latitude   **Longitude**   **Geographic Grid**

(From Darrel Hess, <u>McKnight's Physical Geography: A Landscape Appreciation,</u> (Second California Edition) "Courtesy of Pearson Education."

Latitude- Parallel lines measuring distance North or South of the Equator.
         Latitude ranges from 0° - 90° N or S.

Longitude- Lines converging at the poles measuring distance West or East of the Prime Meridian.
         Longitude ranges from 0° - 180° W or E

Latitude and Longitude are angular measurements expressed in Degrees (°). 1 ° can be divided into 60 Minutes (') and 1'can be divided into 60 Seconds ("). Often times (especially when working with GPS equipment), you will see latitude and longitude expressed in Decimal Degrees instead of Degrees, Minutes, and Seconds. For example, 23° 30' 0" N would be expressed as 23.5° N.

Convert Degrees, Minutes, and Seconds into Decimal Degrees

Example #1: The latitude of San Bernardino expressed in Degrees, Minutes and Seconds is 34° 6' 29" N . To convert this to Decimal Degrees:

Step 1: Divide the Seconds by 60 (29/60 = .48).

Step 2: Add this portion of a minute to the other Minutes (6 + .48 = 6.48).

Step 3: Divide the Minutes by 60 (6.48/60 = .11).

Step 4: Add this portion of a Degree to the Degrees (34 + .11 = 34.11).

The latitude of San Bernardino expressed in Decimal Degrees is **34.11° N.**

Convert Decimal Degrees into Degrees, Minutes, and Seconds.

Example #2: The longitude of San Bernardino expressed in Decimal Degrees is 117.289° W. To convert this to Degrees, Minutes, and Seconds:

Step 1: Multiply the decimal portion of the Degrees by 60 to determine the number of Minutes. (.289*60= 17.34). The whole number is the number of minutes- 17.

Step 2: Multiple the decimal portion of the Minutes by 60 to get Seconds. (.34*60 = 20.4). This is the number of seconds- 20.4.

The longitude of San Bernardino when written as Degrees, Minutes and Seconds is **117° 17' 20" W.**

Assignment:

1. Use an atlas to find the following locations. Remember that by convention, latitude is always listed first, longitude second.

A) New York City _____   E) San Bernardino, CA _____

B) Washington D.C., USA _____   F) Mount Whitney _____

C) Buenos Aires, Argentina _____   G) Mount Everest _____

D) Brussels, Belgium _____   H) Hilo, Hawaii _____

2. Use an atlas to find the name of the major city, region or country located at the following coordinates:

	Latitude	Longitude	
A) city-	30° N	31° E	_____
B) region-	34° N	44° E	_____
C) city-	12° S	77° W	_____
D) country-	30° S	25° E	_____
E) city-	61° N	150° W	_____

3. On the World map located at the end of this lab, plot the following coordinates with a dot. Label each dot with the corresponding letter:

Point A- 20° N, 60° E

Point B- 60° S, 90° E

Point C- 40° S, 20° W

Point D- 0°, 0°

Point E- 30° N, 90° W

Point F- 10° N, 70° W

4. On the World map located at the end of this lab, draw and label the following important lines of latitude and longitude:

North Pole

Arctic Circle

Tropic of cancer

Equator

Tropic of Capricorn

Antarctic Circle

South Pole

Prime Meridian

5. You are halfway between the Equator and the South Pole, and an eighth of the way around the earth to the west of the Prime Meridian. What is your latitude and longitude?"

6. If you began a trip at 60° east, 20° south and traveled 120° farther east and 60° north, your new position would be
    A) the International Dateline at 80° south latitude.
    B) the International Dateline at 40° north latitude.
    C) the Greenwich meridian at 80° south latitude.
    D) the Greenwich meridian at 40° north latitude.

7. Express the latitude of 45° 15' 45" as Decimal Degrees: _____

8. Express the longitude of 111.458° as Degrees, Minutes, and Seconds: _____

Part 2: Time-- "Sun" time versus "Clock" time

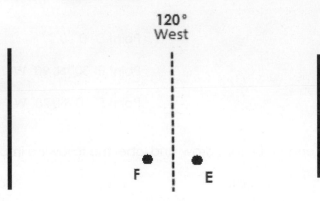

120°
West

Only along the controlling meridian will the sun reach its highest peak (zenith) when the clock reads noon. All other locations within the time zone will experience this earlier or later depending on where they are located within the time zone.

Since the earth rotates 1 degree of longitude every 4 minutes, two locations 1 degree of longitude apart will see the sun rise, reach its zenith and set 4 minutes apart.

Example #3: The diagram above shows the Pacific Standard Time Zone. Locations E and F are 2° of longitude apart. If Location E sees the sun rise at 6:02 am, what time will Location F see the sun rise?

> $\dfrac{4 \text{ minutes}}{1 \text{ degree}}$ * 2 ~~degrees~~ = 8 minutes   Note: the degree units cancel each other.

> Will Location F see the sun rise 8 minutes EARLIER or LATER?
> Later because Location F is farther west then Location E.   [6:02 + 8 = 6:10]

> Answer: Location F will see the sun rise at 6:10 am (8 minutes later than Location E)

Assignment:
9. Within the Pacific Standard Time Zone, Los Angeles (based on 118° W) reports sunrise at 6:20 A.M., what time will the sun rise in San Bernardino (based on 117° W)?

10. Within the Pacific Standard Time Zone, Los Angeles (based on 118° W) reports sunset at 6:36 p.m., what time will the sunset in Santa Barbara (based on 120° W)?

Part 3: Time-- Standard Time

The world is divided into 24 time zones; each time zone spans 15° of longitude. If you know the controlling meridians (the meridian on which time zones are based) for two locations, you can determine the difference in time between these locations.

To mathematically determine how many hours separate two locations, follow these steps:

Step 1: Determine how many degrees (°) of longitude separate these locations?

Step 2: Determine how many time zones separate these locations by dividing the result in Step 1 by 15° (the width of 1 time zone).

Step 3: Determine if you should add or subtract the number of time zones.
All locations to the EAST are "ahead" in time, so you add the number of time zones.
All locations to the WEST are "behind" in time, so you subtract the number of time zones.

The diagram below can help you visualize this process. The inner disk notes every 15° of longitude (controlling meridians) radiating out from the North Pole. The Outer Disk notes every hour within a 24 hour period. You can determine the time at any location by matching the meridian with the time noted on the outer ring.

Example #4, If it is 9 a.m. at Location A (45° West), what time is it at Location B (0°)?

Step 1: Determine how many degrees (°) of longitude separate these locations?

Location A	Location B	Longitudinal Difference
45° West	0°	45° - 0° = **45°**

Step 2: Determine how many time zones separate these locations by dividing the result in Step 1 by 15° (the width of 1 time zone).

45° / 15° = 3   **3 time zones separate these two locations.**
In other words, 3 hours separate these locations.

Step 3: Determine if you should add or subtract the number of time zones.
Since Location B is EAST of Location A, they are three hours "ahead". **9 a.m. + 3 = 12 p.m.**

Answer: It is 12 p.m. (noon) in Location B when it is 9 a.m. at Location A.

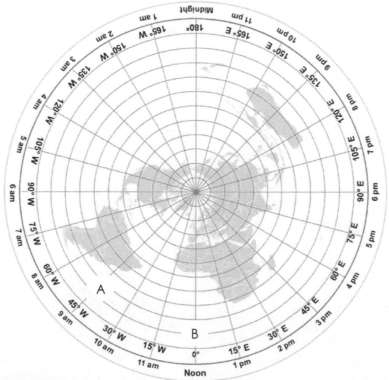

17

Time Continued -- International Date Line (IDL)

When crossing the International Date Line (IDL) the hour portion of time is calculated just like the previous example. However, when crossing the IDL, the date (day of week) portion of time also changes.

Crossing the IDL going from the Western Hemisphere to the Eastern Hemisphere- **add a calendar day**

Crossing the IDL going from the Eastern Hemisphere to the Western Hemisphere- **subtract a day**

To determine the day and time between two locations, follow these steps:

Step 1: Determine how many degrees (°) of longitude separate these locations?

Step 2: Determine how many time zones separate these locations.

Step 3: Determine if you should add or subtract the number of time zones.

Step 4: Determine the day of the week. This step is only required if you pass the IDL.

The diagram below can help you visualize this problem. You may want to turn your paper around so that the 180° meridian is pointing towards you. This helps if you cross the IDL. Remember each meridian on the diagram represents a time zone.

Example #5, If it is 6 a.m. at Location C (135° West), what time is it at Location D (165° East)?

Step 1: Determine how many degrees (°) of longitude separate these locations?

Location C	Location D	Longitudinal Difference
135° West	165° East	(180°- 165° E) + (180°- 135°W) = 15° + 45°= **60°**

Step 2: Determine how many time zones separate these locations.

60° / 15° = 4   **4 time zones separate these two locations.**
In other words, 4 hours separate these locations.

Step 3: Subtract the number of time zones because Location D is **WEST** (across the Pacific Ocean) of Location C.   6 a.m. – 4 (number of time zones) = 2 a.m.

Step 4: Determine the day of the week. Since we crossed the IDL going from the Western Hemisphere to the Eastern Hemisphere, we need to add a Day—so Monday becomes Tuesday.

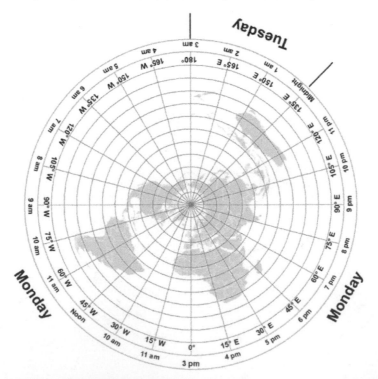

Assignment:

Use the longitude of the time zone's controlling meridian (which has been provided for you) to answer the following questions. I have also included a blank diagram to help you visualize time zones.

11. If it is 7:00 P.M. in Houston (based on 90° W), what time is it in New York City (based on 75° W)?

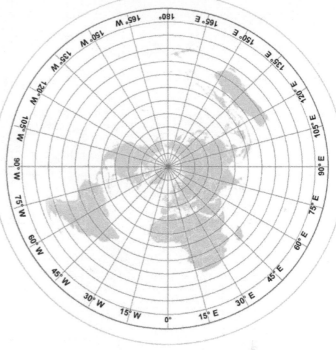

12. If it is 4:00 A.M. Thursday in Denver, Colorado (based on 105° W), what time and day is it in Beijing, China (based on 120° E)?

13. If it is 1:00 P.M. Tuesday in San Bernardino (based on 120° W), what time and day is it in Helsinki, Finland (based on 30° E)?

14. Your plane leaves Seattle, Washington (based on 120° W) at 10:00 P.M. on Friday, bound for Orlando, Florida (based on 75° W). The flight takes 6 hours. What is the time and day when you arrive in Orlando? Hint: Calculate difference in time then add flight time.

15. Your plane leaves Los Angeles (based on 120° W) at 11 P.M. on Monday bound for Sydney, Australia (based on 150° E). The flight takes 13 hours. What is the time and day when you arrive in Sydney? Hint: Calculate difference in time then add flight time.

16. On your return flight from Sydney, you leave at 3 P.M. on Sunday. The flight takes 14 hours. What time and day is it when you arrive in Los Angeles? Hint: Calculate difference in time then add flight time.

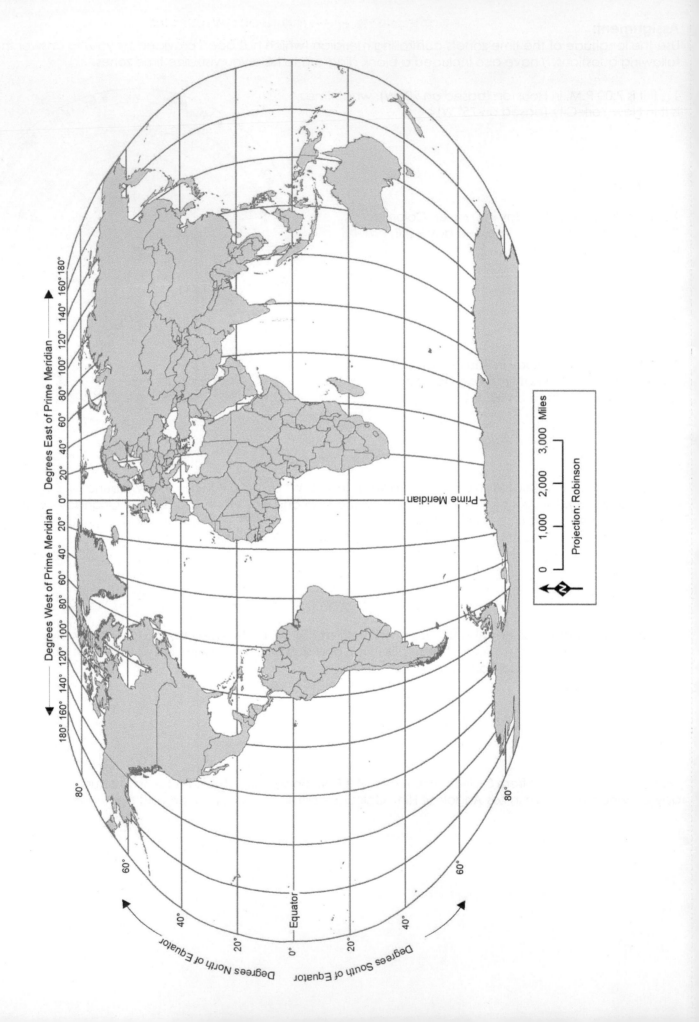

Geography 111: Physical Geography Lab
Lab Four: Isolines and Contours

This lab is designed to introduce you to an important method for displaying information on map- isolines. Isolines are special lines used to connect points of equal value. For example, an isoline used to connect points of equal elevation is a contour line. Isolines are also used on weather maps to show temperatures (isotherms) and atmospheric pressure (isobars). In this lab we will be focused on interpreting contour lines from U.S.G.S. Topographic maps. Contour lines give you insight into the topography (difference in relief) of an area without needing a three dimensional model.

Materials:
San Bernardino North Topographic Map

Objectives:
- Interpret & construct isolines
- Interpret contour lines
  - Determine elevation using contour interval
  - Assess gradient based on contour line spacing
  - Identify landforms based on contour line patterns

Part 1: Interpreting and Constructing Isolines.
Basic characteristics of isolines:
- Isolines are closed lines having no ends. Note: The line may close outside the margins of the map.
- Isolines represent gradations in quantities so they very rarely touch or cross.
- Isolines are drawn at regular intervals (numeric difference between one isoline and the next). If more than one interval is used on the same map, a different line symbol will be used to display those lines having different intervals.
- How close together the isolines are drawn depends on the gradient (change in the interval). Isolines drawn close together indicate a rapid horizontal change in the interval (steep gradient). Whereas, isolines drawn far apart, indicate a gradual horizontal change in the interval (gentle gradient).
- Values inside a closed isoline are either higher or lower than those outside the closed isolines.

Cartographers use isolines to make it easier to interpret what otherwise would appear as random data points. Look at Diagram A below; at first glance it seems like randomly place elevations points (expressed in feet). It isn't until isolines are drawn that an elevation pattern emerges (Diagram B). Note that the elevation increases as you travel from the right side of the map to the left side. The process by which isolines are constructed is called interpolation. The Interval displayed below is 100 feet.

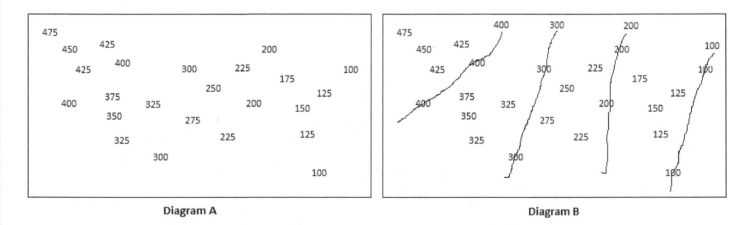

Diagram A   Diagram B

Part 2: Interpreting and Constructing Contours.

Throughout the course of the semester we will be using U.S.G.S Topographic Maps to interpret Earth's surface and to take measurements on Earth's Surface. U.S.G.S. Topographic maps use contours (lines joining points of equal elevation) to portray the topography or shape of the land. In addition to adhering to the basic characteristics of isolines, here are some general rules to follow when working with contours:

> **Contour lines** are drawn as solid brown lines which never cross since they connect points of equal elevation.

> **Contour Interval**- the <u>vertical</u> distance between two successive contours. The contour interval is usually noted at the bottom of U.S.G.S. Topographic Maps.

> **Index Contours** – Index Contours are drawn as thicker and darker contour lines and are marked with the elevation. Usually every 5th contour line is an Index Contour.

> **Supplementary Contours**- In flat regions, additional contours will sometimes be drawn. These are usually half the contour interval and are drawn as dotted lines.

- To determine the elevation of a point on a contour line, find the nearest Index Contour and increase or decrease the elevation by the Contour Interval. Remember, elevations on either side of a contour line will either be higher or lower in elevation. Look at the surrounding contour lines to get a feel for the direction of the slope.

- To determine the elevation of a point between contours lines, you must estimate the elevation.

- The spacing of the contour lines tells you about the shape of the land.
    - Equal spacing indicates uniform slope.
    - Close spacing indicates a steep slope
    - Wide spacing indicates a gentler slope.

- Closed unhactured contours enclose an isolated high area (hill, mountain or peak).
    - To estimate the elevation on a hill top or ridge top **add half the Contour Interval** to the elevation of the inner-most closed contour line representing the hill or ridge top.

- Closed hachured contours (called depression contours) indicate the presence of a closed depression.
    - To estimate the elevation at the bottom of the depression, **subtract half the Contour Interval** from the elevation of the inner-most closed, hactured depression contour.

- Blue lines drawn on U.S.G.S Topographic Maps represent streams.

- Contour lines crossing rivers or valleys always bend upstream or upvalley creating "V"s. In other words, the V is always points up towards the higher elevation.

- Contour lines crossing ridges always bend down slope creating "U"s. In other words, the U always points towards the lower elevation.

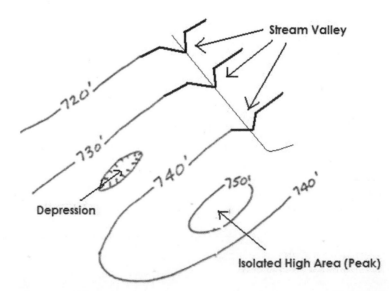

Assignment:
The map below shows 17 spot elevations. The elevations are shown in feet. Draw contours on this map starting at Point A. Note: The **Contour Interval** for this map is 100 ft. Points G and Q represent a depression on this map.

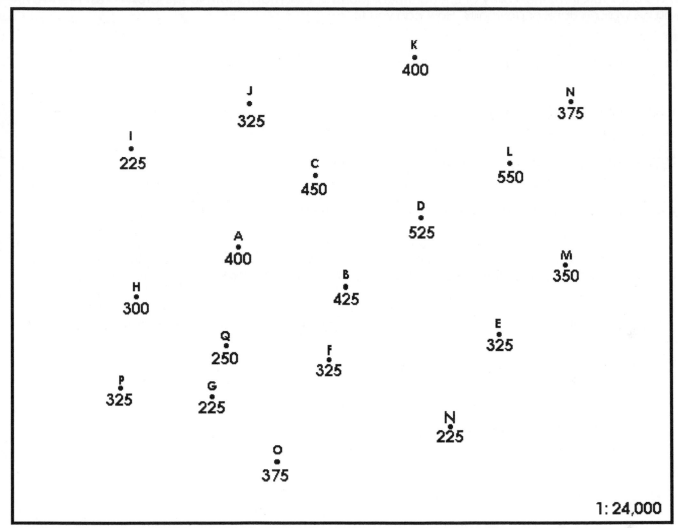

After constructing the contour lines answer the following questions.
1. What is the **horizontal** distance **in feet** between Points J and D?

2. What is the **vertical** distance **in feet** between Points J and D?

3. What is the **horizontal** distance **in feet** between Points D and E?

4. What is the **vertical** distance **in feet** between Points D and E?

5. If you were to walk up both slopes, which would be steeper? Path J to D or Path D to E? Explain your reasoning.

6. Using the Pine Hill contour map found in the following <u>Contour Lines</u> lab, answer <u>Contour Lines Problems</u>-Questions 1 – 18, except 17. Attach Lab Sheet.

Using the San Bernardino North Quadrangle, answer the following questions:

7. What is the Contour Interval on the San Bernardino North Quadrangle map?

8. If you were to walk from the Valley of Enchantment (north side of map) south to the Crest Forest Highway, would you be walking uphill or downhill? How can you tell?

9. What is the elevation at the Water Tank southeast of the Valley of Enchantment?

10. What is the Supplementary Contour Interval on this map?

11. Are Supplementary Contours drawn as solid or dashed lines?

12. What is the elevation of the Rialto Fire Station (located in the southwest corner of the map)?

13. Find Arrowhead Peak on the east side of the map. This is an example of contour lines forming complete, uninterrupted circles. What is the elevation of this peak? Note: Elevation is noted to the left of the triangle.

14. Note the spacing of the contours around this mountain. Which slope is steeper? North side or south side? How can you tell?

15. Find the 1400 foot contour in the southwest corner of the map. Does it close in on itself or is it interrupted by the edge of the map?

16. Draw an example of a depression contour.

17. What is the approximate elevation at the bottom of the Gravel Pit found in Lytle Creek Wash (look south of the word Creek in the southwest corner of the map)?

18. Locate East Twin Creek on the northeast side of the map. Which compass direction is it flowing?

Lab 4a

CONTOUR LINES

> **Objective:** To learn to interpret elevation contour lines.
>
> **Reference:** Hess, Darrel. *McKnight's Physical Geography;* 10th ed.; chapter, "Portraging Earth"; section, "Isolines"; and "Appendix: U.S. Geological Survey Topographic Maps."

CONTOUR LINES

We used **isolines** to illustrate the distribution of various phenomena. We used isotherms to show patterns of temperature and isobars to show patterns of pressure. In the study of landforms, we often use maps showing elevation with isolines known as **contour lines**.

Contour lines are lines that connect points of equal elevation. Contour lines enable us to study the topography of a region from a two-dimensional map. Figure 1 shows a simple contour line map and a profile cross section through the landscape.

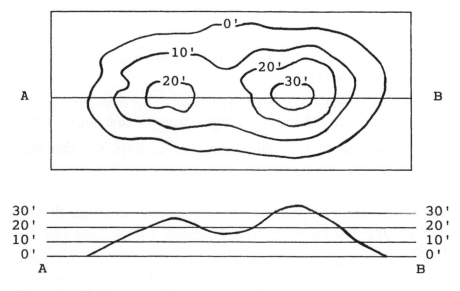

Figure 1: Simple contour line map and profile.

SAMPLE CONTOUR LINE MAP

Figure 2 shows a fictitious landscape and a contour line map of the same landscape with various elevations and features labeled.

CONTOUR LINE RULES

The following rules will help you interpret contour lines:

1. A contour line connects points of equal elevation.

2. The difference in elevation between two contour lines is known as the **contour interval**.

3. Usually every fifth contour line is a wider, darker **index contour**. (On some maps, every fourth line is an index contour.)

4. Elevations on one side of a contour line are higher than on the other side.

5. Contour lines never cross one another, although they may touch at a vertical cliff.

6. Contour lines have no beginning or end. Every line closes on itself, either on or off the map.

7. Uniformly spaced contours indicate a uniform slope.

8. If spaced far apart, contour lines indicate a gentle slope. If spaced close together, they represent a steep slope.

9. When crossing a valley, gully, or "draw," a contour line makes a "V" pointing up-hill.

10. When crossing a spur or a ridge running down the side of a hill, a contour line makes a "V" pointing downhill.

11. A contour line that closes within the limits of the map represents a hill or rise. The land within the closed contour is higher than the land outside the closed contour.

12. The top of a hill shown with closed contour lines is higher than the uppermost closed contour, but lower than the next highest contour that hasn't been shown on the map.

13. A small depression is represented by a closed contour line that is hachured on the side leading into the depression. Hachured contours are called **depression contours**.

Contour Lines

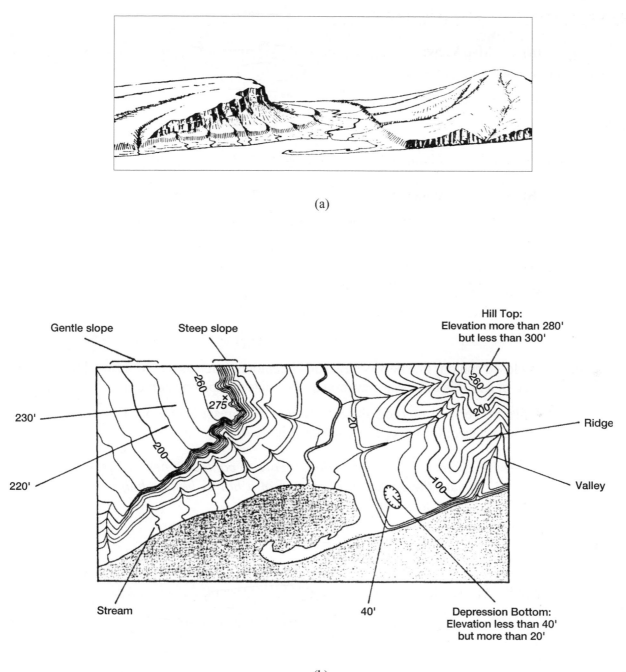

(a)

(b)

Figure 2: (a) Fictitious landscape; (b) Sample contour line map (contour interval 20'; adapted from U.S. Geological Survey).

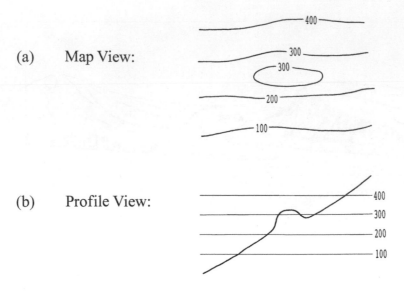

(a) Map View:

(b) Profile View:

Figure 3: Map view and profile view of a closed contour line on a slope.

14. A closed contour line between two other contours (such as would show a bump on the side of a hill) is the same elevation as the adjacent upslope contour line (Figure 3).

15. Unless otherwise marked, the elevation of a depression contour is the same as that of the adjacent lower regular contour (Figure 4).

Note: Unless otherwise noted, estimate elevations between contour lines to the nearest half-contour interval, and estimate the elevation of the top of a hill to be one-half-contour interval higher than the highest contour line shown.

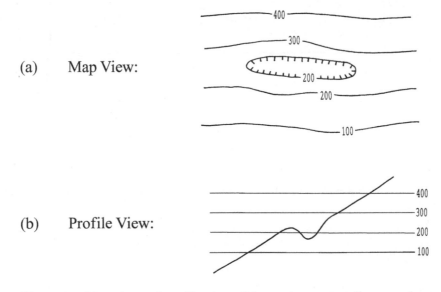

(a) Map View:

(b) Profile View:

Figure 4: Map view and profile view of depression contour line on a slope.

Name _____   Section _____

PROBLEMS

The questions in this exercise are based on this contour line map with elevations shown in feet.

- North is to the top of the map.
- Streams are shown with dashed lines.
- A graphic scale for measuring horizontal distances is shown below the map.
- Estimate elevations between contour lines to the nearest half-contour interval; assume that the top of a hill is one-half-contour interval higher than the highest contour line shown.

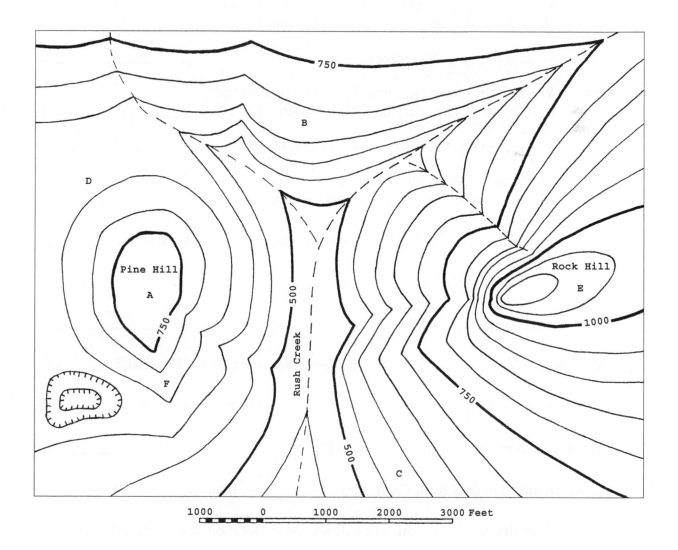

Contour Lines

1. What is the contour interval? _____ feet

2. What is the elevation of Point A? _____ feet

3. What is the elevation of Point B? _____ feet

4. What is the elevation of Point C? _____ feet

5. Which lettered point has the highest elevation? _____

6. Which lettered point has the lowest elevation? _____

7. (a) Where is the highest elevation shown in this landscape?
(It may not be a location marked with a letter.) _____

   (b) What is the elevation of this highest location? _____ feet

8. (a) Where is the lowest elevation shown in this landscape?
(It may not be a location marked with a letter.) _____

   (b) What is the elevation of this lowest location? _____ feet

9. What is the "local relief" of this landscape (the difference
in elevation between the highest and lowest locations)? _____ feet

10. Which lettered point is most clearly on a spur or ridge running down the side of a hill? ____

11. Is it possible to see D from F? _____

12. Is it possible to see D from B? _____

13. What is the elevation at the bottom of the depression southwest of Pine Hill? _____ feet

14. How deep is the depression (from the lip of the depression to its bottom)? _____ feet

15. What is the horizontal distance from C to B? _____ feet

16. In which direction does Rush Creek flow? From _____ to _____

17. Draw a 1 centimeter ($^1/_2$") diameter circle around the location of the steepest slope shown
on the map.

18. Draw in three more streams as indicated by the contour pattern (but not shown on the map
with dashed lines).

Geography 111: Physical Geography Lab
Lab Five: Topographic Maps and U.S. Public Land Survey

This lab is designed to further your understanding of U.S.G.S. Topographic Maps. We have worked with topographic maps to calculate scale and elevations, this week we will focus on understanding the standard features found on topographic maps. In addition, you will familiarize yourself with the Public Land Survey System, which is a grid system developed by the federal government to track land ownership.

Materials:
Red Pencil
Antelope Peak, Arizona Topographic Map- lab manual
San Bernardino North Quadrangle Map

Objectives:
- Identify features on standard U.S. Geological Survey topographic maps.
  - Types of U.S.G.S Topographic Map
  - Marginal Information
  - Map Symbol Key
- Utilize the public land survey system.
  - Identify Township & Range of map features
  - Identify Sections

Part 1: Topographic Maps.

The U.S. Geologic Survey is the federal government agency responsible for providing scientific information (i.e., biology, geography, geology and hydrology) about the United States. They are also responsible for providing geospatial information including the mapping of the United States. The U.S.G.S offers several maps series depicting the United States at various scales. Each series is named after its angular dimensions and is often referred to as a quadrangle map because the map depicts a rectangular portion of earth's surface with each corner of the map representing the intersection of latitude and longitude.
For example,

1° x 2° -	Scale: 1:250,000	1" = 4 miles
30- Minute Series – 30' x 30'	Scale: 1:125,000	1" = 2 miles
15 Minute Series -- 15' x 15'	Scale: 1:62,500	1" = 1 mile
7.5 Minute Series – 7.5' x 7.5'	Scale: 1:24,000	1" = .38 miles

The most popular and widely used U.S.G.S. quadrangle maps are called topographic maps because they show the shape of the land (slope and relief) through the use of contour lines. While we've used the 7.5 Minute Series and the 15 Minute Series when working with map scale and contour line interpretation, this lab will focus on the information in the margins of the maps.

Below is a portion of a U.S.G.S. Topographic map with marginal information identified.

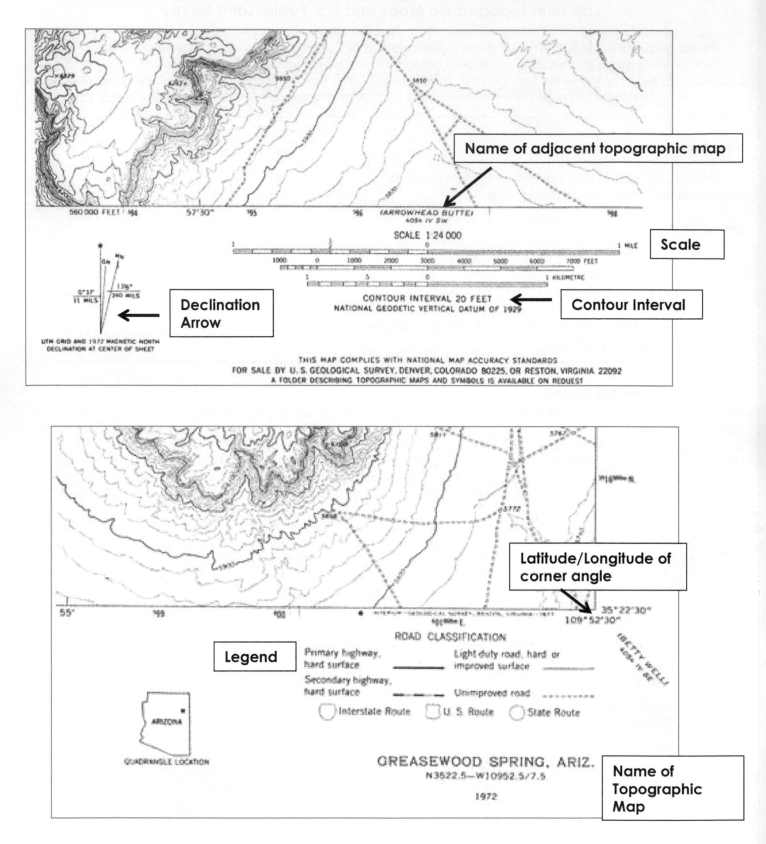

Assignment:

Using the San Bernardino North Quadrangle map, answer the following questions:

1. What is the difference in elevation between Index Contours?

2. What is the elevation of the bench mark at the top of Monument Peak (northwest corner of map)?

3. Draw the symbol used to represent a dirt road on this map.

4. What is the name of the adjacent quadrangle to the northwest?

5. What is the name of the adjacent quadrangle to the east?

6. What is the latitude/ longitude of the northeast corner of the map?

7. At the time this map was printed, what was the difference in degrees between magnetic north and true north?

8. Using the graphic map scales, determine the maximum width of the Shandin Hills. Measure the width from the 1600 foot contour line on the northwest to the 1400 foot contour line on the southeast.

_____ feet   _____ kilometers

Part 2: Public Land Survey System (PLSS)

The public land survey system was established in 1785 as a way to track public lands. The PLSS describes the location of a parcel of land relative to a grid system called Township and Range. This grid system is based on a Principal Meridian and Baseline.

The rows in this system are called Townships and are described as their position north of south of the Baseline. Each row spans 6 miles.

The columns in this system are called Ranges and are described as their position east or west of the Principal Meridian. Each column is 6 miles wide.

The example to the right, describes the shaded township (the generic term for the 6 x 6 mile square) as:
 Township 3 North (T3N) AND Range 4 West (R4W)

This means that the township is located 3 positions north of the Baseline and 4 positions west of the Principal Meridian.

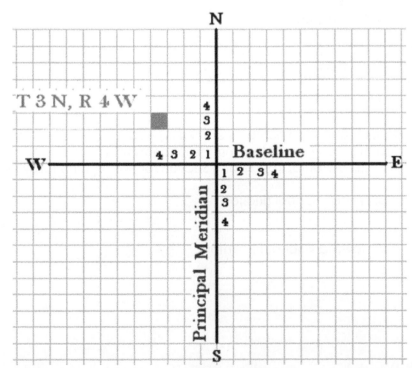

33

The PLSS subdivides each 6 mile square townships into 36 one mile Sections. Below is an example of a township with its 36 Sections:

Each number represents one Section and is 1 mile by 1 mile in size.

Within a Section, the land is further described by its position within this 1 mile by 1 mile square. Each section is divided into quadrants (NW 1/4, NE 1/4, SW 1/4, SE 1/4).

Each quadrant is also divided into quadrants.

For example, the shaded area to the right, can be described as:

West 1/2 of the Southwest 1/4 of Section 7.

Section

NE 1/4

TOWNSHIP

6	5	4	3	2	1
7	8	9	10	11	12
18	17	16	15	14	13
19	20	21	22	23	24
30	29	28	27	26	25
31	32	33	34	35	36

Assignment:

9. Using the USGS "Antelope Peak, Arizona" quadrangle found in the following U.S. Public Land Survey System lab, answer U.S. Public Land Survey System Problems- Questions 4 -6. Attach Lab Sheet.

Using the San Bernardino North Quadrangle map, answer the following questions:
10. Note the Township, Range and Section for each of the following features, the first one has been completed for you:

     a. Lake Gregory (NE)- **T2N   R4W   Section 23**

     b. Arrowhead Peak (E)-

     c. Panorama Point (N)-

Sometimes the section numbers are not printed everywhere on the map, but enough information has been provided that you can determine the location with a little investigative work.
11. Note the Township, Range and Section for each of the following features.

     a. Preston School (Rialto)-

     b. Newmark School (Center)

12. Each section can be further subdivided into "quadrants 1/4". Use the figure below to identify the subdivisions within each section. The first one has been done for you.

A. *S 1/2 of the NW 1/4, Section 27*

B.

C.

D.

E.

F.

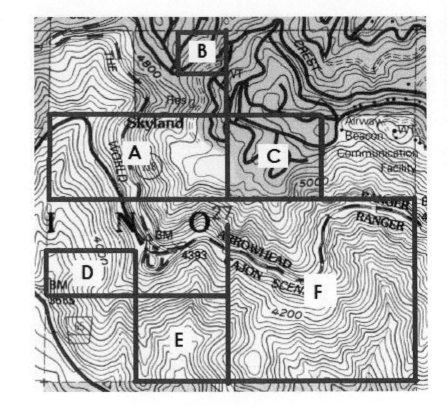

Lab 5a

Lab 5a

U.S. PUBLIC LAND SURVEY SYSTEM

Objective: To learn to use the Public Land Survey System.

PUBLIC LAND SURVEY SYSTEM

The **Public Land Survey**, or **township grid**, was established by the federal government in 1785 in order to keep track of land ownership in the American frontier. This grid covers most of the continental United States west of the Mississippi and Ohio rivers, with the exception of some regions such as those under old Spanish land grants.

The starting point for the grid is a series of parallels known as **base lines**, and a series of **principal meridians** (Figure 1). Note that most sets of base lines and principal meridians are named after the same reference point, such as the *Boise Base Line* and the *Boise Principal Meridian* in Idaho. Beginning at the intersection of a base line and a principal meridian, rows of 36-square-mile tracts of land known as **townships** were established (Figure 2a).

TOWNSHIP AND RANGE

Each township is a square tract of land, 6 miles to a side, and is identified by its position north or south of a base line and east or west of a principal meridian. The first position north of a base line is called "Township 1 North" (T1N), the second position north is T2N, and so on. The first position south is T1S.

The first position west of a principal meridian is called "Range 1 West" (R1W), and the first position east is R1E. Each 36 square-mile township is identified by both a **township** and a **range**. For example, one of the townships would be designated "Township 3 North, Range 2 East" (see Figure 2a).

(Note: The term "township" has two meanings in the context of the Public Land Survey—a 36-square-mile tract of land, as well as the positions of these tracts north and south of a base line. It may help to think of "T1N" and "T2N" as referring to "Tier" 1 North, "Tier" 2 North, and so on.)

A township is divided into 36 **sections**. Each section is 1 square mile (640 acres) in area and is given a number, from 1 to 36. Notice the specific numbering pattern of sections within a township (Figure 2b). Each section is subdivided into "quarter sections" (160 acres), and each quarter section is further divided into "quarters of quarter sections" (40 acres), or as shown in Figure 2c, into even smaller tracts of land. The shaded 10-acre plot shown in Figure 2c would be called the "Southeast Quarter of the Southwest Quarter of the Northeast Quarter, Section 24, Township 2 South, Range 3 West" (SE$^1/_4$, SW$^1/_4$, NE$^1/_4$, Sec. 24, T2S, R3W).

From Exercise 27 of *Physical Geography Laboratory Manual,* Tenth Edition, Darrel Hess. Copyright © 2011 by Pearson Education, Inc. Published by Pearson Prentice Hall. All rights reserved.

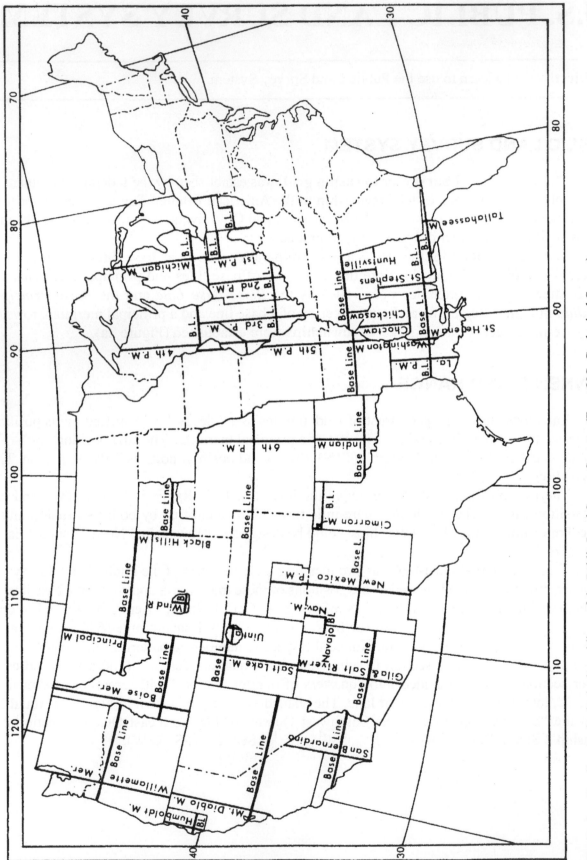

Figure 1: Baselines and principal meridians of the Public Land Survey System. (From U.S. Geological Survey)

Figure 2: Public Land Survey System.

(a) Township & Range Grid

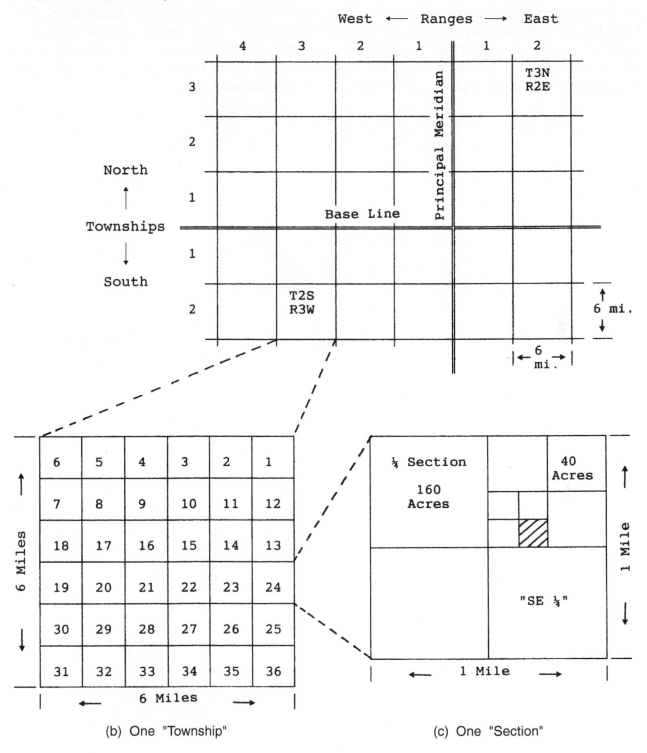

(b) One "Township"

(c) One "Section"

TOWNSHIP GRID ON TOPOGRAPHIC MAPS

On USGS topographic maps, the public land survey grid is usually shown with red lines and section numbers (for example, look at Map T-11, the "Whitewater, Wisconsin," quadrangle). The township and range numbers are shown around the margins of the map. The base line and principal meridian are often not identified. You will also notice that a row of townships is occasionally offset relative to the row to the north or south. This is to compensate for the constriction of a township that would result from the convergence of the meridians as latitude increases.

Name _____   Section _____

PROBLEMS

The following questions are based on Figure 3 on the following page, showing a portion of the "Antelope Peak, Arizona," quadrangle (scale 1:62,500; contour interval 25 feet). The map's marginal information is visible along the left and top margins ("T.5S," "R.2E," etc.). On the original USGS map, this information was printed in red.

1.   The word "Hidden" appears on the map within which township?

       Township _____, Range _____

2.   The words "Vekol Wash" appear within which township?

       Township _____, Range _____

3.   The "Booth Hills" are found within which section and township?

       Section _____, Township _____, Range _____

4.   Find the hill in Sec. 8, T6S, R2E. This hill covers
       approximately how many acres?   _____ acres

5.   With a red pencil, carefully mark off and shade in:

       (a)   The Northeast Quarter of Section 25, T5S, R1E.

       (b)   The Northwest Quarter of the Southeast Quarter of Section 5, T6S, R2E.

6.   Describe two kinds of human/cultural features that follow the Public Land Survey grid.

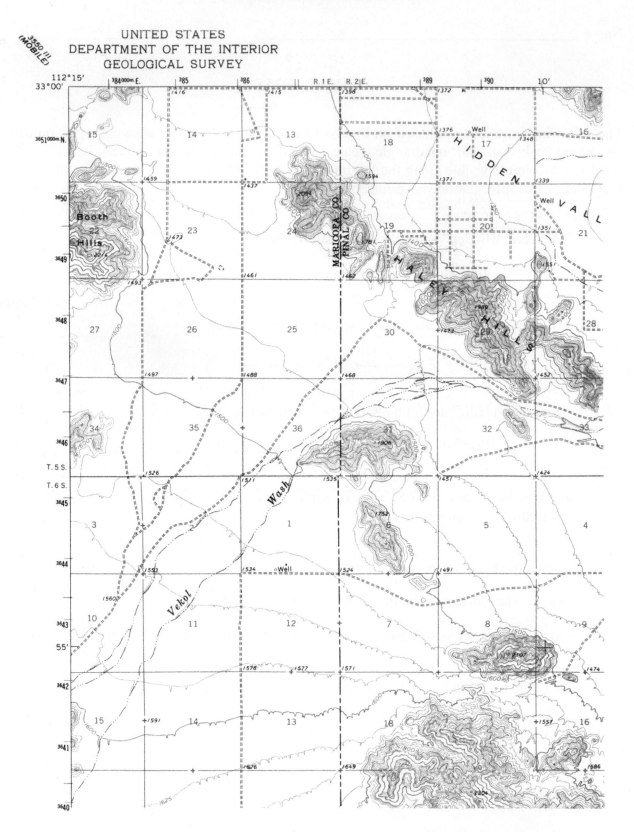

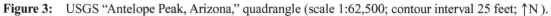

Figure 3: USGS "Antelope Peak, Arizona," quadrangle (scale 1:62,500; contour interval 25 feet; ↑N).

Geography 111: Physical Geography Lab
Lab Six: Earth/Sun Relationship and Solar Angle

This lab is designed to introduce you to the complex relation between the Earth and Sun. The geometry between the Earth and the Sun changes as the Earth orbits the sun, this coupled with the fact that the Earth is tilted relative to the plane of ecliptic and the rotational axis is always pointed to Polaris.

Materials:

Colored Pencils

Protractor

Analemma Chart (attached)

Earth/Sun Diagrams (attached)

Objectives:
- Identify the reasons for the change of seasons.
- Identify Earth-Sun Relations during solstices & equinoxes.
    - Diagram vertical and tangent rays for given day.
    - Identify seasonal variations in solar declination and length of day.
- Use an analemma to determine solar altitude for any given location and to determine the declination of the Sun for any given day.
- Calculate the solar altitude of San Bernardino on solstices, equinoxes, and selected additional days.

Part 1: Visualizing the Inclination of Earth's Rotational Axis

1. Using a protractor draw and label the following items on the diagram below:
- Line up the protractor so that the 0° lines up with the Plane of Ecliptic.
- Mark the Earth's axial tilt of 23.5° to the **right of the 90° line**. With your ruler connect this point with the center of the circle and draw a line completely through the circle. Label this the Earth's Rotational Axis.
- Reposition the protractor so that the 90° lines up with the Rotational Axis. Mark the 0° lines. With your ruler connect these new points and draw a line. Label this the Equator.

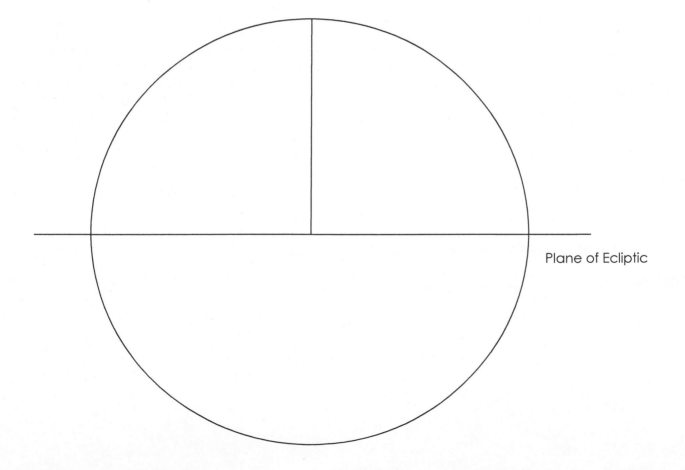

Plane of Ecliptic

Part 2: Earth/Sun Relationship

      Equinox- Occurs on March 20 (1st day of spring*) and September 22 (1st day of fall*)

              12 hours of day and night around the globe

              Circle of Illumination passes through the poles

              Declination (latitude of the direct rays) is at the Equator

      Solstice- Occurs on June 21 (1st day of summer*) and December 22 (1st day of winter*)

              June Solstice: Declination (latitude of the direct rays) is at the Tropic of Cancer

                        24 hours of day north of Arctic Circle

                        24 hours of darkness south of Antarctic Circle

              December Solstice: Declination (latitude of the direct rays) is at the Tropic of Capricorn

                        24 hours of day south of Antarctic Circle

                        24 hours of darkness north of Arctic Circle

2. On the Earth/ Sun Diagrams attached to this lab, draw in the following lines using colored pencils:

      Hint: To fill in the figures, start with the Circle of Illumination which is a straight line drawn through the center of the circle and perpendicular to the direct rays. Next add the lines of latitude based on their relationship to the direct rays and 24 hours of darkness and light. Note: None of the diagrams will contain all of the lines of latitude.

Equator (already drawn on figure- just label)	Tropic of Cancer
North Pole (already drawn on figure- just label)	Tropic of Capricorn
South Pole (already drawn on figure-just label)	Arctic Circle
Circle of Illumination (shade in "dark" side)	Antarctic Circle

After completing the figures, answer the following questions:

3.   What is the latitude receiving the tangent rays on the following days:

      a.   March/ September Equinox

      b.   June Solstice

      c.   December Solstice

4. The amount of incoming solar radiation (insolation) is determined primarily by the angle at which the Sun's rays hit the Earth's surface. If the Sun's rays strike the surface at a 90° angle, the Sun's energy is concentrated in a small area. Conversely, if the Sun's rays strike the Earth at an oblique angle, then the energy is diffused over a larger area. List the time of year (June Solstice, Equinox, December Solstice) that the following locations receive the maximum insolation.

a) Nome, Alaska _____

b) Sydney, Australia _____

c) London, England _____

d) Mbandaka, Dem. Republic of the Congo _____

e) Falkland islands _____

Part 3: Analemma

An analemma is a chart that allows you to determine the declination for any given day of the year. To determine the declination, locate a day of the year and follow it across the graph to the left hand side where the declination is listed. For example, on August 20, the declination is at 12° N.

Using the analemma, answer the following questions:

5. What is the declination of the Sun on the following dates? Indicate whether the declination is north latitude or south latitude.

Date	Declination
a) September 28	_____
b) October 4	_____
c) November 20	_____
d) December 10	_____

Part 4. Solar Altitude

Solar altitude helps us understand the angle at which the Sun's rays strike the Earth's surface. Solar altitude is the height of the Sun above the horizon; therefore, the higher the solar altitude, the more direct the Sun's rays.

Solar Altitude is determined by the following equation:

Solar Altitude at Location A= 90° - Arc Distance

Arc Distance = the difference in latitude between Location A and the latitude receiving the Sun's direct rays (declination).

6. Determine the solar altitude at San Bernardino Valley College (34° N) on the events given:

Date	Latitude	Declination of Sun	Arc Distance	Solar Altitude
Equinox	34° N	0°		
June Solstice	34° N	23.5° N		
December Solstice	34° N	23.5° S		

7. During which event (June Solstice, Equinox, December Solstice) will San Bernardino experience the highest solar altitude and maximum insolation? _____

7. Using the analemma calculate the solar altitude at the various locations on the dates given:

	Date	Latitude	Declination of Sun	Arc Distance	Solar Altitude
a) Seattle, WA	February 5				
b) Cape Town, South Africa	July 30				
c) Quito, Ecuador	March 21				

Earth/Sun Diagrams

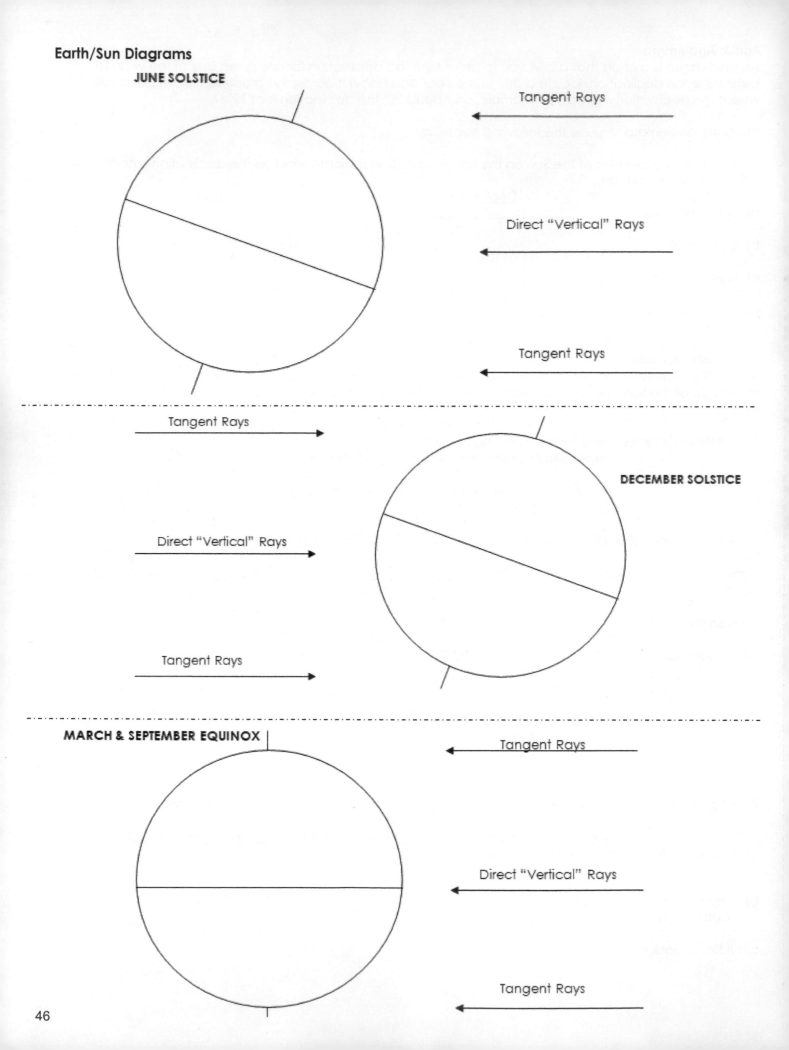

JUNE SOLSTICE

Tangent Rays

Direct "Vertical" Rays

Tangent Rays

Tangent Rays

DECEMBER SOLSTICE

Direct "Vertical" Rays

Tangent Rays

MARCH & SEPTEMBER EQUINOX

Tangent Rays

Direct "Vertical" Rays

Tangent Rays

Analemma

"Courtesy of Pearson Education."

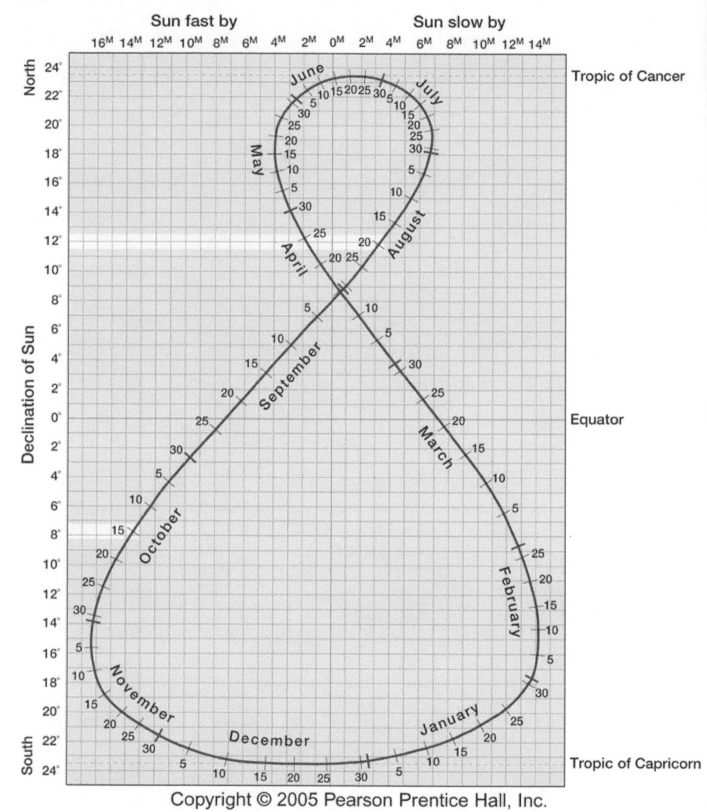

Geography 111: Physical Geography Lab
Lab Seven: Insolation and Temperature

This lab is designed to introduce you to the number of factors that influence temperature at Earth's surface. First we will begin by studying how the amount of insolation received at the Earth's surface varies from place to place. The variation of insolation leads to variations in temperature. Other factors, such as, land-water contrasts, ocean currents, and wind patterns and air masses also influence temperatures. In addition, we will explore how altitude affects temperatures.

Materials:
Red, Blue and Green Pencils
Thermometers
Temperature Graph (attached)
Map of North America (attached)

Objectives:
- Measure surface variation in temperature
- Construct a temperature graph
- Calculate temperature range
- Calculate average annual temperature
- Identify global temperature patterns and to explore the reasons for these patterns.
- Calculate the Average Lapse Rate

Part 1: Incoming Solar Radiation & Surface Variations

The amount of incoming solar radiation (insolation) varies by latitude and by season. Since the sun's energy is our primary source of energy, this radiation imbalance leads to temperature differences. Why do we see this variation in insolation received?

Insolation received depends on:

Angle of Incidence**- the angle at which the sun's rays hit the Earth's surface- direct vs oblique angles.
Day Length**- the amount of time the sun is above the horizon
Atmospheric Obstruction- clouds, haze, etc.
Albedo- the ability of an object to reflect radiation
Low Albedo surfaces: asphalt, aged concrete, dark roof/paint , dark soil, dark rock, forests, grass
High Albedo surfaces: snow/ ice, new concrete, light roof/ paint, sand/desert

** Both of these factors vary by latitude and by season

Assignment:

A. Classify the following locations as having a low or high albedo.

1. Antarctica (ice sheet) _____

2. Lava Flow in Hawaii (black) _____

3. Aged Concrete Sidewalk _____

4. Greek Village with white houses _____

B. Each lab group will select **either full sun or full shade** and measure the temperature for **3 surfaces** listed below. Before you collect the data, hypothesize whether or not each location has a high or low albedo. When measuring the surface temperature, hold the thermometer one inch above the surface- it will take a few minutes to record.

Data Locations	Albedo (high vs. low)	Measured temperature (°C)	Converted temperature (°F) $°F = (°C * 1.8°) + 32°$
Select either FULL SHADE or FULL SUN			
Asphalt			
Black Car			
Cement			
Grass/Vegetation			
Artificial Turf (Football Field)			
White Car			
Soil (light or dark)			

1. Compare the temperatures recorded to the albedo for each surface. Explain how your data does or does not illustrate the relationship between temperature and albedo.

Part 2: Annual Temperature Variations

Temperature - sensible heat (energy that you feel)

Air is heated from the ground up by outgoing longwave radiation emitted from the Earth, not by incoming shortwave insolation.

There is a lag time between the Earth receiving the shortwave insolation and remitting the energy as longwave radiation.

Temperature Range = Maximum Temperature – Minimum Temperature

Assignment:

A. Using the temperature graphs provided in the following Temperature Patterns Lab, calculate the Temperature Range for the following locations. Note: the temperatures displayed on the graphs are the average temperatures for each month. St. Louis has been completed for you.

	Warmest Month- Average Temperature	Coldest Month- Average Temperature	Temperature Range
St. Louis, MO	78° F	30° F	78° - 30° =**48°**
Nome, Alaska			
Fairbanks, Alaska			
Oakland, California			
Lihue, HI			
Kilauea, Hi			

1. Plot these locations on the map provided and label them. Note: You'll have to plot the Hawaiian locations at the correct latitude and then draw an arrow pointing west because this map doesn't include the location of the Hawaiian Islands.

2. Answer Temperature Patterns- Problems- Part III- Questions 5,7, and 8. Consider the *one* temperature control factor that is the *most* responsible for the patterns shown (choose from latitude, land-water contrasts, wind patterns and air masses, or altitude).

Question 5:

Question 7:

Question 8:

Part 3: Coastal Versus Continental Locations

Land heats and cools faster than water for the following reasons:

LAND	WATER
Lower Specific heat	Higher Specific Heat
Immobile – prevents mixing	Mobile- allows mixing
Less Evaporation	More Evaporation
Radiation concentrated at surface	Radiation penetrates below surface

Specific Heat: Amount of energy needs to raise 1 gram of a substance 1 degree of Celsius.

Results: Continental locations experience greater seasonal extremes- hotter summers and colder winters (larger temperature range).

Coastal locations experience more moderate, uniform temperatures (lower temperature range.

Average Annual Temperature = Sum of the temperatures/ Number of temperatures

Assignment:

A. Average Monthly Temperatures for 3 Cities:

San Francisco, CA-- 37.6°N, 122.4°W

	J	F	M	A	M	J	J	A	S	O	N	D
Temperature (° F)	49	52	53	56	58	61	63	64	64	61	55	49

Wichita, Kansas-- 37.7°N, 97.4°W

	J	F	M	A	M	J	J	A	S	O	N	D
Temperature (° F)	30	33	44	56	65	74	80	79	70	58	44	34

Norfolk, Virginia-- 36.9°N, 76.2°W

	J	F	M	A	M	J	J	A	S	O	N	D
Temperature (° F)	39	41	49	57	66	74	78	77	72	61	52	44

1. Plot the cities on the map provided and label them.

2. Construct a temperature graph by plotting the Average Monthly Temperatures on the Graph provided. Use **red** to plot San Francisco, **blue** for Wichita, and **green** for Norfolk.

3. Compute the following statistics. Round your answers to one decimal place.

	Average Annual Temperature	Temperature Range
San Francisco, CA		
Wichita, Kansas		
Norfolk, Virginia		

4. Based on the statistics computed in Question 3, describe the relationship between location and maximum range in temperature.

5. Why does Wichita have colder winters than Norfolk?

6. Why does San Francisco have a smaller temperature range than Norfolk, Virginia, even though both are located on coasts? Keep in mind that the prevailing winds are from the west.

7. Looking back at the temperatures listed in Part 2, answer <u>Temperature Patterns- Problems- Part III-</u> Question 6.

Part 4: Average Lapse Rate- change in temperature as a result in altitude change.

Average Lapse Rate: 3.6° F/ 1000 feet or 6.5° C/ 1000 meters

Steps for calculating the Lapse Rate

Example: If the temperature is 93.6° F at 1000 feet, what would the temperature be like at 5000 feet?

Step 1: Find the Elevation Difference: Maximum – Minimum

5000- 1000 = 4000 feet

Step 2: Set up equivalent fractions and cross multiply:
(Temp) $\dfrac{3.6° F}{1000 ft} = \dfrac{X}{4000 ft}$
(Elevation)

(4000 * 3.6)/1000 =14.4° F

Step 3: If calculating for a higher elevation, subtract degrees from starting temperature. If calculating for a low elevation, add degrees to starting temperature.

93.6° F – 14.4° F = 79.2° F at 5000 ft

Assignment:
Calculate the temperature using the average lapse rate for the locations listed below. Round your answers to one decimal place.

Location	Elevation	Temperature
Fullerton	150 feet	72° F
San Bernardino	1200 feet	
San Gorgonio Peak	11,499 feet	

1. Looking back at the temperatures listed in Part 2, do the temperatures between Lihue and Kilauea follow the average lapse rate?

Annual Temperature Graph

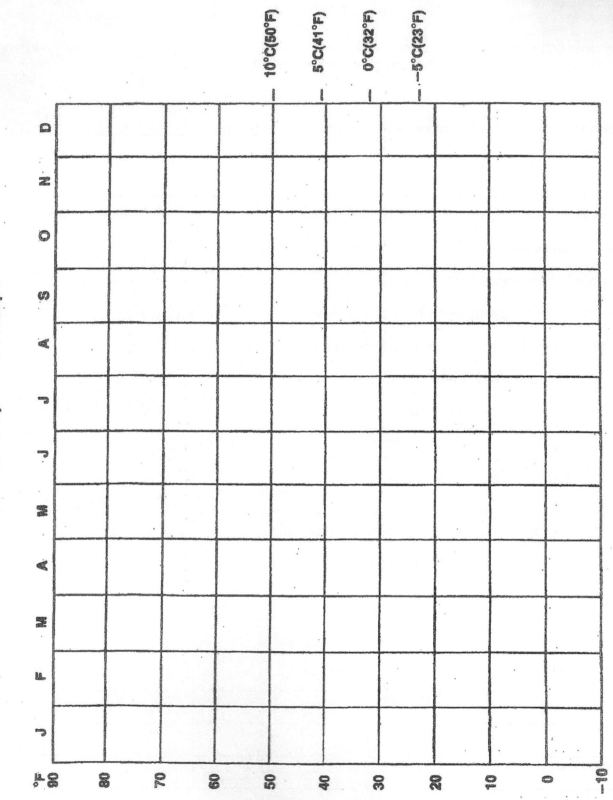

43

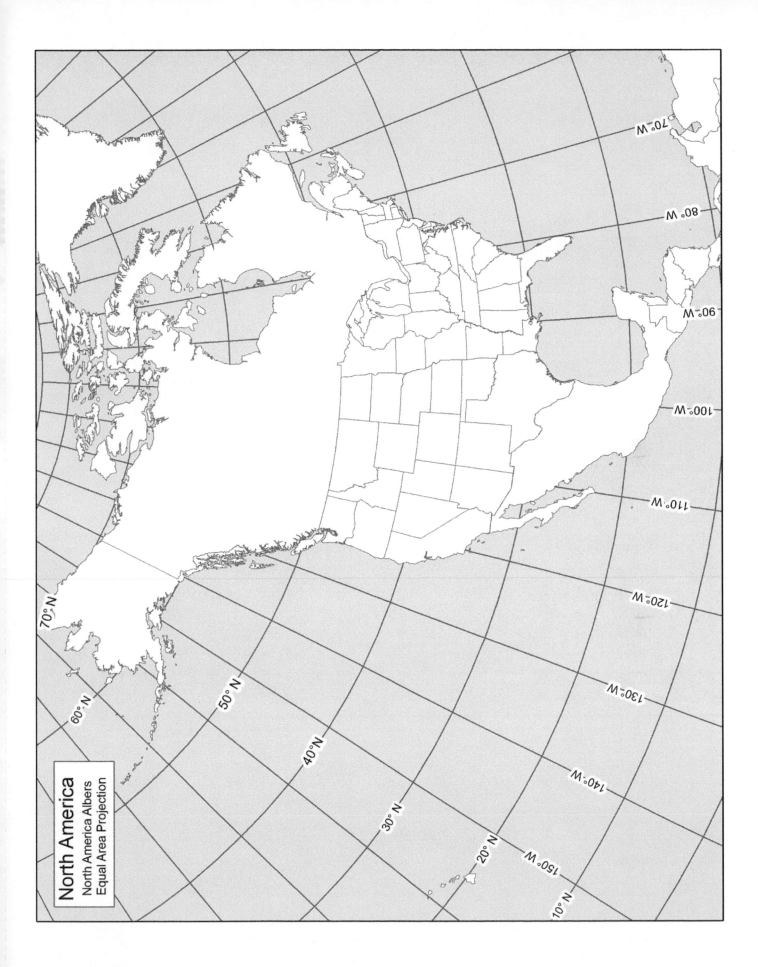

North America

North America Albers
Equal Area Projection

70° N

60° N

50° N

40° N

30° N

20° N

10° N

150° W

140° W

130° W

120° W

110° W

100° W

90° W

80° W

70° W

Lab 7a

TEMPERATURE PATTERNS

Objective:	To study global temperature patterns and to explore the reasons for these patterns.
Reference:	Hess, Darrel. *McKnight's Physical Geography;* 10th ed.; chapter, "Insolation and Temperature"; sections, "Land and Water Contrasts" through "Global Temperature Patterns."

FACTORS INFLUENCING TEMPERATURE PATTERNS

A number of factors influence the temperature regime of a location. The following factors are among the most important:

Latitude: Latitude is the most basic control of temperature. In general, because of the lower total insolation received at high latitudes compared with low latitudes, temperature decreases as we move away from the equator and toward the poles. In addition, the tropics generally show little temperature change during the year, while the mid- and high latitudes experience variation in temperature from summer to winter. These basic global patterns are apparent in Figure 1, showing average sea-level temperatures in January mapped with isotherms, and in Figure 2, showing average sea-level temperatures in July.

Were latitude the only control of temperature, the isotherms would run exactly east to west, parallel to the lines of latitude. However, this hypothetical pattern is altered by a number of additional factors.

Land-Water Contrasts: Land and water react differently to solar heating, and this exerts a strong influence on the atmosphere. In general, land heats up and cools off faster and to a greater extent than water. This means that the interiors of continents will be hotter in summer and colder in winter than maritime regions at the same latitude. The ocean also significantly moderates the temperatures of the coastal regions of a continent.

In addition to the lower annual temperature range associated with maritime regions, the ocean also exhibits a lag in reaching its coolest point in winter and its warmest point in summer. This means that coastal regions often reach their temperature extremes several months after interior regions.

Ocean Currents: The general circulation of the ocean is a significant mechanism of global heat transfer. Major surface ocean currents move warm water from the equatorial regions toward the poles, and bring cool water from the poles back toward the equator. In each of the main ocean basins, warm water is moving toward the poles off the east coasts of continents, while cool water is moving toward the equator off the west coasts of continents.

Wind Patterns: In many regions of the world, the dominant wind direction strongly influences local temperature patterns. For example, in the midlatitudes the dominant wind direction is from the west, meaning that air masses will tend to move from west to east. As a consequence, the temperature patterns of midlatitude locations along the east coast of a continent can be quite "continental"—the westerlies can bring the seasonal warmth or coldness of the interior of the continent all the way to the east coast.

Altitude: In general, temperature decreases with increased altitude. A high elevation station will have a very similar annual temperature pattern to a nearby lowland station, although the high elevation station will be consistently cooler throughout the year. On average, temperature in the **troposphere** decreases by approximately 6.5°C per 1000 meters of elevation increase (3.6°F/1000 feet)—this is known as the **average lapse rate**.

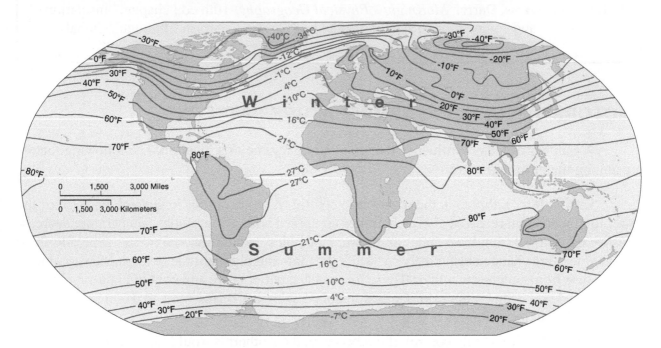

Figure 1: Average January sea-level temperatures. (From McKnight and Hess, *Physical Geography*, 9th ed.)

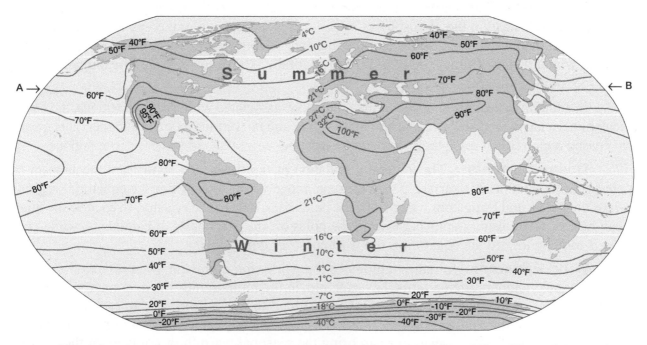

Figure 2: Average July sea-level temperatures. (Adapted from McKnight and Hess, *Physical Geography*, 9th ed.)

Name _____   Section _____

PROBLEMS—PART I

The following questions are based on the maps of average January sea-level temperatures (Figure 1) and average July sea-level temperatures (Figure 2):

1.   Is the temperature contrast between the equator and the
     Arctic region greatest in the winter or summer?   _____

2.   (a)   Were latitude the only control of temperature, the isotherms would run straight
           across the maps from east to west. Describe one region of the world where this hy-
           pothetical isotherm pattern is actually observed:

     (b)   Why is the hypothetical pattern seen here?

3.   (a)   Is the influence of cool ocean currents on coastal
           temperatures more pronounced in summer or winter?   _____

     (b)   Why?

4.   (a)   Comparing the January map with the July map, describe one region of the world
           that exhibits a large annual temperature range (the difference between the January
           and July average temperatures):

     (b)   What explains this large annual temperature range?

     (c)   Describe one region of the world that exhibits a small annual temperature range.

     (d)   What explains this small annual temperature range?

Name _____   Section _____

PROBLEMS—PART II

Using a straightedge, draw a line across the July temperature map (Figure 2) from point "A" to point "B." This reference line can be thought of as the "hypothetical" position of the 16°C (60°F) isotherm were there no land–water contrasts, ocean currents, and so on. Compare the actual 16°C isotherm, with the line you have just drawn. In places where the actual 16°C isotherm is south of the hypothetical line temperatures are lower than expected; in places where the actual 16°C isotherm is north of the hypothetical line, temperatures are higher than expected.

Begin in the west and move across the map to the east, briefly explaining why the actual 16°C (60°F) isotherm deviates from the hypothetical:

Name _____ Section _____

PROBLEMS—PART III

Six charts showing the average monthly temperature (in °C and °F) for seven U.S. cities are provided below. For each of the cities, the latitude and longitude, as well as the elevation, are provided.

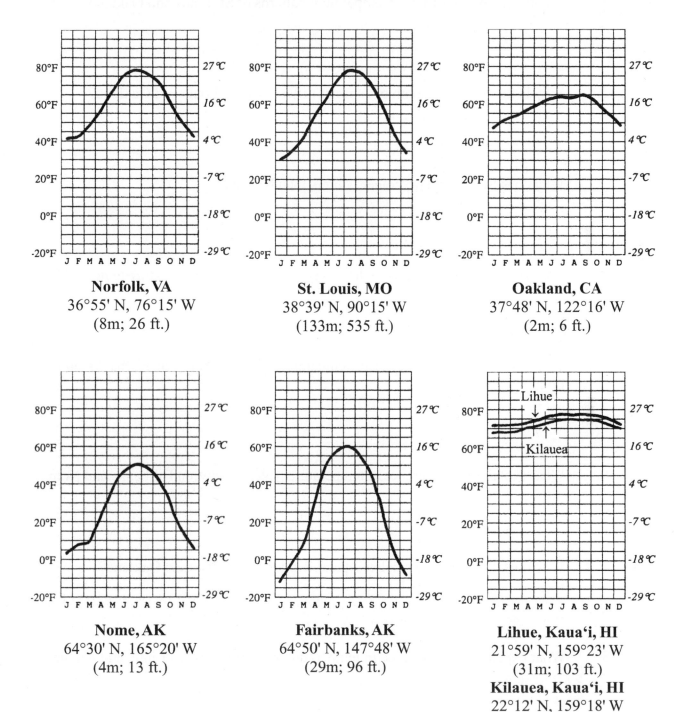

Norfolk, VA
36°55' N, 76°15' W
(8m; 26 ft.)

St. Louis, MO
38°39' N, 90°15' W
(133m; 535 ft.)

Oakland, CA
37°48' N, 122°16' W
(2m; 6 ft.)

Nome, AK
64°30' N, 165°20' W
(4m; 13 ft.)

Fairbanks, AK
64°50' N, 147°48' W
(29m; 96 ft.)

Lihue, Kaua'i, HI
21°59' N, 159°23' W
(31m; 103 ft.)
Kilauea, Kaua'i, HI
22°12' N, 159°18' W
(346m; 1134 ft.)

Answer the following questions by comparing the temperature charts on the previous page. In your answers, consider the *one* **temperature control factor that is** *most* **responsible** for the patterns shown (choose from latitude, land–water contrasts, wind patterns, or altitude). You may use the same answer for more than one question. You should locate each of the cities on a world map before trying to answer the questions. *If altitude is the main factor cited, calculate the expected temperature difference between the two cities based on the average lapse rate.*

1.   What explains the different temperature patterns of St. Louis and Oakland?

2.   Why is the warmest month of summer different in St. Louis and Oakland?

3.   Why does St. Louis have colder winters than Norfolk?

4.   Compared to Oakland, Norfolk has a very "continental" temperature pattern. Why?

5.   What explains the difference in temperature patterns between Fairbanks and St. Louis?

6.   What explains the difference in temperature patterns between Fairbanks and Nome?

7.   Why does Lihue have a smaller annual temperature range than Oakland?

8.   What explains the difference in temperature patterns between Lihue and Kilauea?

Geography 111: Physical Geography Lab
Lab Eight: Humidity and the Adiabatic Process

This lab is designed to help you understand the relationship between water vapor content, temperature and humidity. In addition, we will review the adiabatic process and discuss what happens to a parcel of air as it is forced to rise or descend.

Materials:
Thermometers/ Sling Psychrometer

Objectives:
- Calculate relative humidity
- Find relative humidity using sling psychrometer
- Determine dew point temperature based on water vapor content
- Calculate depression of wet bulb using sling psychrometer

- Calculate Dry Adiabatic Rate and Saturated (Wet) Adiabatic Rate
- Understand what happens to rising air after the dew point temperature has been reached.

Part 1: Relative Humidity and Dew Point Temperature

Relative Humidity: describes how close the air is to saturation. It is expressed as a ratio of water vapor content (Mixing Ratio) to the total amount of water vapor the air mass can hold (Saturation Mixing Ratio)

Mixing Ratio: <u>actual</u> amount of water vapor present in a given parcel of air. Expressed as grams of water vapor/kilogram of dry air (g/kg).

Saturation Mixing Ratio: amount of water vapor (grams) a parcel of air can hold at a given temperature. Expressed as grams of water vapor/kilogram of air (g/kg).

Relative Humidity (%): Mixing Ratio (Actual)/ Saturation Mixing Ratio (Capacity) x 100

Dew Point Temperature: the temperature to which a given parcel of air must cool, so that relative humidity is 100%

Assignment:
A. Use the Saturation Mixing Ratio Table (found in the following <u>Humidity</u> Lab) to find the amount of water vapor a parcel of air can hold at a given temperature. Then calculate the relative humidity of the parcel of air and the dew point temperature. Round off humidity to the nearest percent.

Station	Mixing Ratio (ACTUAL)	Temperature (DETERMINES CAPACITY)	Saturation Mixing Ratio (CAPACITY)	Relative Humidity [(ACTUAL/CAPACITY)* 100]	Dew Point Temperature (TEMP @ WHICH CAPACITY = ACTUAL)
EX	3.5 g/kg	10° C	7.6 g/kg	46%	-1.1° C
1	7.6 g/kg	15.6° C			
2	22.3 g/kg	37.8° C			
3	6.2 g/kg	26.7° C			
4	1.9 g/kg	-6.7° C			
5	11.1 g/kg	32.2° C			
6	13.2 g/kg	21.1° C			

2. What would happen to the Relative Humidity of Station 1, if the temperature decreased to 12.8° C?

3. What would happen to the Relative Humidity of Station 4, if the temperature increased to 35° C?

4. In the following <u>Humidity</u> Lab, answer <u>Humidity- Problems- Part I (SI Units)-</u> Questions 2 and 3.

    2 a.

      b.

      c.

    3a.

      b.

      c.

      d.

5. Based on your observations above, write a statement describing the relationship between temperature, capacity and relative humidity. Specifically, what happens to relative humidity, with an increase or a decrease in temperature, if the actual water vapor content remains the same?

Part 2: Sling Psychrometer- Wet Bulb and Dry Bulb

Dry Bulb: air temperature

Wet Bulb: shows the amount of evaporation-
if air is dry – more evaporation; if air is moist – less evaporation

Wet Bulb Depression: Dry Bulb – Wet Bulb

How to use the Sling Psychrometer:
Step 1:   Check the temperature of two thermometers to ensure they are the same.

Step 2:   Wet cloth and place over the end of one thermometer- this is the Wet Bulb.

Step 3:   Gently spin the psychrometer overhead for a full minute. Check temperature. Continue spinning overhead for another 30 seconds. Once the temperature no longer decreases, record the temperature of the Wet Bulb and the Dry Bulb.

Step 4:   Make sure the cloth is still wet and that the thermometers are once again the same temperature. Repeat steps 1 -3 with the next location.

A. Make a general observation about the current atmospheric conditions. Is it warm? Cloudy? Windy?

B. In addition to measuring the humidity within the classroom, select three sites from the list used for measuring temperatures in Lab 7. Find the Wet Bulb and Dry Bulb temperature following the steps above. Fill in the location and site characteristics, including sunlight, surface, and albedo.

Data Locations	Site Characteristics	Dry Bulb Temp (°C)	Wet Bulb Temp (°C)	Wet Bulb Depression
1 Inside Classroom				
2				
3				
4				

C. Use the Humidity and Dew Point Psychrometer Tables (found in the following Humidity Lab) to find Relative Humidity and Dew Point Temperatures. Once you have found the Dew Point temperature, use the Saturation Mixing Ration Table (also found in the Humidity Lab) to find the Mixing Ratio.

Data Locations	Relative Humidity	Dew Point Temperature	Mixing Ratio
1 Inside Classroom			
2			
3			
4			

Part 3: Adiabatic Processes

Air that is forced to ascend will adiabatically cool and air that is forced to descend will adiabatically heat; this temperature change results from a chance in pressure. As the air rises, the external pressure decreases and the air expands which lowers the temperature of the parcel of air. As air descends, the external pressure increases and the air is compressed which causes warming.

Dry Adiabatic Rate = 10° C/ 1000 meters (5.5° F/ 1000 ft)
Use for *rising* air masses that have not yet reached the dew point temperature.

Saturated Adiabatic Rate = 6° C/ 1000 meters (3.3° F/ 1000 ft).
Use for *rising* air masses that have cooled to the dew point temperature.

Lifting Condensation Level – the altitude at which the dew point temperature has been reached.

Windward – the side of the mountain where the air is rising, cooling and precipitating.

Leeward- the side of the mountain where air is descending and warming- no precipitation.

Assignment:

A. Assume that at sea level a parcel of air has a temperature of 40° C, and a dew point temperature of 20° C.

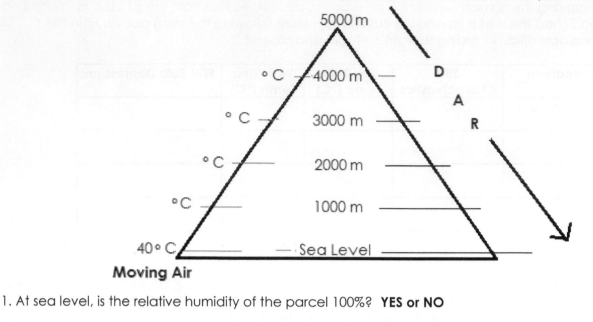

Moving Air

1. At sea level, is the relative humidity of the parcel 100%? **YES or NO**

2. Assume the air is forced upward by a mountain range, it will cool at the _____ (**dry; saturated**) adiabatic rate.

3. What is the temperature of the parcel of air at 2000 m? _____

4. At 2000 m, is the relative humidity of the parcel of air 100%? **YES or NO**

5. What do you call the altitude corresponding to the Dew Point Temperature?

6. Above this level the rising air will begin cooling at the _____(**dry; saturated**) adiabatic rate.

7. What is the temperature at 5000 m? _____

If the air is forced to descend it will warm at the Dry Adiabatic Rate.

8. What is the temperature at sea level on the leeward side of the mountain? _____

Compare the temperature of the parcel on the windward side and the leeward side.

9. Which side has the warmer temperature? _____

10. Is descending air conducive to cloud formation? **YES or NO**

The leeward side of a mountain range tends to be drier and warmer than the windward side. This is called the rain shadow effect.

B. In the following <u>Adiabatic Processes</u> Lab, answer <u>Adiabatic Processes- Problems- Part I (SI Units)</u>- Questions 1 – 4:

1a. _____	b. _____	c._____
2a. _____	b. _____	
3a. _____	b. _____	
4a. _____	b. _____	

Lab 8a

HUMIDITY

Objective:	To study the relationship between the water vapor content of the air, temperature, and relative humidity.
Materials:	Sling Psychrometer (optional).
Reference:	Hess, Darrel. *McKnight's Physical Geography;* 10th ed.; chapter, "Atmospheric Moisture"; sections, "Measures of Humidity"; and "Appendix: Meteorological Tables."

HUMIDITY

In order to understand cloud formation and precipitation, we must begin by studying water vapor in the atmosphere. There are several ways to describe the **humidity**—the amount of **water vapor** in the air—but two are important for us here.

Mixing Ratio: The **mixing ratio** describes the actual amount of water vapor in the air. The mixing ratio is expressed as the mass ("weight") of water vapor in a given mass of dry air, described in grams of water vapor per kilogram of air (g/kg).

In addition to the mixing ratio, there are other ways to describe the actual amount of water vapor in the air. For example, the **specific humidity** is similar to the mixing ratio, except that it describes the number of grams of water vapor per kilogram of air, including water vapor. The **absolute humidity** describes the mass of water vapor in a given volume of air, expressed in grams of water vapor per cubic meter of air (g/m^3).

In many cases, the mixing ratio is more useful to meteorologists than the absolute humidity since the mixing ratio does not change as the volume of air changes (as happens when air rises). As a very rough comparison, at sea level one cubic meter of air at room temperature has a mass of about 1.4 kilograms.

Relative Humidity: **Relative humidity** does not describe the actual amount of water vapor in the air. Rather, it is a ratio that compares the actual amount of water vapor in the air (the mixing ratio) to the maximum amount of water vapor that can be in the air at a given temperature—also called the **capacity**:

$$\text{Relative Humidity} = \frac{\text{Actual water vapor content}}{\text{Water vapor capacity}}$$

The relative humidity (RH) expresses this degree of **saturation** as a percentage. For example, 50% RH means that the air contains half of the water vapor necessary for saturation; 75% RH means that the air has three-quarters of the water vapor necessary for saturation; 100% RH means that the air is saturated. When air is saturated, **condensation**, and therefore cloud formation, can take place.

The water vapor capacity of air at a given temperature is also called the **saturation mixing ratio**, since it is the mixing ratio of a saturated parcel of air. The water vapor capacity of air depends

From Exercise 13 of *Physical Geography Laboratory Manual,* Tenth Edition, Darrel Hess. Copyright © 2011 by Pearson Education, Inc. Published by Pearson Prentice Hall. All rights reserved.

Temperature		Saturation Mixing Ratio ("capacity") g/kg
°F	°C	
15°F	−9.4°C	1.9
20°F	−6.7°C	2.2
25°F	−3.9°C	2.8
30°F	−1.1°C	3.5
35°F	1.7°C	4.3
40°F	4.4°C	5.2
45°F	7.2°C	6.2
50°F	10.0°C	7.6
55°F	12.8°C	9.3
60°F	15.6°C	11.1
65°F	18.3°C	13.2
70°F	21.1°C	15.6
75°F	23.9°C	18.8
80°F	26.7°C	22.3
85°F	29.4°C	26.2
90°F	32.2°C	30.7
95°F	35.0°C	36.5
100°F	37.8°C	43.0

Figure 1: Approximate saturation mixing ratios in g/kg at various temperatures (°F and °C). (Note: at temperatures below freezing over ice, the saturation mixing ratios will be slightly lower than indicated here.)

almost entirely on temperature. As temperature increases, the water vapor capacity of the air also increases. Figure 1 shows the capacity (the saturation mixing ratio) of air at different temperatures.

In popular terms, it is said that warm air can "hold" more water vapor than cold air, but this is somewhat misleading. The air doesn't actually hold water vapor as if it were a sponge. Water vapor is simply one of the gaseous components of the atmosphere—the water vapor capacity of the air is determined by the temperature, which determines the rate of vaporization of water.

CALCULATING RELATIVE HUMIDITY

In this exercise, we will use the mixing ratio to describe the actual water vapor content of the air, and the saturation mixing ratio to describe the water vapor capacity of the air. Relative humidity is calculated with a simple formula:

$$RH = \frac{Mixing\ Ratio}{Saturation\ Mixing\ Ratio} \times 100$$

For example, if the mixing ratio is 13.5 g/kg and the saturation mixing ratio is 22.5 g/kg, the relative humidity is:

$$\frac{13.5 \text{ g/kg}}{22.5 \text{ g/kg}} \times 100 = 60\% \text{ RH}$$

The key to understanding relative humidity is recognizing the relationship between temperature and the water vapor capacity of air. When temperature changes, relative humidity changes. For example, as the temperature of the air decreases, water vapor capacity decreases. This means that as the temperature decreases, the relative humidity increases. If a parcel of air is cooled enough, its mixing ratio will match its capacity and the air will be saturated (100% relative humidity) and condensation can take place. If cooling continues after a parcel of air has become saturated, the relative humidity will tend to remain at 100%—as the capacity continues to decrease, more and more water vapor will condense out of the air, keeping the mixing ratio of the parcel the same as its capacity and so maintaining 100% relative humidity.[1]

THE DEW POINT TEMPERATURE

The temperature at which a parcel of air reaches 100% relative humidity is called the **dew point** (or dew point temperature). This is the temperature at which the water vapor capacity of the air (the saturation mixing ratio) is the same as the actual water vapor content of the air (the mixing ratio). Notice that the dew point is determined by the mixing ratio. For example, the dew point of a parcel of air with a mixing ratio of 11.1 g/kg is always 15.6°C (60°F). Conversely, a parcel of air with a dew point of 15.6°C has a mixing ratio of 11.1 g/kg. This relationship lets us use the table of saturation mixing ratios (Figure 1) in several ways:

(1)   If the temperature is known, you can determine the water vapor capacity of the air: read the "Saturation Mixing Ratio" directly from the table.

(2)   If the mixing ratio is known, you can determine the dew point temperature of the air: find the value of the mixing ratio in the "Saturation Mixing Ratio" column—the dew point is the "Temperature" (remember, at the dew point temperature the air is at 100% RH, so the mixing ratio and the saturation mixing ratio are the same).

(3)   If the dew point temperature is known, you can determine the mixing ratio of the air: find the value of the dew point in the "Temperature" column—the mixing ratio is the same as the "Saturation Mixing Ratio" (again, remember that at the dew point temperature, the mixing ratio, and saturation mixing ratio are the same).

THE SLING PSYCHROMETER

One common method of determining relative humidity is with an instrument called a **sling psychrometer**. The sling psychrometer consists of two thermometers mounted next to each other. One of the thermometers is an ordinary one that is used to measure the air temperature and is called

---

[1]It is possible for air have a relative humidity greater than 100% without condensation taking place. Such air is called "supersaturated." We make the simplifying assumption that condensation begins when air reaches 100% relative humidity.

the **dry-bulb thermometer**. The bulb of the other thermometer is wrapped in cloth that is saturated with room-temperature distilled water before use and is called the **wet-bulb thermometer**.

The instrument is called a "sling" psychrometer since it has a handle that is used to whirl the apparatus around for several minutes. The whirling of the sling psychrometer promotes the evaporation of water from the wet-bulb thermometer. Since evaporation is a cooling process, the temperature of the wet-bulb will decrease. If the air is dry, there will be rapid evaporation and greater cooling, and the temperature of the wet-bulb thermometer will decline more than if the air is relatively moist. In other words, if the temperature of the wet-bulb thermometer is much lower than that of the dry-bulb thermometer, the relatively humidity is low. If the temperature of the wet-bulb thermometer is only slightly lower than that of the dry-bulb thermometer, the relatively humidity is high. If there is no difference in temperature, the air is saturated, since no net evaporation took place.

After using the sling psychrometer, the relative humidity is determined with a table, shown in Figure 2 (°C) or Figure 4 (°F). The dry-bulb temperature is the "Air Temperature" (read along the left side of the chart). The "Depression of Wet-Bulb Thermometer" is the difference (in degrees) between the dry-bulb and wet-bulb temperature. Match the "Air Temperature" with the appropriate wet-bulb depression to find the relative humidity, expressed as a percentage.

For example, after spinning the psychrometer, if the dry-bulb temperature is 20°C, and the wet-bulb temperature is 14°C, the wet-bulb depression is 6°C. From the chart in Figure 2, under an air temperature of 20° and a depression of 6°, you read that the relative humidity is 51 percent.

A sling psychrometer can also be used to determine the temperature of the dew point. The table in Figure 3 (°C) or Figure 5 (°F) provides the dew points for various "Dry-Bulb" and "Depression of the Wet-Bulb" readings from a psychrometer. For example, with an air temperature of 20°C and a wet-bulb depression of 6°, the temperature of the dew point is 10°C.

Tips on Using Sling Psychrometers: After moistening the wet bulb (and being careful not to spill any water on the dry bulb), whirl around the sling psychrometer for about one or two minutes. Stop briefly to check the wet-bulb temperature and begin whirling again. After another minute, stop again to check the wet-bulb temperature. If the temperature is the same as when you first checked, the wet-bulb temperature has stabilized and you can use the reading; if the temperature has continued to decrease, whirl again until the wet-bulb temperature stabilizes. Be sure that the wet bulb has not completely dried out in the process—if so, moisten again and take a new set of readings.

Air Temp. °C	Depression of Wet-Bulb Thermometer (°C)																					
	1	2	3	4	5	6	7	8	9	10	11	12	13	14	15	16	17	18	19	20	21	22
-4	77	54	32	11																		
-2	79	58	37	20	1																	
0	81	63	45	28	11					Relative Humidity (%)												
2	83	67	51	36	20	6																
4	85	70	56	42	27	14																
6	86	72	59	46	35	22	10	0														
8	87	74	62	51	39	28	17	6														
10	88	76	65	54	43	33	24	13	4													
12	88	78	67	57	48	38	28	19	10	2												
14	89	79	69	60	50	41	33	25	16	8	1											
16	90	80	71	62	54	45	37	29	21	14	7	1										
18	91	81	72	64	56	48	40	33	26	19	12	6	0									
20	91	82	74	66	58	51	44	36	30	23	17	11	5									
22	92	83	75	68	60	53	46	40	33	27	21	15	10	4	0							
24	92	84	76	69	62	55	49	42	36	30	25	20	14	9	4	0						
26	92	85	77	70	64	57	51	45	39	34	28	23	18	13	9	5						
28	93	86	78	71	65	59	53	45	42	36	31	26	21	17	12	8	4					
30	93	86	79	72	66	61	55	49	44	39	34	29	25	20	16	12	8	4				
32	93	86	80	73	68	62	56	51	46	41	36	32	27	22	19	14	11	8	4			
34	93	86	81	74	69	63	58	52	48	43	38	34	30	26	22	18	14	11	8	5		
36	94	87	81	75	69	64	59	54	50	44	40	36	32	28	24	21	17	13	10	7	4	
38	94	87	82	76	70	66	60	55	51	46	42	38	34	30	26	23	20	16	13	10	7	5

Figure 2: Relative Humidity Psychrometer Tables (°C).

Air Temp. °C	Depression of Wet-Bulb Thermometer (°C)																					
	1	2	3	4	5	6	7	8	9	10	11	12	13	14	15	16	17	18	19	20	21	22
-4	-7	-17	-22	-29																		
-2	-5	-8	-13	-20																		
0	-3	-6	-9	-15	-24					Dew Point (°C)												
2	-1	-3	-6	-11	-17																	
4	1	-1	-4	-7	-11	-19																
6	4	1	-1	-4	-7	-13	-21															
8	6	3	1	-2	-5	-9	-14															
10	8	6	4	1	-2	-5	-9	-14	-28													
12	10	8	6	4	1	-2	-5	-9	-16													
14	12	11	9	6	4	1	-2	-5	-10	-17												
16	14	13	11	9	7	4	1	-1	-6	-10	-17											
18	16	15	13	11	9	7	4	2	-2	-5	-10	-19										
20	19	17	15	14	12	10	7	4	2	-2	-5	-10	-19									
22	21	19	17	16	14	12	10	8	5	3	-1	-5	-10	-19								
24	23	21	20	18	16	14	12	10	8	6	2	-1	-5	-10	-18							
26	25	23	22	20	18	17	15	13	11	9	6	3	0	-4	-9	-18						
28	27	25	24	22	21	19	17	16	14	11	9	7	4	1	-3	-9	-16					
30	29	27	26	24	23	21	19	18	16	14	12	10	8	5	1	-2	-8	-15				
32	31	29	28	27	25	24	22	21	19	17	15	13	11	8	5	2	-2	-7	-14			
34	33	31	30	29	27	26	24	23	21	20	18	16	14	12	9	6	3	-1	-5	-12	-29	
36	35	33	32	31	29	28	27	25	24	22	20	19	17	15	13	10	7	4	0	-4	-10	
38	37	35	34	33	32	30	29	28	26	25	23	21	19	17	15	13	11	8	5	1	-3	-9

Figure 3: Dew Point Psychrometer Tables (°C).

Air Temp. °F	Depression of Wet-Bulb Thermometer (°F)																													
	1	2	3	4	5	6	7	8	9	10	11	12	13	14	15	16	17	18	19	20	21	22	23	24	25	26	27	28	29	30
0	67	33	1																											
5	73	46	20																											
10	78	56	34	13	15																									
15	82	64	46	29	11																									
20	85	70	55	40	26	12																								
25	87	74	62	49	37	25	13	1																						
30	89	78	67	56	46	36	26	16	6							Relative Humidity (%)														
35	91	81	72	63	54	45	36	27	19	10	2																			
40	92	83	75	68	60	52	45	37	29	22	15	7																		
45	93	86	78	71	64	57	51	44	38	31	25	18	12	6																
50	93	87	74	67	61	55	49	43	38	32	27	21	16	10	5															
55	94	88	82	76	70	65	59	54	49	43	38	33	28	23	19	11	9	5												
60	94	89	83	78	73	68	63	58	53	48	43	39	34	30	26	21	17	13	9	5	1									
65	95	90	85	80	75	70	66	61	56	52	48	44	39	35	31	27	24	20	16	12	9	5	2							
70	95	90	86	81	77	72	68	64	59	55	51	48	44	40	36	33	29	25	22	19	15	12	9	6	3					
75	96	91	86	82	78	74	70	66	62	58	54	51	47	44	40	37	34	30	27	24	21	18	15	12	9	7	4	1		
80	96	91	87	83	79	75	72	68	64	61	57	54	50	47	44	41	38	35	32	29	26	23	20	18	15	12	10	7	5	3
85	96	92	88	84	81	77	73	70	66	63	59	57	53	50	47	44	41	38	36	33	30	27	25	22	20	17	15	13	10	8
90	96	92	89	85	81	78	74	71	68	65	61	58	55	52	49	47	44	41	39	36	34	31	29	26	24	22	19	17	15	13
95	96	93	89	86	82	79	76	73	69	66	63	61	58	55	52	50	47	44	42	39	37	34	32	30	28	25	23	21	19	17
100	96	93	89	86	83	80	77	73	70	68	65	62	59	56	54	51	49	46	44	41	39	37	35	33	30	28	26	24	22	21
105	97	93	90	87	84	81	78	75	72	69	66	64	61	58	56	53	51	49	46	44	42	40	38	36	34	32	30	28	26	24

Figure 4: Relative Humidity Psychrometer Tables (°F).

Air Temp. °F	Depression of Wet-Bulb Thermometer (°F)																													
	1	2	3	4	5	6	7	8	9	10	11	12	13	14	15	16	17	18	19	20	21	22	23	24	25	26	27	28	29	30
0	-7	-20																												
5	-1	-9	-24																											
10	5	-2	-10	-27																										
15	11	6	0	-9	-26																									
20	16	12	8	2	-7	-21																								
25	22	19	15	10	5	-3	-15	-51																						
30	27	25	21	18	14	8	2	-7	-25							Dew Point (°F)														
35	33	30	28	25	21	17	13	7	0	-11	-41																			
40	38	35	33	30	28	25	21	18	13	7	-1	-14																		
45	43	41	38	36	34	31	28	25	22	18	13	7	-1	-14																
50	48	46	44	42	40	37	34	32	29	26	22	18	13	8	0	-13														
55	53	51	50	48	45	43	41	38	36	33	30	27	24	20	15	9	1	-12	-59											
60	58	57	55	53	51	49	47	45	43	40	38	35	32	29	25	21	17	11	4	-8	-36									
65	63	62	60	59	57	55	53	51	49	47	45	42	40	37	34	31	27	24	19	14	7	-3	-22							
70	69	67	65	64	62	61	59	57	55	53	51	49	47	44	42	39	36	33	30	26	22	17	11	2	-11					
75	74	72	71	69	68	66	64	63	61	59	57	55	54	51	49	47	44	42	39	36	32	29	25	21	15	8	-2	-23		
80	79	77	76	74	73	72	70	68	67	65	63	62	60	58	56	54	52	50	47	44	42	39	36	32	28	24	20	13	6	-7
85	84	82	81	80	78	77	75	74	72	71	69	68	66	64	62	61	59	57	54	52	50	48	45	42	39	36	32	28	24	19
90	89	87	86	85	83	82	81	79	78	76	75	73	72	70	69	67	65	63	61	59	57	55	53	51	48	45	43	39	36	32
95	94	93	91	90	89	87	86	85	83	82	80	79	78	76	74	73	71	70	68	66	64	62	60	58	56	54	52	49	46	43
100	99	98	96	95	94	93	91	90	89	87	86	85	83	82	80	79	77	76	74	72	71	69	67	65	63	61	59	57	55	52
105	104	103	101	100	99	98	96	95	94	93	91	90	89	87	86	84	83	82	80	78	77	75	74	72	70	68	67	65	63	61

Figure 5: Dew Point Psychrometer Tables (°F).

Name _____   Section _____

PROBLEMS—PART I *(S.I. Units)*

1. Complete the following chart (round off relative humidity to the nearest percent):

	Mixing Ratio (g/kg)	Air Temperature (°C)	Saturation Mixing Ratio (g/kg)	Relative Humidity (%)
(a)	2.8	−1.1°C		
(b)	2.8	32.2°C		
(c)	11.1		13.2	
(d)	22.3		36.5	

2. The air inside a room is at a temperature of 18.3°C and has a mixing ratio of 5.2 g/kg:

   (a) What is the relative humidity?   _____ %

   (b) What is the dew point?   _____ °C

   (c) If the mixing ratio remains the same, but the temperature of
        the room increases to 26.7°C, what is the new relative humidity?   _____ %

3. The air inside a room is at a temperature of 35°C and has a mixing ratio of 7.6 g/kg:

   (a) What is the relative humidity?   _____ %

   (b) What is the dew point?   _____ °C

   (c) If the room temperature decreases by 5°C per hour, how many
        hours will it take for the air to reach saturation?   _____ hours

   (d) After reaching saturation, if the temperature of the room
        continues to decrease for one more hour, approximately how
        many grams of water vapor (per kg of air) will have had to
        condense out of the air to maintain a relative humidity of 100%?   _____ g/kg

Name _____   Section _____

PROBLEMS—PART II *(S.I. Units)*

Using the psychrometer tables (Figures 2 and 3) and the table of saturation mixing ratios (Figure 1), answer the following questions about determining relative humidity with a sling psychrometer:

1. If the dry-bulb temperature is 32°C, and the wet-bulb temperature is 26°C:

    (a) What is the relative humidity?   _____ %

    (b) What is the dew point?   _____ °C

    (c) What is the mixing ratio?
         (Estimate from Figure 1)   _____ g/kg

2. If the dry-bulb temperature is 14°C, and the wet-bulb temperature is 12°C:

    (a) What is the relative humidity?   _____ %

    (b) What is the dew point?   _____ °C

    (c) What is the mixing ratio?
         (Estimate from Figure 1)   _____ g/kg

OPTIONAL:

3. If a sling psychrometer is available in class, determine the following both indoors (in the classroom) and outdoors. Be sure to include the correct units (%, g/kg, etc.) in each answer.

	Indoors	Outdoors
Dry-Bulb Temperature		
Wet-Bulb Temperature		
Depression of Wet-Bulb Thermometer		
Relative Humidity		
Dew Point		
Mixing Ratio (Estimate from Figure 1)		

Humidity

Name _____   Section _____

PROBLEMS—PART III *(English Units)*

1. Complete the following chart (round off relative humidity to the nearest percent):

	Mixing Ratio (g/kg)	Air Temperature (°F)	Saturation Mixing Ratio (g/kg)	Relative Humidity (%)
(a)	2.8	30°F		
(b)	2.8	90°F		
(c)	11.1		13.2	
(d)	22.3		36.5	

2. The air inside a room is at a temperature of 65°F and has a mixing ratio of 5.2 g/kg:

   (a) What is the relative humidity?   _____ %

   (b) What is the dew point?   _____ °F

   (c) If the mixing ratio remains the same, but the temperature of
        the room increases to 80°F, what is the new relative humidity?   _____ %

3. The air inside a room is at a temperature of 70°F and has a mixing ratio of 7.6 g/kg:

   (a) What is the relative humidity?   _____ %

   (b) What is the dew point?   _____ °F

   (c) If the room temperature decreases by 10°F per hour, how many
        hours will it take for the air to reach saturation?   _____ hours

   (d) After reaching saturation, if the temperature of the room
        continues to decrease for one more hour, how many grams
        of water vapor (per kg of air) will have had to condense
        out of the air to maintain a relative humidity of 100%?   _____ g/kg

Name _____   Section _____

PROBLEMS—PART IV *(English Units)*

Using the psychrometer tables (Figures 4 and 5) and the table of saturation mixing ratios (Figure 1), answer the following questions about determining relative humidity with a sling psychrometer:

1. If the dry-bulb temperature is 90°F, and the wet-bulb temperature is 79°F:

    (a)   What is the relative humidity?   _____ %

    (b)   What is the dew point?   _____ °F

    (c)   What is the mixing ratio?   _____ g/kg

2. If the dry-bulb temperature is 55°F, and the wet-bulb temperature is 52°F:

    (a)   What is the relative humidity?   _____ %

    (b)   What is the dew point?   _____ °F

    (c)   What is the mixing ratio?   _____ g/kg

OPTIONAL:

3. If a sling psychrometer is available in class, determine the following both indoors (in the classroom) and outdoors. Be sure to include the correct units (%, g/kg, etc.) in each answer.

	Indoors	Outdoors
Dry-Bulb Temperature		
Wet-Bulb Temperature		
Depression of Wet-Bulb Thermometer		
Relative Humidity		
Dew Point		
Mixing Ratio (Estimate from Figure 1)		

Lab 8b

ADIABATIC PROCESSES

Objective:	To study adiabatic processes in the atmosphere, and to calculate temperature and humidity changes in parcels of moving air.
Reference:	Hess, Darrel. *McKnight's Physical Geography*; 10th ed.; chapter, "Atmospheric Moisture"; section, "Adiabatic Processes."

ADIABATIC PROCESSES

As the temperature of a parcel of air decreases, the relative humidity increases. When a parcel of air has cooled to the **dew point temperature**, it becomes saturated and **condensation** can take place. The most common way that a parcel of air is cooled enough to form clouds and precipitation is through **adiabatic cooling**.

As a parcel of air rises, it comes under lower pressure and expands. As the air expands, it cools adiabatically ("adiabatic" means without the gain or loss of heat). Rising air always cools adiabatically. Conversely, as air descends, it comes under higher pressure and compresses. As the air compresses, it warms adiabatically. Descending air always warms adiabatically.

If a parcel of rising air is unsaturated (the relative humidity is less than 100%) it will cool at the **dry adiabatic rate** (DAR; also called the "dry adiabatic lapse rate") of about 10°C per 1000 meters (5.5°F per 1000 feet). As the air rises and cools, its relative humidity increases. At some point, the parcel of air will have cooled enough to reach its dew point. The elevation at which a parcel of air reaches its dew point temperature is called the **lifting condensation level** (LCL), and at this point, condensation and cloud formation can begin.

If a parcel of air keeps rising while condensation is taking place, the air will continue to cool adiabatically, but at a slower rate. Saturated air cools at the **saturated adiabatic rate** (SAR; also called the "wet" or "saturated adiabatic lapse rate") of about 6°C per 1000 meters (3.3°F per 1000 feet). The SAR varies, however, and the rate of cooling may be as slow as 4°C per 1000 meters (2.0°F per 1000 feet).

Rising saturated air cools more slowly than rising unsaturated air because of the release of **latent heat** during condensation. **Evaporation** is, in effect, a cooling process since heat is stored when water changes from liquid to gas. When the water vapor condenses back to liquid water, this heat is released. As saturated air rises, it expands and cools adiabatically, but the latent heat released during condensation counteracts some of this cooling.

Figure 1 shows the temperature changes in a parcel of air as it rises up and over a 4000-meter-high mountain. In this hypothetical example, the dew point of the parcel is 5°C and the lifting condensation level is 2000 meters.

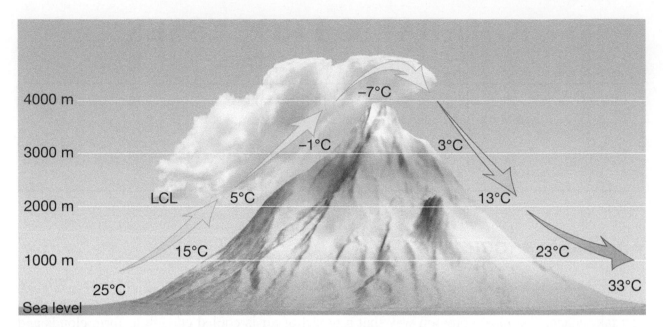

Figure 1: Temperature changes in a hypothetical parcel of air passing over a 4000-meter-high mountain (assuming no evaporation as the air descends down the lee side of the mountain). The lifting condensation level of the parcel is 2000 meters, the dry adiabatic rate is 10°C/1000 m, and the saturated adiabatic rate is 6°C/1000 m. Notice that because of the release of latent heat during condensation on the windward side of the mountain, by the time the air has descended back down to sea level on the leeward side, it is warmer than before it started up the windward side. (From Hess, *McKnight's Physical Geography*, 10th ed.)

Notice that the air descending down the lee side of the mountain warms at the DAR. Descending air generally warms at the DAR, because as air warms, its capacity increases and so it cannot be saturated.[1]

Adiabatic temperature changes may lead to changes in both the relative humidity and the **water vapor** content—the **mixing ratio**—of a parcel of air. For example, as unsaturated air rises or descends (and the temperature decreases or increases), its capacity changes. Because of this, the relative humidity of the parcel will change.

On the other hand, as rising saturated air cools adiabatically, the relative humidity of the parcel generally remains at about 100% as condensation takes place. As the air continues to rise and water vapor is lost through condensation, the water vapor content (the mixing ratio) of the parcel will change.

---

[1]Although descending air usually warms at the dry adiabatic rate, there is a circumstance when this may not be the case. If air descends through a cloud, some water droplets may evaporate and the evaporative cooling will counteract some of the adiabatic warming. As a result, such descending air can warm at a rate very close to the saturated adiabatic rate. As soon as evaporation of water droplets ceases, this descending air will warm at the dry adiabatic rate as usual.

Name _____   Section _____

PROBLEMS—PART I *(S.I. Units)*

Assume that a parcel of air is forced to rise up and over a 4000-meter-high mountain (shown below). The initial temperature of the parcel at sea level is 30°C, and the lifting condensation level (LCL) of the parcel is 2000 meters. The DAR is 10°C/1000 m and the SAR is 6°C/1000 m. Assume that condensation begins at 100% relative humidity and that no evaporation takes place as the parcel descends.

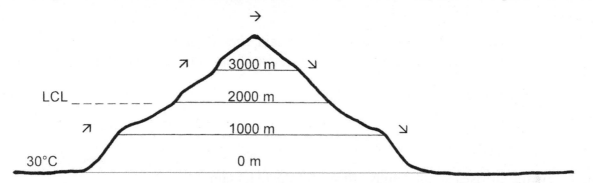

1. Calculate the temperature of the parcel at the following elevations as it rises up the windward side of the mountain:

   (a) 1000 m _____ °C   (b) 2000 m _____ °C   (c) 4000 m _____ °C

2. (a) After the parcel of air has descended down the lee side of the mountain to sea level, what is the temperature of the parcel?   _____ °C

   (b) Why is the parcel now warmer than it was at sea level on the windward side (what is the source of the heat energy)?

3. (a) On the windward side of the mountain, is the relative humidity of the parcel increasing or decreasing as it rises from sea level to 2000 meters?   _____

   (b) Why?

4. (a) On the lee side of the mountain, is the relative humidity of the parcel increasing or decreasing as it descends from 4000 meters to sea level?   _____

   (b) Why?

Name _____   Section _____

PROBLEMS—PART II *(S.I. Units)*

Answer the following questions after completing the problems in Part I. You will also need to refer to the chart of Saturation Mixing Ratios in Figure A; interpolate from the chart as needed. Assume that condensation begins at 100% relative humidity and that no evaporation takes place as the parcel descends.

5. (a) On the windward side of the mountain, should the relative
         humidity of the parcel change as it rises from 2000 m to 4000 m? _____

    (b) Why?

6. As the air rises up the windward side of the mountain:

    (a) What is the capacity (saturation mixing ratio) of the
         rising air at 2000 meters?   _____ g/kg

    (b) What is the capacity of the air at 4000 meters?   _____ g/kg

7. What is the capacity of the air after it has descended back down to
    sea level on the lee side of the mountain?   _____ g/kg

8. (a) Assuming that *no* water vapor is added as the parcel descends
         down the lee side of the mountain to sea level, is the water vapor
         content (the mixing ratio) of the parcel higher or lower than
         before it began to rise over the mountain?   _____

    (b) Why?

    (c) What is the lifting condensation level of this parcel now?   _____ meters

Name _____   Section _____

PROBLEMS—PART III *(English Units)*

Assume that a parcel of air is forced to rise up and over a 6000-foot-high mountain (shown below). The initial temperature of the parcel at sea level is 76.5°F, and the lifting condensation level (LCL) of the parcel is 3000 feet. The DAR is 5.5°F/1000' and the SAR is 3.3°F/1000'. Assume that condensation begins at 100% relative humidity and that no evaporation takes place as the parcel descends. Indicate calculated temperatures to one decimal place.

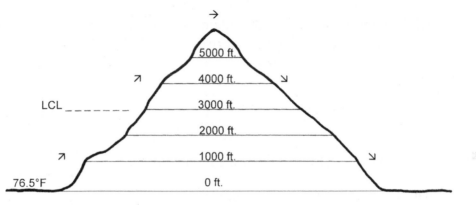

1. Calculate the temperature of the parcel at the following elevations as it rises up the windward side of the mountain:

    (a) 1000' _____ °F   (b) 3000' _____ °F   (c) 6000' _____ °F

2. (a) After the parcel of air has descended down the lee side of the
         mountain to sea level, what is the temperature of the parcel?   _____ °F

    (b) Why is the parcel now warmer than it was at sea level on the windward side (what
         is the source of the heat energy)?

3. (a) On the windward side of the mountain, is the relative humidity
         of the parcel increasing or decreasing as it rises from sea level
         to 3000 feet?   _____

    (b) Why?

4. (a) On the lee side of the mountain, is the relative humidity
         of the parcel increasing or decreasing as it descends from
         6000 feet to sea level?   _____

    (b) Why?

Name _____   Section _____

PROBLEMS—PART IV *(English Units)*

Answer the following questions after completing the problems in Part III. You will also need to refer to the chart of Saturation Mixing Ratios in Figure A; interpolate from the chart as needed. Assume that condensation begins at 100% relative humidity and that no evaporation takes place as the parcel descends.

5. (a) On the windward side of the mountain, should the relative humidity of the parcel change as it rises from 3000' to 6000'?   _____

    (b) Why?

6. As the air rises up the windward side of the mountain:

    (a) What is the capacity (saturation mixing ratio) of the rising air at 3000 feet?   _____ g/kg

    (b) What is the capacity of the air at 6000 feet?   _____ g/kg

7. What is the capacity of the air after it has descended back down to sea level on the lee side of the mountain?   _____ g/kg

8. (a) Assuming that *no* water vapor is added as the parcel descends down the lee side of the mountain to sea level, is the water vapor content (the mixing ratio) of the parcel higher or lower than before it began to rise over the mountain?   _____

    (b) Why?

    (c) What is the lifting condensation level of this parcel now?   _____ feet

Temperature		Saturation Mixing Ratio ("capacity") g/kg
°F	°C	
15°F	−9.4°C	1.9
20°F	−6.7°C	2.2
25°F	−3.9°C	2.8
30°F	−1.1°C	3.5
35°F	1.7°C	4.3
40°F	4.4°C	5.2
45°F	7.2°C	6.2
50°F	10.0°C	7.6
55°F	12.8°C	9.3
60°F	15.6°C	11.1
65°F	18.3°C	13.2
70°F	21.1°C	15.6
75°F	23.9°C	18.8
80°F	26.7°C	22.3
85°F	29.4°C	26.2
90°F	32.2°C	30.7
95°F	35.0°C	36.5
100°F	37.8°C	43.0

Figure A: Approximate saturation mixing ratios in g/kg at various temperatures (°F and °C). (Note: at temperatures below freezing over ice, the saturation mixing ratios will be slightly lower than indicated here.)

Geography 111: Physical Geography Lab
Lab Nine: Weather Maps and Midlatitude Cyclones

This lab is designed to help you identify the air masses that affect North America and to recognize the fronts associated with the interaction among these air masses. In addition, you will learn how to read station model information and to apply this knowledge to hypothetical and real weather maps. While using the weather maps you will be describing the atmospheric changes that occur within a midlatitude cyclone.

Materials:
Weather map (provided)   Red, blue and purple pencils

Objectives:
- Identify air masses that affect North America
- Identify low pressure and high pressure on a weather map
- Identify cold fronts and warm fronts on a weather map
- Read a weather station model to determine the weather at a given location.
- Read a weather map to determine how the weather is changing at various points in a midlatitude cyclone.

Part 1: Air Masses
Midlatitude cyclones are the result of unlike air masses meeting. There a several air masses that affect North America, each with different temperature and moisture characteristics. Air masses get their temperature and moisture characteristics based on their source regions. For example, air masses that originate over water are characterized as moist.

Assignment:
A.   Classify the moisture characteristics (dry or moist) for the following locations:

   a. Continental (c)   _____

   b. Maritime   (m)   _____

   Classify the temperature characteristics (cool or warm) for the following locations:

   c. Polar (P)   _____

   d. Tropical (T)   _____

B.   Fill in the chart with air mass characteristics.

Air Mass	Characteristics
cP	
mP	
cT	
mT	

C.   Identify the source regions for the air masses that affect North America on the map provided (Attachment A).
         a. Outline the air mass based on temperature (warm = red and cool = blue)

Part 2: Fronts

When two unlike air masses meet, a low pressure cell forms due to the mixing. In the northern hemisphere, the wind will circulate in a counterclockwise direction around the low pressure cell. As a result, cold air moves into an area containing warm air and warm air will move into an area containing cold air. This results in the development of a cold and warm front.

Assignment:

A. Draw the symbols for the following fronts using conventional colors (blue, red and purple)

Cold Front	**Warm Front**
Stationary Front	**Occluded Front**

Part 3: Weather Station Model

Weather information is collected at many stations around the world. That data is then plotted on weather maps in a standard format and code. This format is called a station model. Appendix I, Figure I-1 at the end of this lab manual is an example of the standard station model. In addition, we will look at wind speed and direction which is not displayed on this sample model.

Appendix I, Figure I-2 at the end of this lab manual is the same station model, but the codes have been replaced by sample data. When using the station model, it is important to understand data is placed in a specific location relative to the circle at the center. You need to understand where this data is in relation to the model in order to properly read the model.

Assignment:

Looking at the station model for San Francisco, complete the table:

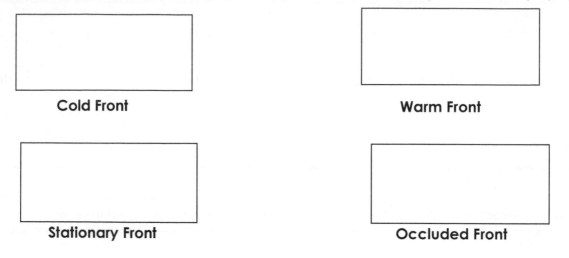

Temperature		°F
Dewpoint Temperature		°F
Pressure* You must include the initial 9 or 10 in your answer		mb
Pressure Change		mb
Wind Speed		knots
Wind Direction		
Total Amount of Clouds		

Part 4: Weather Maps I

A. Draw in the type of front that is shown on the hypothetical weather map below. Use the appropriate weather map symbol for the front.

Hint: Look at the station model information for temperature and wind direction.

Note: This is also found in the following Midlatitude Cyclone lab – Problems – Part II- Question 1- Weather Map B.

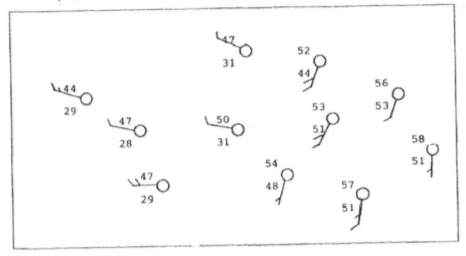

B. Midlatitude Cyclones-- Using this hypothetical weather map (located in the southeastern United States) answer the following questions.

Note: This map is also found in the following Midlatitude Cyclone lab – Problems – Part I.

Weather Map:

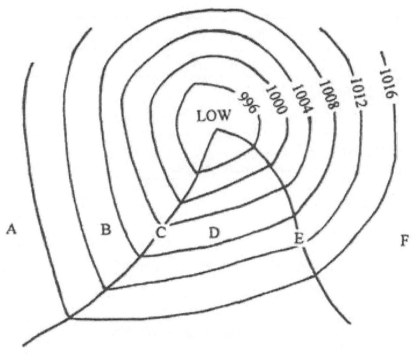

1. Label the following features:
   a. Cold front (use standard weather map symbols)
   b. Warm front (use standard weather map symbols)
   c. Cold air section of midlatitude cyclone
   d. Warm air section of midlatitude cyclone
   e. Flow of wind circulation around midlatitude cyclone. Use arrows to denote wind flow patterns.

Part 5: Weather Maps II

A.	Using the surface weather map for February 9, 1962, answer the following questions. Don't forget to write the proper units of measurement.

	Mobile, Alabama	Lake Charles, Louisiana	Fort Worth, Texas	Dodge City, Kansas	Phoenix, Arizona	Winnipeg, Canada
Temperature						
Dewpoint Temperature						
Pressure* You must include the initial 9 or 10 in your answer						
Pressure Change						
Wind Speed						
Wind Direction					N/A	
Total Amount of Clouds						

B.	Answer the following questions:

1. Describe the following weather conditions in *Mobile, Alabama*-

	a. What explains the change in pressure?

	b. What will happen to the air pressure after the cold front passes?

	c. Mobile lies in which section of the middle latitude cyclone? Warm or Cold

	d. What type of air mass is present?		cA		mT		mP		cT

	e. What is the relative humidity at Mobile? _____%

2. Describe the following weather conditions in *Lake Charles, Louisiana*.

    a. Is the air pressure rising or falling in Lake Charles, Louisiana?

    b. What kind of weather do you think Lake Charles will experience in the next day or so?

3. Describe the following weather conditions in *Dodge City, Kansas*.

    a. Dodge City lies in which section of the middle latitude cyclone? Warm or Cold

    b. What kind of air mass is present at Dodge City?   cA   mT   mP   cT

4. Which city Phoenix or Hudson Bay has more water vapor in the air? Hint: Think about the Dew Point

Temperature, what information does it give regarding water vapor?

5. Between which two cities on the map (not in the table above) has the cold front overtaken the warm front?

    a. What is the name for this type of a front?

6. Where will the low pressure system be the next day? Hint: which direction is it moving?

7. Revisit the hypothetical weather map found in Part 4- Weather Maps I, Question B- Midlatitude Cyclones. Summarize the atmospheric conditions at Point B and Point D.

Atmospheric Conditions	Point D – Pre-Cold Front	Point B- Post-Cold Front
Temperature: Warm or Cold		
Pressure: Rising or Falling		
Winds: Northern or Southern		
Skies: Clear or Cloudy		

Attachment A: North American Air Masses

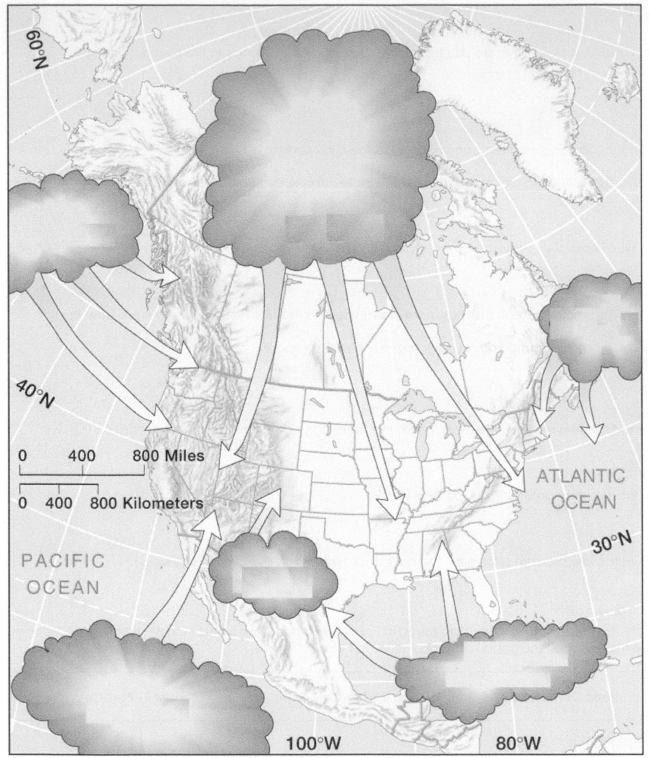

Lab 9a

MIDLATITUDE CYCLONES

Objective:	To study the pressure, wind, and temperature patterns of midlatitude cyclones.
Resources:	Internet access (optional).
Reference:	Hess, Darrel. *McKnight's Physical Geography*; 10th ed.; chapter, "Atmospheric Disturbances"; section, "Fronts" through "Midlatitude Cyclones."

THE MIDLATITUDE CYCLONE

The **midlatitude cyclone** is the most important storm of the midlatitudes. At the heart of a midlatitude cyclone is an area of low pressure, as much as 1600 kilometers (1000 miles) across.

The low pressure cell produces a converging counterclockwise wind flow that pulls together two unlike **air masses** (the wind flow is converging clockwise in the Southern Hemisphere). Relatively cool air from the high latitudes is brought together with relatively warm air from the subtropics. These unlike air masses do not mix readily. Instead, abrupt transition zones known as **fronts** develop between the air masses. At the surface, a mature midlatitude cyclone has a "cool sector" and a "warm sector," separated by a **cold front** (cold air advancing under the warm) and a **warm front** (warm air advancing over the cold).

Figure 1 shows a typical well-developed midlatitude cyclone in the Northern Hemisphere, mapped with **isobars**. The lowest pressure is at the heart of the storm, but a **trough** of low pressure extends down the length of the cold front as well. As the whole storm migrates eastward in the flow of the **westerlies** (left to right in this diagram), air converges counterclockwise into the low. The cold front typically advances faster than the storm itself and eventually catches up with the warm front. A cross section through the storm is shown in Figure 1b.

Figure 2 shows the life cycle of a midlatitude cyclone, beginning with the early development of the storm along the **polar front**, through maturity, and finally the process of **occlusion**, in which the cold front catches up with the warm front, lifting all of the warm air off the ground. After occlusion, the storm generally begins to lose strength and die.

The cross sections shown in Figure 2 help illustrate the reasons for the weather typically brought by these storms. Generally, the heaviest precipitation is associated with the cold front. The abrupt uplift of the warm air along the advancing, steeply sloping cold front causes the **adiabatic cooling** needed to produce clouds and precipitation. Because of the more gentle slope of the warm front, this region of the storm is usually associated with more widespread but less intense precipitation than the cold front.

FRONTS ON WEATHER MAPS

There are four common kinds of fronts. Cold fronts develop where the cold air is actively advancing under warm air. Warm fronts occur when the warm air is actively advancing over cold air. **Occluded fronts** develop when the cold front catches up with a warm front. **Stationary fronts** represent boundaries between unlike air masses, but neither air mass is actively advancing. Figure 3 shows the commonly used weather map symbols for these four kinds of fronts.

From Exercise 16 of *Physical Geography Laboratory Manual,* Tenth Edition, Darrel Hess. Copyright © 2011 by Pearson Education, Inc. Published by Pearson Prentice Hall. All rights reserved.

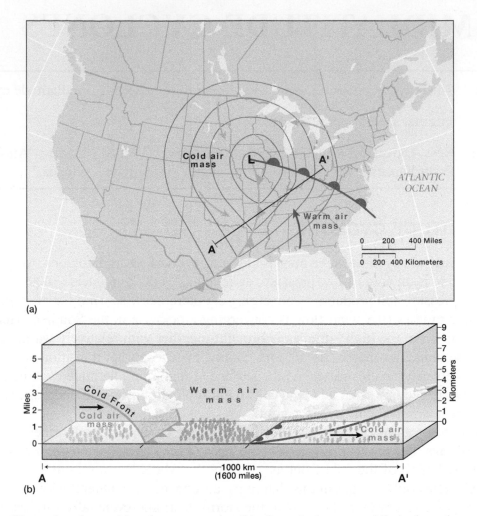

(a)

(b)

Figure 1: A map (a) and a cross section (b) of a typical mature midlatitude cyclone. Arrows in (b) indicate the direction of frontal movement. (From McKnight and Hess, *Physical Geography*, 9th ed.)

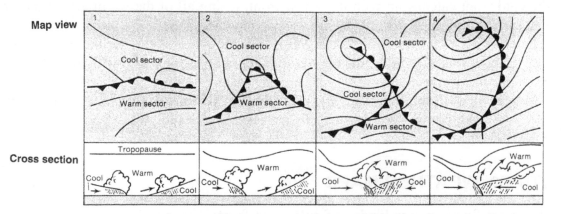

Figure 2: Stages in the life of a midlatitude cyclone: (1) early development, (2) maturity, (3) partial occlusion, (4) full occlusion. (Adapted from McKnight, *Physical Geography*, 4th ed.)

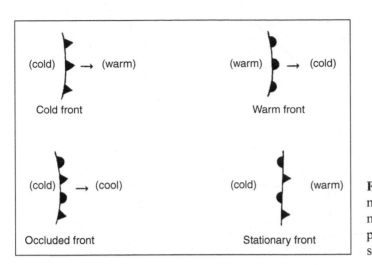

Figure 3: Fronts as shown on weather maps. Arrows indicate the direction of movement of the front. The relative temperature of air masses at the surface is shown in parentheses.

While it might seem that the most obvious way to recognize a front would be an abrupt change in temperature from one meteorological data station to the next, such changes are not always obvious on weather maps. Fronts often represent transition zones that may be 15 kilometers (about ten miles) or more wide. It is quite possible that the spacing of meteorological stations is such that a sharp difference in temperature is not clearly visible on a weather map.

Figure 4 shows a section of a hypothetical weather map in the Northern Hemisphere (top of map is north) showing isobars, a cold front, and 10 meteorological stations. In a simplified form used here, the weather map station model shows the temperature, **dew point**, and wind direction. For example:

In this case, the temperature is 40°F, the dew point is 27°F, and the wind is coming from the northeast at 15 knots (the "feathers" on the wind shaft point *into* the wind).

The pattern of dew points may be helpful in locating the position of a front. Dew points are usually lower in relatively dry cold air than in warm air, and so generally there is a drop in dew points across a front.

Wind direction is another useful indication of the location of a front. Notice in Figure 4 that a wind direction shift is observed from one side of the front to the other. In this example, the wind direction in the cold sector suggests that the cold air is advancing, and therefore, pushing the position of the cold front toward the southeast.

Also notice the "kink" in the isobars at the position of the front. A cold front is associated with a trough of low pressure. As a cold front passes, the pressure trend changes from falling to rising.

METEOGRAMS

Meteograms are charts that plot changes in a wide range of weather conditions for a location over a 25-hour period. Meteograms may appear in several different formats, but all contain the same general information. Figure 5 is a typical meteogram. The top chart shows temperature ("TMPF"), dew point ("DWPF"), and relative humidity ("RELH"). Below the temperature charts, information such as current weather conditions ("WSYM" or "WX")

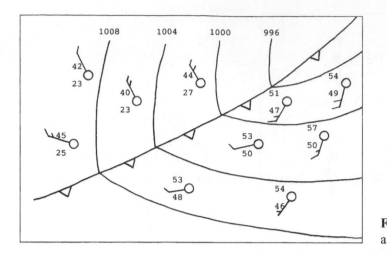

Figure 4: Hypothetical weather map showing a cold front.

and wind direction and speed are shown. A middle chart shows the elevation of the cloud base and visibility ("VSBY"), while precipitation amounts ("P061" or "PREC") are shown below. In the bottom chart, atmospheric pressure ("PMSL") is plotted. The date and time of the meteogram is in **Zulu time** or UTC (Universal Time Coordinated; GMT).

Meteograms clearly show changing trends in weather, such as that associated with the passing of a midlatitude cyclone. For example, in Figure 5 notice the change in wind direction, the drop in temperature, the decreasing visibility and lower cloud cover, and the onset of precipitation associated with the passing of a front. The trough of the front passed through Boothville, Louisiana, at about 1200Z on January 9, 2004.

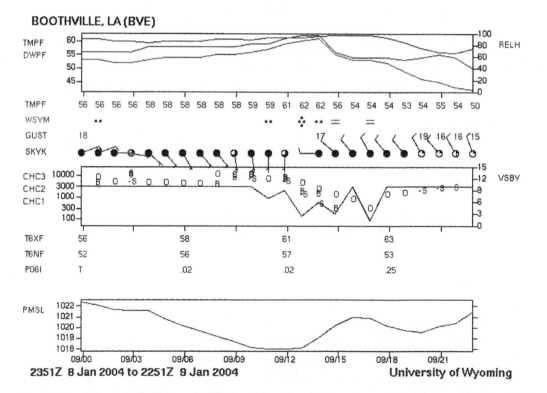

Figure 5: Meteogram for Boothville, Louisiana, on 1/8/04–1/9/04. (Meteogram courtesy of the University of Wyoming)

Name _____   Section _____

PROBLEMS—PART I

The following questions are based on this hypothetical weather map in the Northern Hemisphere showing isobars and the positions of a cold front and a warm front (top of map is north). Six locations are marked on the map (points A, B, C, D, E, and F). A cross-section diagram along points A, B, C, D, E, and F is shown below the map.

Map:

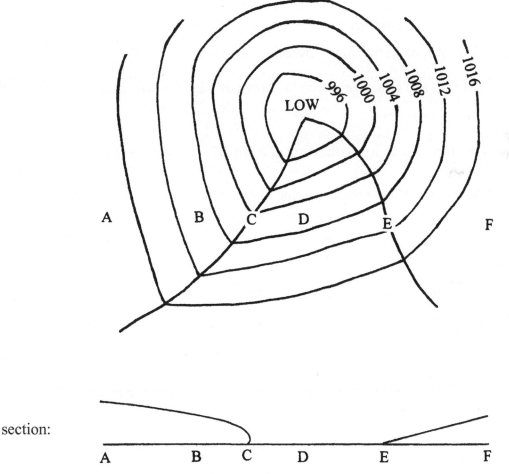

Cross section:

1. On the map above, label the following:

   (a) Cold front (use standard weather map symbols)

   (b) Warm front (use standard weather map symbols)

   (c) Cool sector of storm

   (d) Warm sector of storm

2.   On the map on the previous page, use arrows to show the wind direction in the western, southern, eastern, and northern parts of the storm.

3.   In which direction is the storm as a whole moving? From _____ to _____

4.   On the cross-section diagram, label the following:

         (a)   Cold front

         (b)   Warm front

         (c)   Cold air mass(es)

         (d)   Warm air mass

         (e)   Direction of cold front movement (use arrow)

         (f)   Direction of warm front movement (use arrow)

Using your labeled map and cross section on the previous page for reference, answer the following questions:

5.   What is the most likely wind direction at Point D?   From the _____

6.   (a)   At point D, is the pressure rising or falling?   _____

         (b)   Why?

7.   (a)   Is precipitation more likely at Point D or at Point C?   _____

         (b)   Why?

8.   (a)   At Point C, what general temperature change will take place with the passing of the cold front?

         (b)   Why?

9.   What is the most likely wind direction at Point B?   From the _____

10.   (a)   At point B, is the pressure rising or falling?   _____

         (b)   Why?

Name _____   Section _____

PROBLEMS—PART II

1. Two hypothetical weather maps in the Northern Hemisphere are shown below. Using the appropriate symbols (see Figure 3), draw in the position of the front on each map (one map shows a cold front, and the other a warm front). Top of each map is north. (Hint: Each of the fronts can be drawn with a nearly straight line.)

Map A

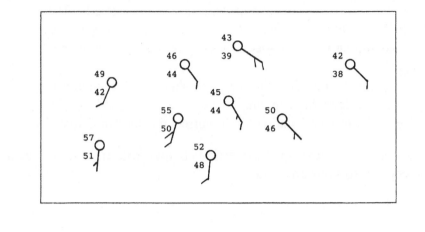

Map B

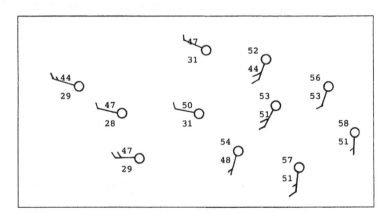

2. Is a cold front or warm front shown in Map A?   _____

3. (a)   In which direction is the front in Map A advancing?   To the _____

    (b)   How can you tell?

4. Is a cold front or warm front shown in Map B?   _____

5. In which direction is the front in Map B advancing?   To the _____

Name _____   Section _____

PROBLEMS—PART III—INTERNET

In this exercise, you will use a meteogram to study the weather changes brought by the passing of a midlatitude cyclone. This exercise will work best about 12 hours after a midlatitude cyclone or front passes through your area. If no storms are currently in your area, your instructor may have you choose another city that has experienced a passing storm within the last day.

- Go to the Hess *Physical Geography Laboratory Manual*, for *McKnight's Physical Geography*, 10th edition, Web site at **http://www.mygeoscienceplace.com**, then select Exercise 16. Then select "Go to *University of Wyoming, Information for United States Cities*" for the Department of Atmospheric Science Web page, **http://weather.uwyo.edu/cities**. (Your instructor may recommend a different Internet site that provides meteograms.)
- Select your region of the United States to see a map showing cities in the area.
- Under "Observations" select "Meteogram."
- Click on the closest city to your location for the current meteogram in that city.

After viewing the meteogram, answer the questions below. Your instructor may ask that you attach a copy of the meteogram to your answers.

1. Which city did you study?   _____

2. What was the date and time of the meteogram studied? (Be sure to also indicate the *local* day and time of the meteogram.)

3. (a) Describe the changes in pressure over the 25-hour period.   _____

   (b) What might explain these pressure changes?

4. (a) Describe the changes in temperature over the 25-hour period.   _____

   (b) What might explain these temperature changes?

5. (a) Describe the changes in wind direction over the 25-hour period.   _____

   (b) What might explain these wind direction changes?

6. Did any precipitation take place during the 25-hour period? If so, how much and when?

7. (a) Based on the information in the meteogram, what time did the front(s) and/or storm pass through your city?   _____

   (b) How can you tell?

Geography 111: Physical Geography Lab
Lab Eleven: Köppen Climate Classification System

The purpose of this exercise is to help you familiarize yourself with the Köppen system of climatic classification. This system was developed early in the 20th century by Köppen, a biogeographer. It has been modified several times and we will use a modified version in this exercise. The system uses temperature and precipitation data to determine a location's climatic region.

Materials:

World map (provided)   2 colored pencils
Climograph (provided)   Köppen Climate Charts (lab manual)

Objectives:
- Graph climate data- climograph
- Classify Climate Data using the Köppen Classification Method
- Locate/identify climates on a map

Part 1: Climographs
Climatic regions are classified based on the following data:

Temperature:
- **Average Monthly Temperature**
- **Average Annual Temperature (T)**

Precipitation:
- **Average Monthly Precipitation**
- **Average Annual Precipitation (P)**

While we can (and will) use this data in a tabular format, it is also useful to visualize the data in the form of a graph called a climograph.

climograph= A graph showing average monthly temperature and average monthly precipitation

temperature is displayed as a line graph

precipitation is displayed as a bar graph

Assignment:
Using the blank climograph provided, graph climate data for the following location: _____

Part 2: Köppen Climate Classification System
Köppen classified various locations in the world into climatic regions based on their temperature and precipitation patterns. Based on these temperature and precipitation patterns, he created 5 major climate groups. An additional "H" climate group was added later.

Assignment:
Write a brief description (including temperature and precipitation characteristics, as well as general location information) for each major climate group:

"A" Climates- Tropical Humid Climates:

"B" Dry Climates:

"C" Mild Midlatitude Climates:

"D" Severe Midlatitude Climates:

"E" Polar Climates:

"H" Highland Climates:

Part 3: Using the Köppen Climate Classification System

You will look at temperature and precipitation data for a series of locations. Using this data and the classification charts found in the following Climate Classification Lab, you will, through a series of steps, determine the Köppen climate for each location. The steps used to classify a given location are found in Attachment A.

Here is an example of the process using the location of Pasadena, California.

Sample Station, Pasadena, California

	J	F	M	A	M	J	J	A	S	O	N	D	Year
Temperature (F°)	53	55	57	59	62	68	73	73	71	66	59	53	62
Precipitation (inches)	4.3	4.3	3.4	1.4	0.5	0.1	0	0.1	0.5	0.7	1.8	3.1	20.3

Average monthly temperatures for January through December are listed in the first row.
The YEAR column shows average annual temperature (T).

Average monthly precipitation values for January through December are listed in the second row.
The YEAR column shows average annual precipitation (P).

Step 1- Are **all** the monthly temperature averages below 50° F?
  NO- All of Pasadena's monthly temperatures are 50° F or above. This is **NOT** an E climate.

Step 2- Is the Average Annual Precipitation (P) **less** than 35 inches?
  YES-- Pasadena's Average Annual Precipitation is 20.3 inches which is less than 35 inches. Proceed to the B Climate chart.

  Dry Climate Boundary Charts-
  1. Average Annual Temperature-- 62° F
     Average Annual Precipitation—20.3 inches

  2. Calculate the precipitation for the "summer" months (April to September in Northern Hemisphere)— 1.4 + 0.5 + 0.1 + 0 + 0.1 + 0.5 = 2.6 inches.

     2a. 2.6 inches/ 20.3 inches indicates that 13 % of the precipitation occurs in the summer. Therefore, 87% occurs in the winter. Pasadena has a **Winter Concentration.**

Step 2 Continued...

3. Using the **Winter Concentration** Chart, plot Average Annual Temperature & Average Annual Precipitation. (See below). This station is Humid, proceed to Step 3.

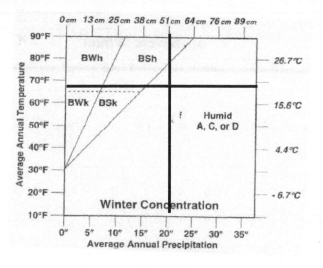

Step 3- Is the average temperature of **every** month above 64.4° F?
NO—Pasadena's coldest month has a temperature of 53° F which is less than 64.4° F. Pasadena is **NOT** an A climate.

Step 4- Is the warmest month above 50° F AND is at **least** one winter month less than 26.6° F?
NO—Pasadena's coldest month is 53 ° F which is more than 26.6° F. Pasadena is **NOT** an D climate.

Step 5- Is the warmest month above 50° F AND is the coldest winter month between 26.6° - 64.4° F?
YES- Pasadena is a **C Climate**. Proceed to the C Climate Chart.

    Step 5a- Determine 2nd letter in classification scheme:
    Does the wettest winter month have at least 3 times the precipitation of driest winter month?
    YES— Driest Winter Month : October-- .7 inches. Wettest Winter Month: January – 4.3 inches. [4.3 > (3 times .7 = 2.1 inches)] The second letter is a "s".

    Step 5b- Determine 3rd letter in classification scheme:
    Is the warmest month above 71.6° F?
    YES—July is the warmest month at 73° F. The third letter corresponds to an "a".

        Pasadena has a Csa climate, which is a mediterranean climate with a hot summer.

Assignment:

A. Using the Modified Köppen System Charts found in the following <u>Climate Classification</u> lab, determine the Köppen climatic classification of each of the 12 mystery stations found on the next two pages.

    Hint: there are two A climates, two B climates, three C climates, three D climates, and two E climates.

    Note: one of the 12 stations is a Highland station meaning altitude is more significant than latitude in determining the climate.

B. Identify the location of the stations on the attached map. Do not label each point with the climate type (for example Dfa), instead label each point Station 1, 2, 3 etc. As an example, I have identified the Sample station as Station 0 on the map.

Mystery Climatic Stations

Station 1_____

	J	F	M	A	M	J	J	A	S	O	N	D	Year
Temperature (F°)	68.4	73.4	82.2	87.2	88.1	86.7	84.5	84.5	84.6	82.1	75.1	69.1	80.5
Precipitation (")	0.55	0.94	1.06	1.69	4.76	10.20	11.85	12.50	11.42	6.30	1.38	0.12	62.28

Station 2_____

	J	F	M	A	M	J	J	A	S	O	N	D	Year
Temperature (F°)	45.1	47.1	51.6	57.8	64.9	72.6	77.5	77.1	71.7	62.8	53.7	47.5	60.8
Precipitation (")	2.97	2.67	1.63	1.73	1.87	1.23	0.38	0.87	2.28	3.82	3.55	3.11	26.13

Station 3_____

	J	F	M	A	M	J	J	A	S	O	N	D	Year
Temperature (F°)	46.4	46.0	45.9	46.0	45.9	45.1	44.8	44.8	45.3	45.7	46	46.4	45.7
Precipitation (")	3.43	3.94	5.55	6.42	4.76	2.91	1.26	1.22	1.77	4.02	3.23	3.15	41.65

Station 4_____

	J	F	M	A	M	J	J	A	S	O	N	D	Year
Temperature (F°)	-48.0	-40.0	-18.0	10.0	37.0	55.0	59.0	52.0	37.0	5.0	-31.0	-41.0	7.0
Precipitation (")	0	0.20	0.20	0.20	0.30	1.00	1.20	1.10	0.60	0.40	0.40	0.30	6.00

Station 5_____

	J	F	M	A	M	J	J	A	S	O	N	D	Year
Temperature (F°)	78.8	80.6	80.6	82.4	82.4	80.6	80.6	80.6	80.6	80.6	78.8	78.8	80.6
Precipitation (")	11.22	6.46	6.01	6.30	5.16	6.97	6.42	7.87	4.80	7.24	9.29	12.05	89.79

Station 6_____

	J	F	M	A	M	J	J	A	S	O	N	D	Year
Temperature (F°)	82.6	81.5	76.4	67.6	59.6	54.2	52.9	57.8	64.7	73.1	77.9	81.4	69.1
Precipitation (")	1.74	1.32	1.09	0.39	0.60	0.52	0.29	0.31	0.28	0.71	1.15	1.53	9.93

Station 7_____

	J	F	M	A	M	J	J	A	S	O	N	D	Year
Temperature (F°)	70.5	72.0	72.3	67.6	63.5	60.1	59.4	59.0	59.7	61.2	63.3	66.4	64.5
Precipitation (")	0.03	0.01	0.03	0.01	0.05	0.13	0.19	0.25	0.18	0.08	0.04	0.02	1.02

Station 8_____

	J	F	M	A	M	J	J	A	S	O	N	D	Year
Temperature (F°)	-13.0	-9.0	1.0	23.0	42.0	55.0	62.0	57.0	45.0	29.0	6.0	-9.0	24.0
Precipitation (")	0.50	0.50	0.40	0.45	0.60	0.80	1.40	1.50	1.10	1.30	0.90	0.70	10.20

Station 9_____

	J	F	M	A	M	J	J	A	S	O	N	D	Year
Temperature (F°)	-15.6	-18.4	-15.1	0.1	18.7	33.6	39.6	38.3	30.5	16.7	-0.1	-11.0	9.8
Precipitation (")	0.19	0.16	0.12	0.12	0.12	0.35	0.89	0.90	0.60	0.56	0.27	0.19	4.47

Station 10_____

	J	F	M	A	M	J	J	A	S	O	N	D	Year
Temperature (F°)	2.0	8.0	21.0	40.0	54.0	62.0	68.0	65.0	54.0	42.0	23.0	7.0	37.0
Precipitation (")	0.80	0.80	1.00	1.30	2.20	3.20	2.90	2.60	2.10	1.40	1.00	0.90	20.2

Station 11_____

	J	F	M	A	M	J	J	A	S	O	N	D	Year
Temperature (F°)	55.2	57.6	63.0	69.3	75.8	81.3	82.7	82.8	79.7	71.6	62.1	56.1	69.8
Precipitation (")	4.53	4.50	5.48	5.32	4.88	5.77	6.98	6.02	5.53	3.35	3.64	4.70	60.70

Station 12_____

	J	F	M	A	M	J	J	A	S	O	N	D	Year
Temperature (F°)	52.0	55.4	61.0	68.2	75.3	81.9	84.0	83.8	78.6	70.6	59.5	53.7	68.7
Precipitation (")	1.74	1.65	1.67	2.82	3.45	2.95	2.09	2.36	3.49	2.50	1.37	1.75	27.84

Attachment A: Köppen Classification Process

Step 1: Determine if station is an E climate.

Are **all** the monthly temperature averages below 50° F?

> **YES**-- Go to the E Climate chart and determine if it is an ET or EF climate. Once you have determined the climate type, you have classified the station.
>
> > *[STOP- you have classified this station. Proceed to next mystery station]*

> **NO** – Proceed to Step 2.

Step 2: Determine if station is a Humid or Dry climate.

Is the average annual precipitation (P) **less** than 35 inches?

> **YES**-- Go to the B Climate Chart to determine seasonality of precipitation and climate.

> If the climate type is Dry, (BWh, BWk, BSh, or BSk), you have classified the station.
>
> > *[STOP- you have classified this station. Proceed to next mystery station]*

> If the climate is Humid, proceed to Step 3.

> **NO** – Proceed to Step 3.

Step 3: Determine if station is an A climate.

Is the average temperature of **every** month above 64.4° F?

> **YES**-- Go to the A Climate Chart and determine the climate type. Once you have determined the climate type, you have classified the station.
>
> > *[STOP- you have classified this station. Proceed to next mystery station]*

> **NO**-- Proceed to Step 4.

Step 4: Determine if a station is a D climate.

Is the warmest month above 50° F AND is at **least** one winter month less than 26.6° F?

> **YES**-- Go to the D Climate chart and further classify the climate based on precipitation and monthly temperature patterns. Once you have determined the subtype of the D Climate, you have classified the station.
>
> > *[STOP- you have classified this station. Proceed to next mystery station]*

> **NO**-- Proceed to Step 5

Step 5: Determine if a station is a C climate.

Is the warmest month above 50° F AND is the coldest winter month between 26.6° F and 64.4° F?

> **YES**-- Go to the C Climate chart and further classify the climate based on precipitation and monthly temperature patterns. Once you have determined the subtype of the C Climate, you have classified the station.
>
> > *[STOP- you have classified this station. Proceed to next mystery station]*

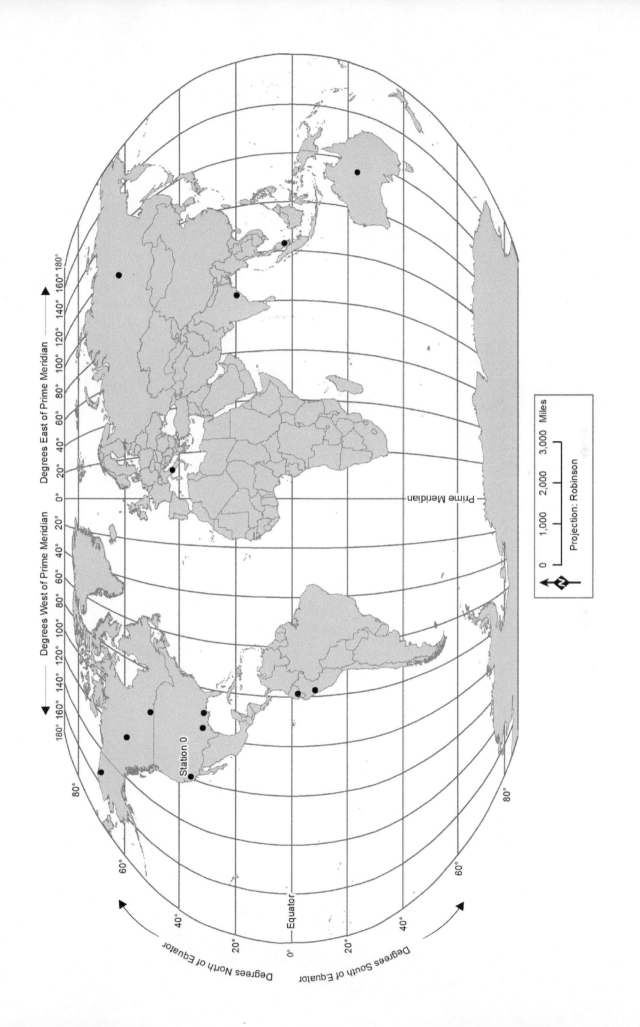

Lab 11a

Lab 14

CLIMATE CLASSIFICATION

> **Objective:** To use average monthly temperature and precipitation data to classify climates with the Köppen climate classification system.
>
> **Resource:** Internet access (optional).
>
> **Reference:** Hess, Darrel. *McKnight's Physical Geography;* 10th ed.; chapter, "Climate and Climate Change"; sections, "Climate Classification" through "Global Patterns Idealized."

KÖPPEN CLIMATE CLASSIFICATION SYSTEM

The modified **Köppen system** is the most widely used climate classification system. With the Köppen system, all climates of the world can be grouped into just 15 types, based simply on **average monthly temperature** and **average monthly precipitation**.

In the Köppen system, each climate type is given a descriptive name, as well as a code based on two or three letters. The first letter refers to the major climate group, the second letter generally refers to the precipitation pattern, and the third letter generally refers to the temperature pattern.

There are actually several different versions of the modified Köppen system in use—the definitions of some climate types vary slightly from version to version. Also, while there are specific boundaries for each climate type, in reality the borders between climates should be thought of as transition zones, rather than sharp boundaries.

CLIMOGRAPHS

One of the key tools used in climate study is the **climograph** or **climatic diagram** (Figure 1). In a single chart, the climatic regime of a location can be summarized. The months of the year are indicated along the bottom. The average monthly temperature is shown with a solid line (the temperature scale is along the left side of chart), and the average monthly precipitation is indicated with bars (the precipitation scale is along the right side of chart).

In the sample diagram, notice that in St. Louis the average temperature in January is about −1°C (30°F), while in July the average temperature is 27°C (80°F). Precipitation is evenly distributed throughout the year, each month receiving approximately 8 to 13 centimeters (3–5 inches).

USING THE MODIFIED KÖPPEN SYSTEM CHARTS

Each of the climate types in the Köppen system has a specific definition. The "Modified Köppen System Charts" on the following pages of the Lab Manual provide concise definitions for 14 climate types (plus the special category of "Highland" climate). *In order to use these charts you must follow the procedure for classifying climates listed below.*

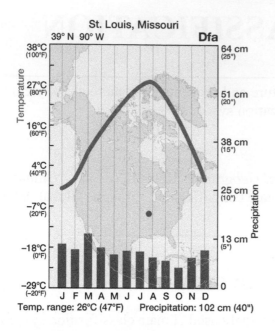

Figure 1: Climograph for St. Louis, Missouri. (From McKnight and Hess, *Physical Geography*, 9th ed.)

At the top of each chart, the basic definition for the major climate group is given. Next, the different climate types found within the major group are listed (in some cases a climate type is represented by several different letter combinations). Finally, the specific definitions of the second and third letters for each climate type are provided. Note that the "C" and "D" climates have been grouped together and that not all second and third letters can be combined with both C and D.

PROCEDURE FOR CLASSIFYING CLIMATES

Construct a climograph for the location by plotting the average monthly temperature and average monthly precipitation (this step is actually optional, but it usually makes classification easier). Then, calculate the average annual temperature and average annual precipitation for the location. (This has been done for you in the problems for this exercise.)

Next, determine the major climate group. If you go through the following steps *in sequence*, you will find the correct major climate group. With experience, you will learn shortcuts to narrow your choices more quickly:

1. If the average temperature of *every* month is below 10°C (50°F), go to the "E" climate chart. (Note: Some "H" climates may also exhibit this temperature pattern.)

2. If the total annual precipitation is *more* than 89 centimeters (35 inches), continue to #4.

3.   If the total annual precipitation is *less* than 89 centimeters (35 inches), determine if it is a dry climate by using the "Dry Climate Boundary Charts" under "B—Dry Climates." If it is a dry climate, continue with the "B" climate chart; if not a dry climate, continue to #4. (A detailed description of dry climates and using these charts is given below.)

4.   If the average temperature of *every* month is above 18°C (64.4°F), go to the "A" climate chart.

5.   If at least one winter month is colder than −3°C (26.6°F), go to the "D" climate chart.

6.   If the coldest winter month is between −3°C (26.6°F) and 18°C (64.4°F), go to the "C" climate chart.

After establishing the major climate group, determine which climate type is correct by checking the definitions of the second, and if necessary, third letters. When assessing seasonal patterns of temperature or precipitation, be sure to consider if the station is in the Northern or Southern Hemisphere. If you are unsure of the hemisphere of the station in question, look at the temperature pattern. If the coolest months are in December, January, and February, it is in the Northern Hemisphere. If the coolest months are in June, July, and August, it is in the Southern Hemisphere.

CLASSIFYING DRY CLIMATES IN THE KÖPPEN SYSTEM

The basic definition of a dry ("B") climate in the Köppen system is one in which the **potential evaporation** exceeds **precipitation**. There is a complex relationship between temperature, precipitation, and the dryness of a region. For example, because of the lower potential for evaporation, a very cold region with an average annual precipitation of 25 centimeters (10 inches) would not be classified as a dry climate, while a hot region receiving 25 centimeters (10 inches) of precipitation would be. These relationships are shown on the "Dry Climate Boundary Charts."

In order to use the "Dry Climate Boundary Charts," you need to know the average annual precipitation, the average annual temperature, and if there is a "seasonal concentration" of precipitation. A seasonal concentration means that more than 70% of the precipitation comes in either the six summer months or six winter months. For purposes of classification, April to September are considered the six summer months in the Northern Hemisphere. (These would be the six winter months in the Southern Hemisphere.)

To determine if a seasonal concentration is present, add up the precipitation amounts for the months April to September and divide this by the total annual precipitation. For example, if a Northern Hemisphere location with annual precipitation of 38 centimeters (15 inches) receives 30 centimeters (12 inches) of rain between April and September, make the following calculation: 30 cm/38 cm = 0.8 or 80% (12"/15" = 0.8 or 80%). Since more than 70% of the precipitation comes between April and September, this location has a summer concentration of rainfall.

Modified Köppen System Charts

To use these charts, go through the following steps *in sequence*:

1.   If average temperature of every month is below 10°C (50°F), go to "E" climate chart.

2.   If total annual precipitation is more than 89 centimeters (35 inches), continue to #4.

3.   If total annual precipitation is less than 89 centimeters (35 inches), determine if it is a dry climate by using "Dry Climate Boundary Charts" under "B—Dry Climates." If a dry climate, continue with "B" climate chart; if not a dry climate, continue to #4.

4.   If average temperature of every month is above 18°C (64.4°F), go to "A" climate chart.

5.   If at least one winter month is colder than −3°C (26.6°F), go to "D" climate chart.

6.   If coldest winter month is between −3°C (26.6°F) and 18°C (64.4°F), go to "C" climate chart.

A—TROPICAL HUMID: Temperature of every month above 18°C (64.4°F).

Group A Climate Types
Af —Tropical Wet
Am—Tropical Monsoon
Aw —Tropical Savanna

Second Letters	**Definition**
f —Wet All Year	Every month has at least 6 cm (2.4") of rainfall.
m—Monsoon Pattern	Short dry season; pronounced rainy season.*
w—Winter Dry	Winter dry season of 3 to 6 months.*

*To calculate boundaries between "Am" and "Aw," determine the average rainfall and the average rainfall of the driest month; then use the chart below. For example, a location with an average annual rainfall of 200 cm (about 80") and 5 cm (2") of rainfall in the driest month is an "Am" climate.

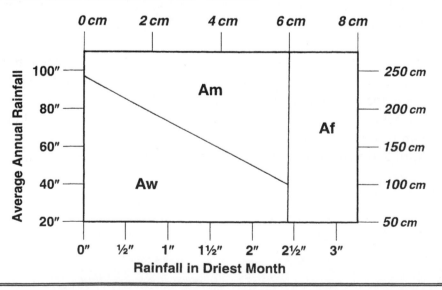

B—DRY CLIMATES: Evaporation exceeds precipitation.

Group B Climate Types

BWh — Subtropical Desert	(Avg. annual temperature above 18°C [64.4°F]).	
BSh — Subtropical Steppe	" " " " "	
BWk — Midlatitude Desert	(Avg. annual temperature below 18°C [64.4°F]).	
BSk — Midlatitude Steppe	" " " " "	

DRY CLIMATE BOUNDARY CHARTS

1. Determine the average annual temperature and average annual precipitation.
2. Determine if the precipitation is distributed evenly during the year:

   (a) If more than 70% of the precipitation comes in the 6 summer months (April to September in Northern Hemisphere), use "Summer Concentration" chart.

   (b) If more than 70% of the precipitation comes in the 6 winter months (October to March in Northern Hemisphere), use "Winter Concentration" chart.

   (c) If precipitation is evenly distributed throughout year (neither a or b), use "Even Distribution" chart.

3. Line up the average annual temperature with the average annual precipitation to find the climate.

Example: If a location has an annual precipitation of 38 cm (15″) with a winter concentration, use the "Winter Concentration" chart. If the average annual temperature is 21°C (70°F), the climate is BSh; if the average annual temperature is 10°C (50°F), it is not a dry climate.

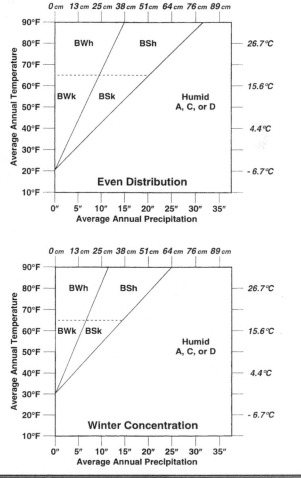

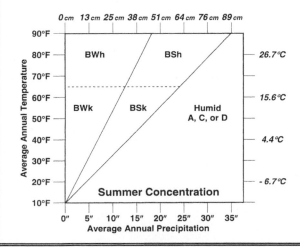

C—MILD MIDLATITUDE:

Temperature of warmest month above 10°C (50°F); coldest month between −3°C (26.6°F) and 18°C (64.4°F).

D—SEVERE MIDLATITUDE:

Warmest month above 10°C (50°F); coldest month below −3°C (26.6°F).

Group C & D Climate Types

Cs	— Mediterranean	(includes Csa and Csb)
Cfa	— Humid Subtropical	(also includes Cwa)
Cfb	— Marine West Coast	(also includes Cfc)
Dfa	— Humid Continental	(also includes Dwa, Dfb, and Dwb)
Dfc	— Subarctic	(also includes Dwc, Dfd, and Dwd)

Second Letters / Definition

s—Summer Dry — Wettest winter month has at least 3× precipitation of driest summer month.

w—Winter Dry — Wettest summer month has at least 10× precipitation of driest winter month.

f—Wet All Year — Neither "s" nor "w" above.

Third Letters / Definition

a—Hot Summer — Warmest month above 22°C (71.6°F).

b—Warm Summer — Warmest month below 22°C (71.6°F); at least 4 months above 10°C (50°F).

c—Cool Summer — Warmest month below 22°C (71.6°F); 1 to 3 months above 10°C (50°F); coldest month above −38°C (−36.4°F).

d—Severe Winter — Coldest month below −38°C (−36.4°F).

E—POLAR CLIMATES: Temperature of every month below 10°C (50°F).

Group E Climate Types
ET—Tundra
EF—Ice Cap

Second Letters	**Definition**
T—Tundra	At least one month above 0°C (32°F).
F—Ice Cap	All months below 0°C (32°F).

H—HIGHLAND CLIMATES: Significant variation or modification of a climate type due to high elevation.

Highland climates are not defined in the same way as other climates in the Köppen system. Rather, these are regions in high mountain areas where the climate has been significantly modified from the adjacent lowlands by high elevation.

FINAL SUGGESTIONS ON CLIMATE CLASSIFICATION

You may also want to compare the climograph of the station in question with those in your textbook. This is a quick way to determine if your classification is reasonable. If you know the location of the station in question, look at a generalized map of climate. This map may help narrow down the climate type to several possibilities. However, because there are local variations in climate, this map alone is *not* enough to accurately determine all climates. You will need to use the charts defining each climate type to verify your answer.

KÖPPEN CLASSIFICATION AND CLIMATE CONTROLS

Köppen climate classification is based solely on temperature and precipitation patterns. Although the Köppen system does not consider the origin of a climate, the location and dominant controls of each climate type are quite predictable.

This regularity is illustrated with the hypothetical continent shown in Figure 2. This idealized distribution pattern predicts quite closely the actual arrangement of climate types on the continents and reflects the dominant controls that produce each of these climates. These dominant controls include latitude, continent–ocean temperature contrasts, ocean currents, the general circulation of the atmosphere, and the most important kinds of storms.

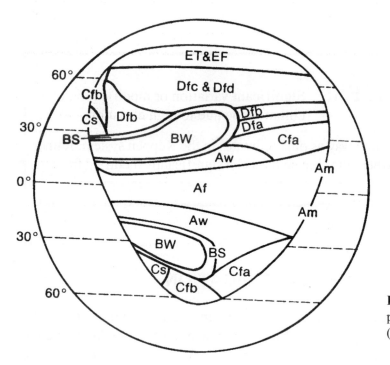

Figure 2: The presumed arrangement of Köppen climatic types on a hypothetical continent. (From McKnight, *Physical Geography*, 4th ed.)

Name _____   Section _____

PROBLEMS—PART I

For each of the following six locations, complete the climograph using the average monthly temperature ("Temp") given in degrees Celsius and Fahrenheit, and the average monthly precipitation ("Precp") given in centimeters and inches. The average annual temperature and precipitation are provided for you. After completing the climographs, answer the questions at the end of Part I. You may plot data on the climographs using either S.I. or English (note that the English unit and S.I. unit scales on the climographs are not exactly equivalent). It may be helpful to locate each of these stations on a map. No "H" climates are given.

1. Cuiabá, Brazil							Average Annual: 26°C (78°F); 138.8 cm (54.6″)					
	JAN	**FEB**	**MAR**	**APR**	**MAY**	**JUN**	**JUL**	**AUG**	**SEP**	**OCT**	**NOV**	**DEC**
Temp	81°F 27°C	80°F 27°C	81°F 27°C	80°F 27°C	75°F 24°C	72°F 22°C	73°F 23°C	75°F 24°C	79°F 26°C	82°F 28°C	81°F 27°C	81°F 27°C
Precp	9.6″ 24.4 cm	8.9″ 22.6 cm	8.1″ 20.6 cm	4.1″ 10.4 cm	2.0″ 5.1 cm	0.3″ 0.8 cm	0.2″ 0.5 cm	1.1″ 2.8 cm	2.0″ 5.1 cm	4.4″ 11.2 cm	6.0″ 15.2 cm	7.9″ 20.1 cm

2. Kashi (Kashgar), China							Average Annual: 12°C (54°F); 8.7 cm (3.4″)					
	JAN	**FEB**	**MAR**	**APR**	**MAY**	**JUN**	**JUL**	**AUG**	**SEP**	**OCT**	**NOV**	**DEC**
Temp	22°F −6°C	34°F 1°C	47°F 8°C	61°F 16°C	70°F 21°C	77°F 25°C	80°F 27°C	76°F 24°C	59°F 15°C	56°F 13°C	40°F 4°C	26°F −3°C
Precp	0.3″ 0.8 cm	0.0″ 0.0 cm	0.2″ 0.5 cm	0.2″ 0.5 cm	0.8″ 2.0 cm	0.4″ 1.0 cm	0.3″ 0.8 cm	0.7″ 1.8 cm	0.3″ 0.8 cm	0.0″ 0.0 cm	0.0″ 0.0 cm	0.2″ 0.5 cm

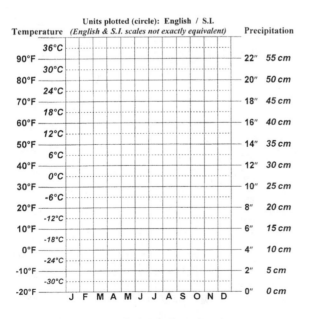

1. Cuiabá, Brazil

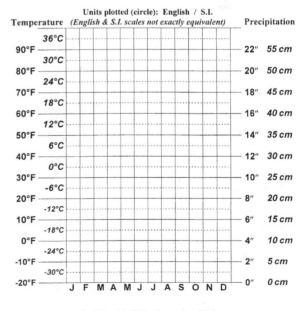

2. Kashi (Kashgar), China

3. New Orleans, Louisiana — Average Annual: 21°C (70°F); 161.8 cm (63.6″)

	JAN	FEB	MAR	APR	MAY	JUN	JUL	AUG	SEP	OCT	NOV	DEC
Temp	56°F 13°C	58°F 14°C	63°F 17°C	70°F 21°C	76°F 24°C	82°F 28°C	83°F 28°C	83°F 28°C	80°F 27°C	73°F 23°C	62°F 17°C	57°F 14°C
Precp	4.8″ 12.2 cm	4.2″ 10.7 cm	6.6″ 16.8 cm	5.4″ 13.7 cm	5.4″ 13.7 cm	5.6″ 14.2 cm	7.1″ 18.0 cm	6.4″ 16.3 cm	5.8″ 14.7 cm	3.7″ 9.4 cm	4.0″ 10.2 cm	4.6″ 11.9 cm

4. Palau, Caroline Islands — Average Annual: 27°C (81°F); 396.2 cm (155.9″)

	JAN	FEB	MAR	APR	MAY	JUN	JUL	AUG	SEP	OCT	NOV	DEC
Temp	81°F 27°C	80°F 27°C	81°F 27°C	82°F 28°C	82°F 28°C	82°F 28°C	81°F 27°C	81°F 27°C	81°F 27°C	81°F 27°C	81°F 27°C	81°F 27°C
Precp	15.3″ 38.9 cm	9.4″ 23.9 cm	6.8″ 17.3 cm	7.6″ 19.3 cm	15.5″ 39.4 cm	12.4″ 31.5 cm	19.9″ 50.5 cm	14.0″ 35.6 cm	15.7″ 39.9 cm	14.8″ 37.6 cm	11.8″ 30.0 cm	12.7″ 32.3 cm

5. Irkutsk, Siberia — Average Annual: 0°C (31°F); 37.0 cm (14.6″)

	JAN	FEB	MAR	APR	MAY	JUN	JUL	AUG	SEP	OCT	NOV	DEC
Temp	−5°F −21°C	1°F −17°C	17°F −8	37°F 3°C	48°F 9°C	59°F 15°C	65°F 18°C	60°F 16°C	48°F 9°C	33°F 1°C	13°F −11°C	1°F −17°C
Precp	0.6″ 1.5 cm	0.5″ 1.3 cm	0.4″ 1.0 cm	0.6″ 1.5 cm	1.2″ 3.0 cm	2.3″ 5.8 cm	2.9″ 7.4 cm	2.4″ 6.1 cm	1.6″ 4.1 cm	0.7″ 1.8 cm	0.6″ 1.5 cm	0.8″ 2.0 cm

6. Dublin, Ireland — Average Annual: 9°C (48°F); 70.4 cm (27.7″)

	JAN	FEB	MAR	APR	MAY	JUN	JUL	AUG	SEP	OCT	NOV	DEC
Temp	40°F 4°C	41°F 5°C	42°F 6°C	45°F 7°C	49°F 9°C	55°F 13°C	58°F 14°C	57°F 14°C	54°F 12°C	48°F 9°C	44°F 7°C	41°F 5°C
Precp	2.2″ 5.6 cm	1.9″ 4.8 cm	1.9″ 4.8 cm	1.9″ 4.8 cm	2.1″ 5.3 cm	2.0″ 5.1 cm	2.6″ 6.6 cm	3.1″ 7.9 cm	2.0″ 5.1 cm	2.6″ 6.6 cm	2.9″ 7.4 cm	2.5″ 6.4 cm

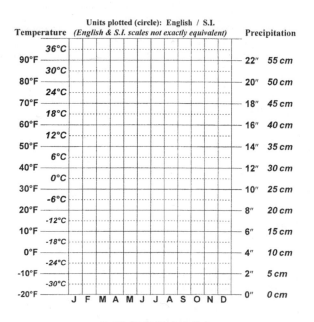

3. New Orleans, LA

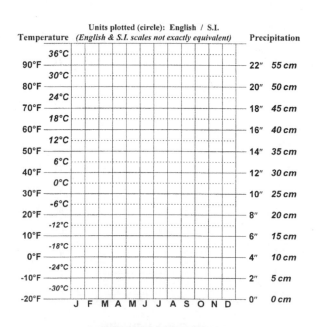

4. Palau, Caroline Islands

Climate Classification

Name _____   (Ex. 21—Part I)

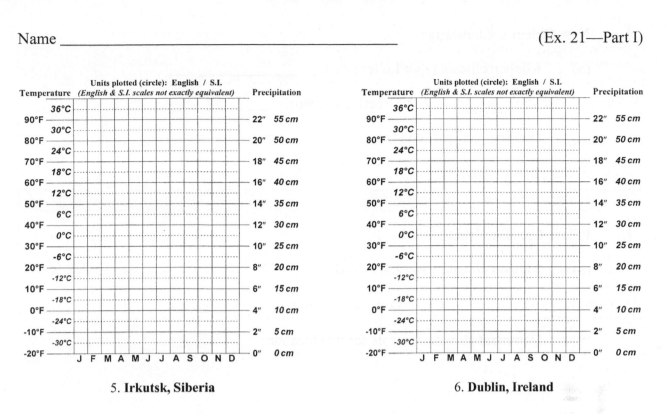

5. **Irkutsk, Siberia**   6. **Dublin, Ireland**

After completing the climographs, answer the following questions about each location:

1.   **Cuiabá, Brazil:**

(a)   Köppen climate type: Letter code: _____

Descriptive name: _____

(b)   Dominant climate controls for this location:

2.   **Kashi (Kashgar), China:**

(a)   Köppen climate type: Letter code: _____

Descriptive name: _____

(b)   Dominant climate controls for this location:

3. **New Orleans, Louisiana:**

    (a) Köppen climate type: Letter code: _____

    Descriptive name: _____

    (b) Dominant climate controls for this location:

4. **Palau, Caroline Islands:**

    (a) Köppen climate type: Letter code: _____

    Descriptive name: _____

    (b) Dominant climate controls for this location:

5. **Irkutsk, Siberia:**

    (a) Köppen climate type: Letter code: _____

    Descriptive name: _____

    (b) Dominant climate controls for this location:

6. **Dublin, Ireland:**

    (a) Köppen climate type: Letter code: _____

    Descriptive name: _____

    (b) Dominant climate controls for this location:

Name _____   Section _____

PROBLEMS—PART II

For each of the following six locations, complete the climograph using the average monthly temperature ("Temp") given in degrees Celsius and Fahrenheit, and the average monthly precipitation ("Precp") given in centimeters and inches. The average annual temperature and precipitation are provided for you. After completing the climographs, answer the questions at the end of Part II. You may plot data on the climographs using either S.I. or English units (note that the English unit and S.I. unit scales on the climographs are not exactly equivalent). No "H" climates are given.

1.   Average Annual: 10°C (50°F); 31.4 cm (12.3″)

	JAN	FEB	MAR	APR	MAY	JUN	JUL	AUG	SEP	OCT	NOV	DEC
Temp	21°F / −6°C	30°F / −1°C	42°F / 6°C	54°F / 12°C	63°F / 17°C	70°F / 21°C	73°F / 23°C	71°F / 22°C	61°F / 16°C	51°F / 11°C	35°F / 2°C	23°F / −5°C
Precp	0.1″ / 0.3 cm	0.1″ / 0.3 cm	0.3″ / 0.8 cm	0.5″ / 1.3 cm	0.7″ / 1.8 cm	1.5″ / 3.8 cm	2.6″ / 6.6 cm	3.6″ / 9.1 cm	2.2″ / 5.6 cm	0.6″ / 1.5 cm	0.1″ / 0.3 cm	0.0″ / 0.0 cm

2.   Average Annual: −12°C (10°F); 13.4 cm (5.2″)

	JAN	FEB	MAR	APR	MAY	JUN	JUL	AUG	SEP	OCT	NOV	DEC
Temp	−20°F / −29°C	−13°F / −25°C	−13°F / −25°C	−2°F / −19°C	22°F / −6°C	35°F / 2°C	41°F / 5°C	39°F / 4°C	32°F / 0°C	16°F / −9°C	0°F / −18°C	−15°F / −26°C
Precp	0.1″ / 0.3 cm	0.4″ / 1.0 cm	0.2″ / 0.5 cm	0.3″ / 0.8 cm	0.3″ / 0.8 cm	0.8″ / 2.0 cm	0.3″ / 0.8 cm	0.9″ / 2.3 cm	0.5″ / 1.3 cm	0.7″ / 1.8 cm	0.3″ / 0.8 cm	0.4″ / 1.0 cm

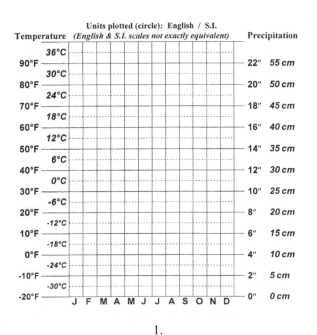

1.

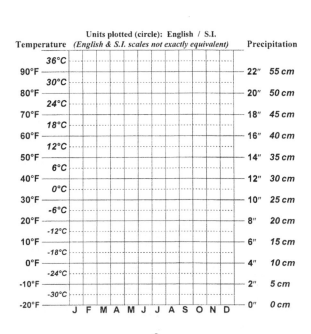

2.

3.

Average Annual: 16°C (61°F); 52.6 cm (20.7″)

	JAN	FEB	MAR	APR	MAY	JUN	JUL	AUG	SEP	OCT	NOV	DEC
Temp	69°F 21°C	68°F 20°C	66°F 19°C	61°F 16°C	57°F 14°C	55°F 13°C	53°F 12°C	54°F 12°C	57°F 14°C	59°F 15°C	64°F 18°C	67°F 19°C
Precp	0.4″ 1.0 cm	0.6″ 1.5 cm	0.5″ 1.3 cm	2.1″ 5.3 cm	3.5″ 8.9 cm	3.3″ 8.4 cm	3.3″ 8.4 cm	2.9″ 7.4 cm	1.8″ 4.6 cm	1.2″ 3.0 cm	0.7″ 1.8 cm	0.4″ 1.0 cm

4.

Average Annual: 27°C (81°F); 291.4 cm (114.7″)

	JAN	FEB	MAR	APR	MAY	JUN	JUL	AUG	SEP	OCT	NOV	DEC
Temp	81°F 27°C	82°F 28°C	84°F 29°C	85°F 29°C	84°F 29°C	80°F 27°C	79°F 26°C	79°F 26°C	80°F 27°C	80°F 27°C	81°F 27°C	81°F 27°C
Precp	0.8″ 2.0 cm	0.8″ 2.0 cm	1.7″ 4.3 cm	3.7″ 9.4 cm	11.4″ 29.0 cm	27.8″ 70.6 cm	25.3″ 64.3 cm	12.5″ 31.8 cm	9.22″ 23.4 cm	12.9″ 32.8 cm	6.7″ 17.0 cm	1.9″ 4.8 cm

5.

Average Annual: 10°C (50°F); 83.6 cm (32.9″)

	JAN	FEB	MAR	APR	MAY	JUN	JUL	AUG	SEP	OCT	NOV	DEC
Temp	25°F −4°C	27°F −3°C	36°F 2°C	48°F 9°C	58°F 14°C	68°F 20°C	74°F 23°C	72°F 22°C	66°F 19°C	54°F 12°C	40°F 4°C	30°F −1°C
Precp	1.9″ 4.8 cm	1.9″ 4.8 cm	2.7″ 6.9 cm	2.9″ 7.4 cm	3.5″ 8.9 cm	3.7″ 9.4 cm	3.3″ 8.4 cm	3.1″ 7.9 cm	3.0″ 7.6 cm	2.6″ 6.6 cm	2.3″ 5.8 cm	2.0″ 5.1 cm

6.

Average Annual: 21°C (70°F); 25.2 cm (9.9″)

	JAN	FEB	MAR	APR	MAY	JUN	JUL	AUG	SEP	OCT	NOV	DEC
Temp	84°F 29°C	82°F 28°C	77°F 25°C	68°F 20°C	60°F 16°C	54°F 12°C	53°F 12°C	58°F 14°C	65°F 18°C	73°F 23°C	79°F 26°C	82°F 28°C
Precp	1.7″ 4.3 cm	1.3″ 3.3 cm	1.1″ 2.8 cm	0.4″ 1.0 cm	0.6″ 1.5 cm	0.5″ 1.3 cm	0.3″ 0.8 cm	0.3″ 0.8 cm	0.3″ 0.8 cm	0.7″ 1.8 cm	1.2″ 3.0 cm	1.5″ 3.8 cm

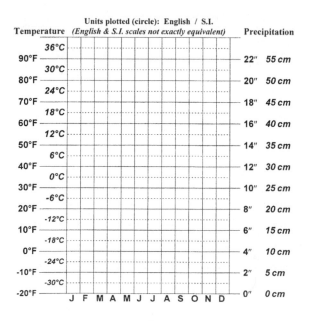

3.

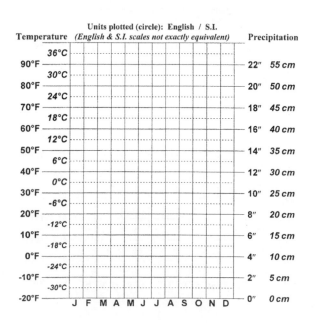

4.

Name _____   (Ex. 21—Part II)

Units plotted (circle): English / S.I.
Temperature *(English & S.I. scales not exactly equivalent)* Precipitation

36°C	
90°F	22″ 55 cm
30°C	
80°F	20″ 50 cm
24°C	
70°F	18″ 45 cm
18°C	
60°F	16″ 40 cm
12°C	
50°F	14″ 35 cm
6°C	
40°F	12″ 30 cm
0°C	
30°F	10″ 25 cm
-6°C	
20°F	8″ 20 cm
-12°C	
10°F	6″ 15 cm
-18°C	
0°F	4″ 10 cm
-24°C	
-10°F	2″ 5 cm
-30°C	
-20°F J F M A M J J A S O N D	0″ 0 cm

5.

Units plotted (circle): English / S.I.
Temperature *(English & S.I. scales not exactly equivalent)* Precipitation

6.

After completing the climographs, assign a Köppen letter code and descriptive climate name to each location:

1.   Köppen climate type: Letter code: _____

        Descriptive name: _____

2.   Köppen climate type: Letter code: _____

        Descriptive name: _____

3.   Köppen climate type: Letter code: _____

        Descriptive name: _____

4.   Köppen climate type: Letter code: _____

        Descriptive name: _____

5.   Köppen climate type: Letter code: _____

        Descriptive name: _____

6.   Köppen climate type: Letter code: _____

        Descriptive name: _____

Name _____   Section _____

PROBLEMS—PART III

Before answering the following questions, assign Köppen climate types to each of the six locations in Part II. Match each of the locations in Part II (1 through 6) with its most likely city from the list below:

Alice Springs, Australia   Cochin, India

Capetown, South Africa   Lanzhou, China

Chicago, Illinois   Barrow, Alaska

1.   (a)   Most likely city: _____

     (b)   Why is this the most likely city?

2.   (a)   Most likely city: _____

     (b)   Why is this the most likely city?

3.   (a)   Most likely city: _____

     (b)   Why is this the most likely city?

4.   (a)   Most likely city: _____

     (b)   Why is this the most likely city?

5.   (a)   Most likely city: _____

     (b)   Why is this the most likely city?

6.   (a)   Most likely city: _____

     (b)   Why is this the most likely city?

Name _____   Section _____

PROBLEMS—PART IV

The following questions are based on the diagram of the Köppen climate distribution on a hypothetical continent (Figure 2). It may also be helpful to compare the hypothetical continent with a map of actual climate distribution. In answering the questions, consider both the characteristics of a climate and the dominant controls producing that climate.

1. Why are Aw (tropical savanna) climates found in bands north and south of the Af (tropical wet) climates?

2. Why do the Af climates extend farther toward the poles along the east coast than along the west coast?

3. What explains the distribution of BW (desert) climates centered at about 25° to 30° north and south latitude along the west coast?

4. On the hypothetical continent, why does the BW climate extend farther inland in the Northern Hemisphere than in the Southern Hemisphere?

5. What explains the distribution of BS (steppe) climates?

6. What explains the narrow coastal band of Cs (mediterranean) climates at about 35° north and south latitude along the west coast?

7. Why do the Cfb (marine west coast) climates, just poleward of the dry summer Cs climates, receive rain all year?

8. Why do Cfa (humid subtropical) climates along the east coast receive rain all year, but at the same latitude along the west coast, the Cs climates have dry summers?

9. Why is the Dfb (humid continental) climate in a band just north of the band of Dfa climate?

10. Why is the high latitude interior of the continent dominated by Dfc and Dfd (subarctic) climates?

11. Why are no D or E climates shown in the Southern Hemisphere?

Name _____   Section _____

PROBLEMS—PART V—INTERNET

In this exercise, you will use the Internet to find the climate record of the city where you live, and then classify its climate with the Köppen system.

- Go to the Hess *Physical Geography Laboratory Manual* for *McKnight's Physical Geography*, 10th edition, Web site at **http://www.mygeoscienceplace.com**, then select Exercise 21. Select "Go to *Regional Climate Centers*" under NOAA: **http://www.ncdc.noaa.gov/oa/climate/regionalclimatecenters.html**. (Your instructor may recommend a different Internet site that provides climate data.)

- From the map of the United States, select the Regional Climate Center for your state, and then look for the historical climate summary for your city.

- To properly classify the climate of your city, you will need the average monthly temperature and average monthly precipitation. (If "Average" or "Mean" Monthly Temperature is not given, it may be calculated by taking the average of a month's "Mean Maximum Temperature" and its "Mean Minimum Temperature.") The averages should be based on weather data over at least a 25-year period. If you choose not to print out the data, write down the information in the chart on the following page. Also note the years on which the averages are based.

- Indicate if your data are in S.I. or English units.

- Note (or calculate) the average annual temperature and precipitation.

- Using the graph on the following page, complete a climograph for your city.

- Use the "Modified Köppen System Charts" to classify the climate of your city.

As an alternative assignment, your instructor may ask that you classify the climate of a city other than where you live.

Climate Classification

City: _____

Years of climate record: From _____ to _____

Units used: S.I. or English (circle)

	JAN	FEB	MAR	APR	MAY	JUN	JUL	AUG	SEP	OCT	NOV	DEC
Temp												
Precp												

Average Annual Temperature: _____

Average Annual Precipitation: _____

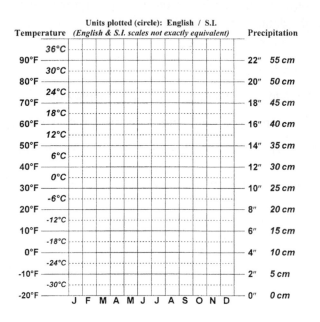

Köppen climate type: Letter code: _____

Descriptive name: _____

Geography 111: Physical Geography Lab
Lab Twelve: Rock Identification

The purpose of this exercise is to help you familiarize yourself with common rocks found at or near Earth's surface. You will be classifying rocks as igneous, metamorphic, or sedimentary, as well as differentiating rocks within a rock class.

Materials:
Rock Samples

Objectives:
- Differentiate between the three types of rock classes (i.e., igneous, sedimentary, metamorphic).
- Differentiate within a rock type:
  - intrusive igneous vs extrusive igneous
  - clastic vs chemically precipitated
  - foliated vs non-foliated

- Describe the process used to classify rocks into different types and within each type.
- Describe the rock cycle.
- Describe where to find various types of rocks.
- Identify rocks when given samples.

Part 1: Rock Cycle

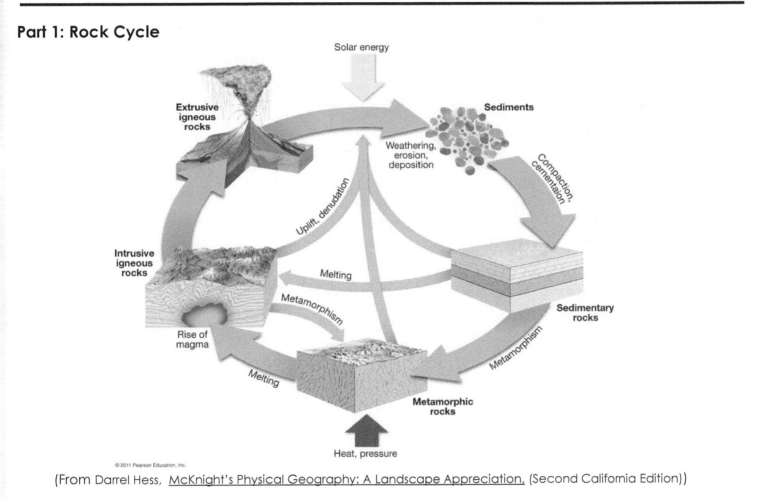

(From Darrel Hess, _McKnight's Physical Geography: A Landscape Appreciation,_ (Second California Edition))

1. Which type of rock is formed by the cooling and solidification of molten rock? Hint: magma is the term for molten rock beneath the surface.

There are two types of igneous rocks- one formed from the cooling of magma and one from the cooling of lava.

2. What is the difference between intrusive and extrusive igneous rocks? Hint: think about where the cooling occurs.

External processes, such as weathering (both chemical and mechanical), cause rock to break down and disintegrate. Running water, waves, wind and ice erode the fragmented rock (sediment) and transport them elsewhere, where they are deposited.

3. Are sediments and sedimentary rocks the same? If not, what processes act upon sediments to form sedimentary rock?

Lithification is the process whereby sediments are converted into solid rock through compaction and cementation.

4. Write the word lithification in the proper spot on the diagram.

Metamorphism alters the rock via heat and pressure, causing its mineral components to recombine and recrystallize.

5. What type of rock is formed through heat and pressure?

Extrusive igneous rocks are not the only type of rock that is weathered into sediments.

6. How are intrusive igneous, metamorphic, and sedimentary rocks subjected to solar energy?

Metamorphic rock isn't the only rock type subjected to melting.
7. Can sedimentary rock become molten rock? Explain.

8. Using a complete sentence, explain how igneous rocks are formed.

9. Using a complete sentence, explain how sedimentary rocks are formed.

10. Using a complete sentence, explain how metamorphic rocks are formed.

Part 2: Rock Identification

Using the rock samples and rock identification tables provided, classify the samples as igneous, metamorphic or sedimentary rocks. In addition, you will further classify the rocks within each class, ultimately determining the name of the rock and its characteristics.

Complete the tables on the following page as you classify the samples. *Hint: Of the 13 samples, 4 are igneous, 5 are sedimentary, and 4 are metamorphic.*

Igneous Rocks:

Specimen number	Texture: Coarse grained or Fine grained	Color: Light or Dark	Dominant Materials	Rock Name

Sedimentary Rocks:

Specimen number	Detrital (Clastic) or Chemical	Texture	Sediment Name or Composition	Rock Name

Metamorphic Rocks:

Specimen number	Foliated or Nonfoliated	Grain size	Parent Rock	Rock Name

Lab 12a

Common Rocks

To an Earth scientist, rocks represent much more than usable substances. They are the materials of the Earth; understanding their origin and how they change allows us to begin to understand Earth and its processes. It is often said that "the history of Earth is written in the rocks"—we just have to be smart enough to read the "words."

In this exercise, you will investigate some of the common rocks that are found on and near Earth's surface. The criteria used to classify a rock as being of either igneous, sedimentary, or metamorphic origin are examined, as well as the procedure for identifying rocks within each of these three families.

Objectives

After you have completed this exercise, you should be able to:

1. Examine a rock and determine if it is an igneous, sedimentary, or metamorphic rock.
2. List and define the terms used to describe the textures of igneous, sedimentary, and metamorphic rocks.
3. Name the dominant mineral(s) found in the most common igneous, sedimentary, and metamorphic rocks.
4. Use a classification key to identify a rock.
5. Recognize and name some of the common rocks by sight.

Materials

metric ruler   hand lens

Materials Supplied by Your Instructor

igneous rocks   dilute hydrochloric acid
sedimentary rocks   streak plate

metamorphic rocks   glass plate
hand lens or binocular   copper penny
   microscope

Terms

rock   weathering   composition
rock cycle   sediment   detrital material
igneous rock   lithification   chemical material
magma   metamorphic   foliation
sedimentary   rock   texture
   rock

Introduction

Most **rocks** are aggregates (mixtures) of minerals. However, there are some rocks that are composed essentially of one mineral found in large impure quantities. The rock limestone, consisting almost entirely of the mineral calcite, is a good example.

Rocks are classified into three types, based on the processes that formed them. One of the most useful devices for understanding rock types and the geologic processes that transform one rock type into another is the **rock cycle**. The cycle, shown in Figure 1, illustrates the various Earth materials and uses arrows to indicate chemical and physical processes. As you examine the rock cycle and read the following definitions, notice the references to the origin of each rock type.

The three types of rock are igneous, sedimentary, and metamorphic.

Igneous Igneous rocks (Figures 2–9) are the solidified products of once molten material called **magma**. The distinguishing feature of most igneous rocks is an interlocking arrangement of mineral crystals that forms as the molten material cools and crystals grow. *Intrusive* igneous rocks form below the surface of Earth, while those that form at the surface from lava are termed *extrusive*.

From *Applications and Investigations in Earth Science*, Fifth Edition, Edward J. Tarbuck, Frederick K. Lutgens, Dennis Tasa, and Kenneth G. Pinzke.

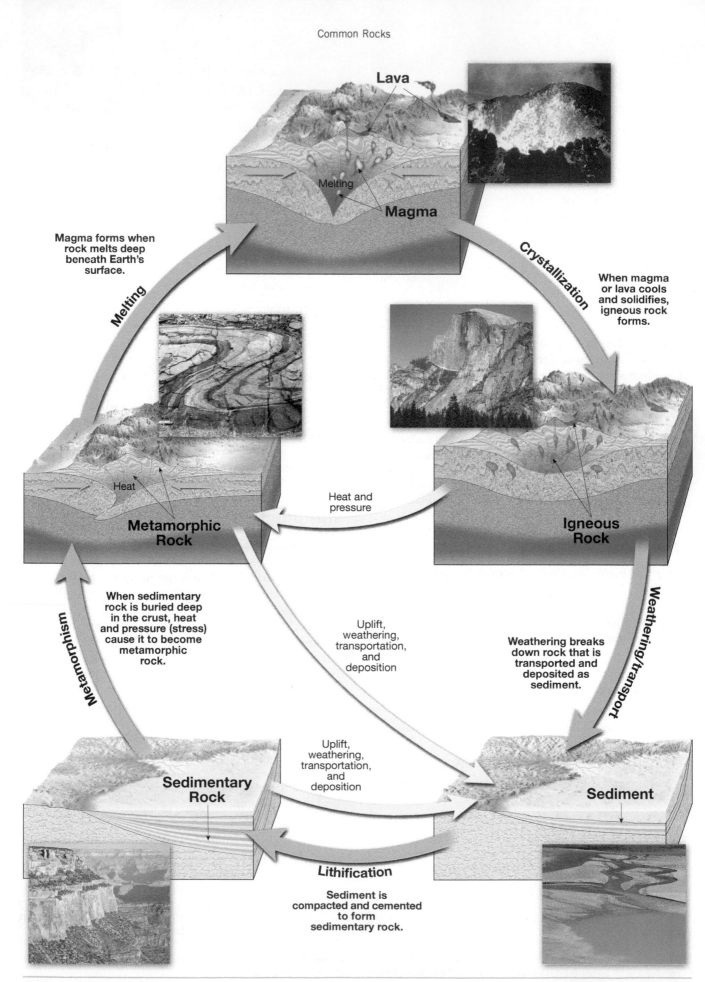

Lava

Melting

Magma

Magma forms when rock melts deep beneath Earth's surface.

Melting

Crystallization

When magma or lava cools and solidifies, igneous rock forms.

Heat and pressure

Metamorphic Rock

Heat

Igneous Rock

Weathering/transport

When sedimentary rock is buried deep in the crust, heat and pressure (stress) cause it to become metamorphic rock.

Metamorphism

Uplift, weathering, transportation, and deposition

Weathering breaks down rock that is transported and deposited as sediment.

Sedimentary Rock

Uplift, weathering, transportation, and deposition

Sediment

Lithification

Sediment is compacted and cemented to form sedimentary rock.

Figure 1 The rock cycle illustrating the role of the various geologic processes that act to transform one rock type into another.

Sedimentary These rocks (Figures 10–17) form at or near Earth's surface from the accumulated products of **weathering**, called **sediment**. These products may be solid particles or material that was formerly dissolved and then precipitated by either inorganic or organic processes. The process of **lithification** transforms the sediment into hard rock. Since sedimentary rocks form at, or very near, Earth's surface, they often contain organic matter, or fossils, or both. The layering (or bedding) that develops as sediment is sorted by, and settled out from, a transporting material (usually water or air) helps make sedimentary rocks recognizable.

Metamorphic These rocks (Figures 18–25) form below Earth's surface where high temperatures, pressures, and/or chemical fluids change preexisting rocks without melting them.

Minerals are identified by using their physical and chemical properties. However, rock types and the names of individual rocks are determined by describing their *textures* and *compositions*. The key to success in rock identification lies in learning to accurately determine and describe these properties.

Texture refers to the shape, arrangement, and size of mineral grains in a rock. The shape and arrangement of mineral grains help determine the type (igneous, sedimentary, or metamorphic) of rock. Mineral grain size is often used to separate rocks within a particular type. Each rock type uses different terms to describe its textures.

Composition refers to the minerals that are found in a rock. Often the larger mineral grains can be identified by sight or by using their physical properties. In some cases, small mineral grains may require the use of a hand lens or microscope. Occasionally, very small grains cannot be identified with the normal magnification of a microscope. Practice and increased familiarity with the minerals will make this assessment easier.

Comparing Igneous, Sedimentary, and Metamorphic Rocks

One of the first steps in the identification of rocks is to determine the rock type. Each of the three rock types has a somewhat unique appearance that helps to distinguish one type from the other.

Examine the specimens of the three rock types supplied by your instructor, as well as the photographs of the rocks in Figures 2–25. Then answer the following questions.

1. Which two of the three rock types appear to be made primarily of intergrown crystals?

   _____ rocks and _____ rocks

2. Which one of the two rocks types you listed in question 1 has the mineral crystals aligned or

arranged so that they are oriented in the same direction in a linear, linelike manner?

   _____

3. Which one of the two rock types you listed in question 1 has the mineral crystals in most of the rocks arranged in a dense interlocking mass with no alignment?

   _____

4. Of the three rock types, (igneous, sedimentary, metamorphic) rocks often contain haphazardly arranged pieces or fragments, rather than crystals. Circle your answer.

Igneous Rock Identification

Igneous rocks form from the cooling and crystallization of magma. The interlocking network of mineral crystals that develop as the molten material cools gives most igneous rocks their distinctive crystalline appearance.

Textures of Igneous Rocks

The rate of cooling of the magma determines the size of the interlocking crystals found in igneous rocks. The slower the cooling rate, the larger the mineral crystals. The five principal textures of igneous rocks are:

Coarse Grained (or *phaneritic*) The majority of mineral crystals are of a uniform size and large enough to be identifiable without a microscope. This texture occurs when magma cools slowly inside Earth.

Fine Grained (or *aphanitic*) Very small crystals, which are generally not identifiable without strong magnification, develop when molten material cools quickly on, or very near, the surface of Earth.

Porphyritic Two very contrasting sizes of crystals are caused by magma having two different rates of cooling. The larger crystals are termed *phenocrysts*; and the smaller, surrounding crystals are termed *groundmass* (or *matrix*).

Glassy No mineral crystals develop because of very rapid cooling. This lack of crystals causes the rock to have a glassy appearance. In some cases, rapidly escaping gases may produce a frothy appearance similar to spun glass.

Fragmental The rock contains broken, angular fragments of rocky materials produced during an explosive volcanic eruption.

Examine the igneous rock photographs in Figures 2–9. Then answer the following questions.

5. The igneous rock illustrated in Figure 2 is made of large mineral crystals that are all about the same size. The rock formed from magma that cooled (slowly, rapidly) (inside, on the surface of) Earth. Circle your answers.

Igneous Rocks

Figure 2 Granite, a common coarse-grained, intrusive igneous rock.

Figure 6 Basalt, a fine-grained igneous rock.

Figure 3 Rhyolite, a fine-grained, extrusive rock.

Figure 7 Gabbro, a coarse-grained, intrusive igneous rock.

Figure 4 Diorite, a coarse-grained igneous rock.

Figure 8 Obsidian, an igneous rock with a glassy texture.

Figure 5 Andesite porphry, an igneous rock with a porphyritic texture.

Figure 9 Pumice, a glassy rock containing numerous tiny voids.

Sedimentary Rocks

Figure 10 Conglomerate, a detrital sedimentary rock.

Figure 11 Sandstone, a common detrital sedimentary rock.

Figure 12 Shale, a detrital sedimentary rock composed of very fine grains.

Figure 13 Breccia, a detrital sedimentary rock containing large, angular fragments.

Figure 14 Fossiliferous limestone, a biochemical sedimentary rock.

Figure 15 Coquina, a biochemical limestone consisting of visible shells and shell fragments, loosely cemented.

Figure 16 Rock salt, a chemical sedimentary rock formed as water evaporates.

Figure 17 Bituminous coal, a sedimentary rock composed of altered plant remains.

135

Metamorphic Rocks

Figure 18 Slate, a fine-grained, foliated metamorphic rock.

Figure 22 Schist, variety mica schist.

Figure 19 Phyllite, a foliated metamorphic rock with barely visible grains.

Figure 23 Marble, a nonfoliated metamorphic rock that forms from the metamorphism of the sedimentary rock limestone.

Figure 20 Schist, a foliated metamorphic rock with visible grains (variety: garnet-mica schist).

Figure 24 Quartzite, a nonfoliated metamorphic rock composed of fused quartz grains.

Figure 21 Gneiss, a foliated-banded metamorphic rock that often forms during intensive metamorphism.

Figure 25 Anthracite coal, often called hard coal, forms from the metamorphism of bituminous coal.

6. The rock shown in Figure 6 is made of mineral crystals that are all small and not identifiable without a microscope. The rock formed from magma that cooled (slowly, rapidly) (inside, on/near the surface of) Earth. Circle your answers.

7. The igneous rock in Figure 5 has a porphyritic texture. The large crystals are called _____, and the surrounding, smaller crystals are called _____.

8. The rocks in Figures 2 and 3 have nearly the same mineral composition. What fact about the mineral crystals in the rocks makes their appearances so different? What caused this difference?

_____

_____

Select a coarse-grained rock from the igneous rock specimens supplied by your instructor and examine the mineral crystals closely using a hand lens or microscope.

9. Sketch a diagram showing the arrangement of the mineral crystals in the igneous rock specimen you examined in the space provided below. Indicate the scale of your sketch by writing the appropriate length within the ( ) provided on the bar scale.

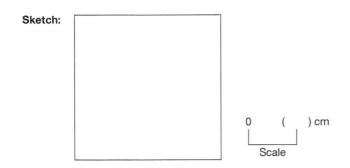

Sketch:

0   (   ) cm

Scale

Composition of Igneous Rocks

The specific mineral composition of an igneous rock is ultimately determined by the chemical composition of the magma from which it crystallized. However, the minerals found in igneous rocks can be arranged into four groups. Each group can be identified by observing the proportion of dark-colored minerals compared to light-colored minerals. The four groups are

Felsic (or *granitic*)—composed mainly of the light-colored minerals quartz and potassium feldspars. Dark-colored minerals account for less than 15% of the minerals in rocks found in this group.

Intermediate (or *andesitic*)—a mixture of both light-colored and dark-colored minerals. Dark minerals comprise about 15% to 45% of these rocks.

Mafic (or *basaltic*)—dark-colored minerals such as pyroxene and olivine account for over 45% of the composition of these rocks.

Ultramafic—composed almost entirely of the dark-colored minerals pyroxene and olivine, these rocks are rarely observed on Earth's surface. However, the ultramafic rock peridotite is believed to be a major constituent of Earth's upper mantle.

10. Estimate the percentage are of dark minerals contained in the igneous rock in Figure 4. The rock's color is (light, medium, dark, very dark). Circle your answer.

11. The rocks shown in Figures 3 and 6 have the same texture. What fact about the mineral crystals makes their appearances so different?

_____

Using an Igneous Rock Identification Key

The name of an igneous rock can be found by first determining its texture and color (an indication of mineral composition), identifying visible mineral grains, and then using an igneous rock identification key such as the one shown in Figure 26 to determine the name.

For example, the igneous rock shown in Figure 2 has a coarse-grained texture and is light-colored (quartz and potassium feldspar dominant). Intersecting the light-colored column with the coarse-grained row on the igneous rock identification key, Figure 26, determines that the name of the rock is "granite."

12. Place each of the igneous rocks supplied by your instructor on a numbered piece of paper. Then complete the igneous rock identification chart, Figure 27, for each rock. Use the igneous rock identification key, Figure 26, to determine each specimen's name.

Sedimentary Rock Identification

Sedimentary rocks, Figures 10–17, form from the accumulated products of weathering called *sediment*. Sedimentary rocks can be made of either, or a combination of, detrital or chemical material.

Detrital material consists of mineral grains or rock fragments derived from the process of mechanical weathering that are transported and deposited as solid particles (sediment). Rocks formed in this manner are called *detrital sedimentary rocks*. The mineral pieces that make

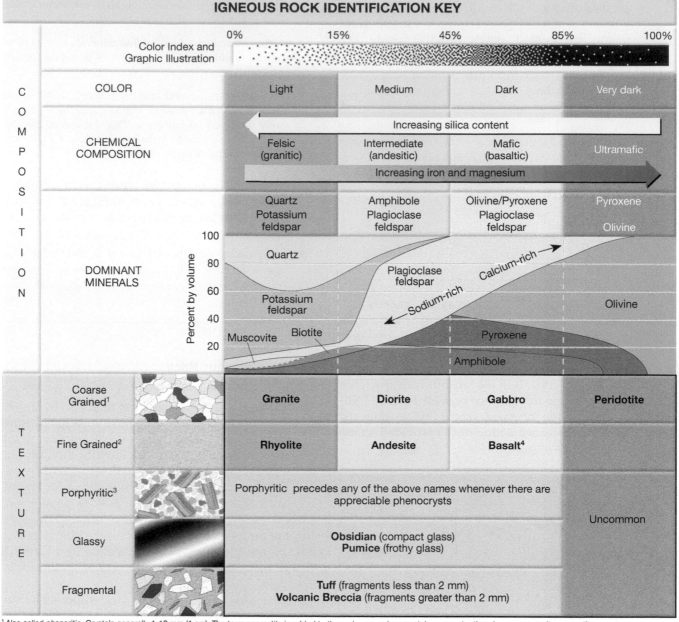

IGNEOUS ROCK IDENTIFICATION KEY

COMPOSITION

	0%	15%	45%	85%	100%
Color Index and Graphic Illustration					
COLOR	Light	Medium	Dark	Very dark	
CHEMICAL COMPOSITION	Felsic (granitic)	Intermediate (andesitic)	Mafic (basaltic)	Ultramafic	
DOMINANT MINERALS	Quartz, Potassium feldspar	Amphibole, Plagioclase feldspar	Olivine/Pyroxene, Plagioclase feldspar	Pyroxene, Olivine	

Increasing silica content

Increasing iron and magnesium

Quartz, Potassium feldspar, Muscovite, Biotite, Plagioclase feldspar (Sodium-rich, Calcium-rich), Pyroxene, Amphibole, Olivine

TEXTURE

Coarse Grained[1]	**Granite**	**Diorite**	**Gabbro**	**Peridotite**
Fine Grained[2]	**Rhyolite**	**Andesite**	**Basalt[4]**	
Porphyritic[3]	Porphyritic precedes any of the above names whenever there are appreciable phenocrysts			Uncommon
Glassy	**Obsidian** (compact glass) **Pumice** (frothy glass)			
Fragmental	**Tuff** (fragments less than 2 mm) **Volcanic Breccia** (fragments greater than 2 mm)			

[1] Also called *phaneritic.* Crystals generally 1-10 mm (1 cm). The term *pegmatite* is added to the rock name when crystals are greater than 1 cm; e.g. *granite-pegmatite.*

[2] Also called *aphanitic.* Crystals generally less than 1 mm.

[3] For example, a granite with phenocrysts is called *porphyritic granite.*

[4] Basalt with a cinder-like appearance that develops from gas bubbles trapped in cooling lava (a texture referred to as *vesicular*) is called *scoria.*

Figure 26 Igneous rock identification key. Color, with associated mineral composition, is shown along the top axis. Each rock in a column has the color and composition indicated at the top of the column. Texture is shown along the left side of the key. Each rock in a row has the texture indicated for that row. To determine the name of a rock, intersect the appropriate column (color & mineral composition) with the appropriate row (texture) and read the name at the place of intersection.

up a detrital sedimentary rock are called *grains* (or *fragments* if they are pieces of rock). The identification of a detrital sedimentary rock is determined primarily by the size of the grains or fragments. Mineral composition of the rock is a secondary concern.

Chemical material was previously dissolved in water and later precipitated by either inorganic or organic processes. Rocks formed in this manner are called *chemical sedimentary rocks.* If the material is the result of the life processes of water-dwelling organisms—for example, the formation of a shell—it is said to be of biochemical origin. Mineral composition is the primary consideration in the identification of chemical sedimentary rocks.

Sedimentary rocks come in many varieties that have formed in many different ways. For the purpose of examination, this investigation divides the sedimentary rocks into the two groups, *detrital* and *chemical,* based upon the type of material found in the rock.

Specimen Number	Texture	Color (light-intermediate-dark)	Dominant Minerals	Rock Name

Figure 27 Igneous rock identification chart. See Figure 1 in color image atlas.

Examining Sedimentary Rocks

Examine the sedimentary rock specimens supplied by your instructor. Separate those that are made of pieces or fragments of mineral, rock material, or both. They are the detrital sedimentary rocks. Do *not* include any rocks that have abundant shells or shell fragments. You may find the photographs of the detrital sedimentary rocks in Figures 10–13 helpful. The remaining sedimentary rocks, those with shells or shell fragments and those that consist of crystals, are the chemical rocks.

Pick up each detrital rock specimen and rub your finger over it to feel the size of the grains or fragments.

13. How many of your detrital specimens feel rough like sand? How many feel smooth like mud or clay?

_____ specimens feel rough and _____ feel smooth.

Use a hand lens or microscope to examine the grains or fragments of several coarse detrital rock specimens. Notice that they are not crystals.

14. Sketch the magnified pieces and surrounding material, called *cement* (or *matrix*), of a coarse detrital rock in the space provided on the following page. Indicate the scale of your sketch by writing the appropriate length within the ( ) provided on the bar scale.

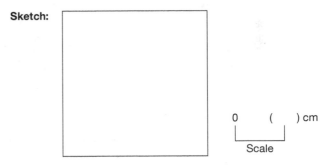

Sketch:

a. Observe the material surrounding the grains or fragments in the rock specimen closely with a hand lens or microscope. The material is (course, fine). Circle your answer.

b. Write a brief description of the detrital rock specimen you have examined.

_____

_____

Two of the minerals that often comprise the grains of detrital sedimentary rocks are quartz, a hard (hardness = 7) mineral with a glassy luster, and clay, a soft, fine mineral that consists of microscopic platy particles. The difference in appearance and hardness of quartz and clay is helpful in distinguishing them.

15. How many of your detrital specimens are made of quartz, and how many appear to be made of clay?

_____ specimens have quartz grains and

_____ have clay grains.

As a result of their method of formation, many chemical sedimentary rocks are fine-to-coarse crystalline, while others consist of shells or shell fragments.

16. How many of your chemical sedimentary rocks are crystalline, and how many contain abundant shells or shell fragments?

_____ specimens are crystalline and

_____ contain shells or shell fragments.

Limestones, Figures 14 and 15, are the most abundant chemical sedimentary rocks. They have several origins and many different varieties; however, one thing that all limestones have in common is that they are made of the calcium carbonate mineral called *calcite*. Calcite can precipitate directly from the sea to form limestone or can be used by marine organisms to make shells. After the organisms die, the shells become sediment and eventually the sedimentary rock limestone.

Calcite is a mineral that reacts with dilute hydrochloric acid and effervesces (fizzes) as carbon dioxide gas is released. Most limestones react readily when a small drop of acid is placed on them, thus providing a good test for identifying the rock. Many limestones also contain fragments of seashells, which also aid in their identification.

17. Follow the directions of your instructor to test the specified sedimentary rock(s) with the dilute hydrochloric acid provided and observe the results. (*Note:* Several detrital sedimentary rocks have calcite surrounding their grains or fragments (calcite cement) that will effervesce with acid and give a *false* test for limestone. Observe the acid reaction closely.)

Using a Sedimentary Rock Identification Key

The sedimentary rock identification key in Figure 28 divides the sedimentary rocks into detrital and chemical types. Notice that the primary subdivisions for the detrital rocks are based upon grain size, whereas composition is used to subdivide the chemical rocks.

Detrital Sedimentary Rocks

Texture (particle size)		Sediment Name	Rock Name
Coarse (over 2 mm)		Gravel (rounded particles)	Conglomerate
		Gravel (angular particles)	Breccia
Medium (1/16 to 2 mm)		Sand (if abundant feldspar is present the rock is called **Arkose**)	Sandstone
Fine (1/16 to 1/256 mm)		Mud	Siltstone
Very fine (less than 1/256 mm)		Mud	Shale

Chemical Sedimentary Rocks

Composition	Texture	Rock Name		
Calcite, CaCO₃ (effervesces in HCl)	Fine to coarse crystalline	Crystalline Limestone		
		Travertine		
	Visible shells and shell fragments loosely cemented	Coquina	Biochemical	Limestone
	Various size shells and shell fragments cemented with calcite cement	Fossiliferous Limestone		
	Microscopic shells and clay	Chalk		
Quartz, SiO₂	Very fine crystalline	**Chert** (light colored) **Flint** (dark colored)		
Gypsum CaSO₄•2H₂O	Fine to coarse crystalline	**Rock Gypsum**		
Halite, NaCl	Fine to coarse crystalline	**Rock Salt**		
Altered plant fragments	Fine-grained organic matter	**Bituminous Coal**		

Figure 28 Sedimentary rock identification key. Sedimentary rocks are divided into two groups, detrital and chemical, depending upon the type of material that composes them. Detrital rocks are further subdivided by the size of their grains, while the subdivision of the chemical rocks is determined by composition. See Figure 2 in color image atlas.

Specimen Number	Detrital or Chemical	Texture (grain size)	Sediment Name or Composition	Rock Name

Figure 29 Sedimentary rock identification chart. See Figure 3 in color image atlas.

18. Place each of the sedimentary rocks supplied by your instructor on a numbered piece of paper. Then complete the sedimentary rock identification chart, Figure 29, for each rock. Use the sedimentary rock identification key, Figure 28, to determine each specimen's name.

Sedimentary Rocks and Environments

Sedimentary rocks are extremely important in the study of Earth's history. Particle size and the materials from which they are made often suggest something about the place, or environment, in which the rock formed. The fossils that often are found in a sedimentary rock also provide information about the rock's history.

Reexamine the sedimentary rocks and think of them as representing a "place" on Earth where the sediment was deposited.

19. Figure 11 is the rock sandstone that formed from sand. Where on Earth do you find sand, the primary material of sandstone, being deposited today?

_____

Figure 30 shows a few generalized environments (places) where sediment accumulates. Often, an environment is characterized by the type of sediment and life forms associated with it.

20. Use Figure 30 to name the environment(s) where, in the past, the sediment for the following sedimentary rocks may have been deposited.

	ORIGINAL SEDIMENT	ENVIRONMENT(S)
Sandstone:	(sand)	_____
Shale:	(mud)	_____
Limestone:	(coral, shells)	_____

Metamorphic Rock Identification

Metamorphic rocks were previously igneous, sedimentary, or other metamorphic rocks that were changed by any combination of heat, pressure, and chemical fluids during the process of **metamorphism**. They are most often located beneath sedimentary rocks on the continents and in the cores of mountains.

During metamorphism new minerals may form, and/or existing minerals can grow larger as metamorphism becomes more intense. Frequently, mineral crystals that are elongated (like hornblende) or have a sheet structure (like the micas—biotite and muscovite) become oriented perpendicular to compressional forces. The resulting parallel, linear alignment of mineral crystals perpendicular to compressional forces (differential stress) is called **foliation** (Figure 31). Foliation is unique to many metamorphic rocks and gives them a layered or banded appearance.

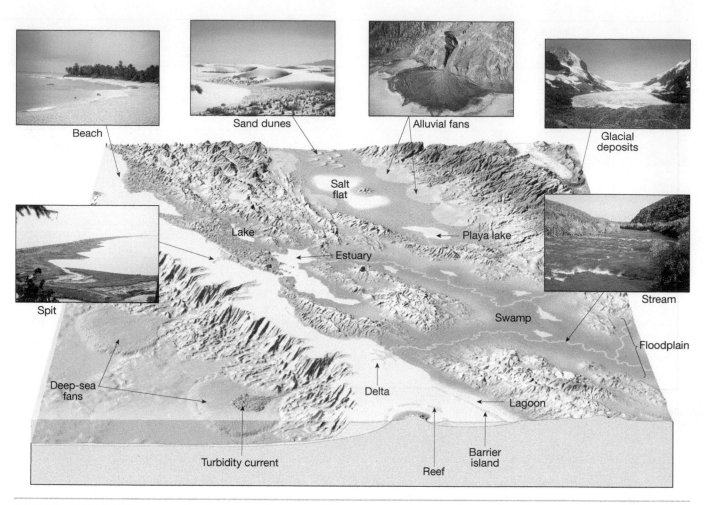

Figure 30 Generalized illustration of sedimentary environments. Although many environments exist on both the land and in the sea, only some of the most important are represented in this idealized diagram. (Photos by E. J. Tarbuck, except alluvial fan, by Marli Miller)

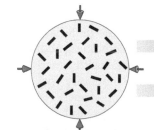

Figure 31 Under directed pressure, planar minerals, such as the micas, become reoriented or recrystallized so that their surfaces are aligned at right angles to the stress. The resulting planar orientation of mineral grains is called **foliation** and gives the rock a foliated texture. If the coarse-grained igneous rock (granite) on the left underwent intense metamorphism, it could end up closely resembling the metamorphic rock on the right (gneiss). (Photos by E. J. Tarbuck) See Figure 4 in color image atlas.

Metamorphic rocks are divided into two groups based on texture—foliated and nonfoliated. These textural divisions provide the basis for the identification of metamorphic rocks.

Foliated Metamorphic Rocks

The mineral crystals in foliated metamorphic rocks are either elongated or have a sheet structure and are arranged in a parallel or "layered" manner. *During metamorphism, increased heat and pressure can cause the mineral crystals to become larger and the foliation more obvious.* (Figure 32) The metamorphic rocks in Figures 18–22 exhibit foliated textures.

21. From the rocks illustrated in Figures 18 and 20, the (slate, schist) resulted from more intensive heat and pressure. Circle your answer.

22. From the metamorphic rocks in Figures 19 and 21, the (phyllite, gneiss) shows the minerals separated into light and dark bands. Circle your answer. (The foliated-banded texture of the rock that you have selected often results

from the most intensive heat and pressure during metamorphism.)

Select several of the foliated metamorphic rock specimens supplied by your instructor that have large crystals and examine them with a hand lens or microscope.

23. Sketch the appearance of the magnified crystals of one foliated metamorphic rock in the space provided below. Indicate the scale of your sketch by writing the appropriate length within the ( ) provided on the bar scale.

Sketch:

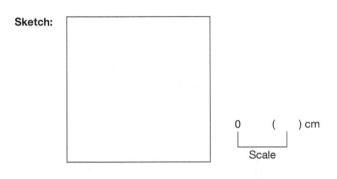

0   (   ) cm

Scale

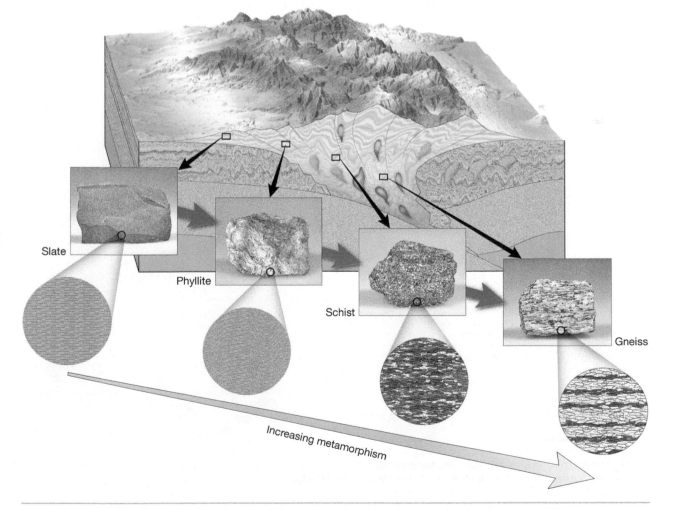

Slate

Phyllite

Schist

Gneiss

Increasing metamorphism

Figure 32   Idealized illustration showing the effect of increasing metamorphism in foliated metamorphic rocks. (Photos by E. J. Tarbuck)

Nonfoliated Metamorphic Rocks

Nonfoliated metamorphic rocks are most often identified by determining their mineral composition. The minerals that comprise them, most often calcite or quartz, are neither elongated nor sheet structured and therefore cannot be as easily aligned. Hence, no foliation develops during metamorphism.

24. Examine the nonfoliated metamorphic rocks supplied by your instructor to determine if any are composed of calcite or quartz. Hardness and the reaction to dilute hydrochloric acid often provide a clue.

CAUTION: Follow the directions of your instructor when using acid to test for calcite.

Using a Metamorphic Rock Identification Key

A metamorphic rock identification key is presented in Figure 33. To use the key, first determine a rock's texture, foliated or nonfoliated, and then proceed to further sub-divisions to arrive at a name. The names of the medium or coarse foliated rocks are often modified with the mineral composition placed in front of the name, e.g., "mica schist."

25. Place each of the metamorphic rocks supplied by your instructor on a numbered piece of paper. Then complete the metamorphic rock identification chart, Figure 34, for each rock. Use the metamorphic rock identification key, Figure 33 to determine each specimen's name.

Rocks on the Internet

Associated with igneous rock, the most abundant rock on Earth, are often geologic hazards related to volcanic activity. Investigate this potentially destructive geologic process by completing the corresponding online activity on the *Applications & Investigations in Earth Science* website at http://prenhall.com/earthsciencelab

Texture	Grain Size	Rock Name	Comments	Parent Rock
Foliated	Very fine	Slate	Excellent rock cleavage, smooth dull surfaces	Shale, mudstone, or siltstone
Foliated	Fine	Phyllite	Breaks along wavey surfaces, glossy sheen	Slate
Foliated	Medium to Coarse	Schist	Micas dominate, scaly foliation	Phyllite
Foliated	Medium to Coarse	Gneiss	Compositional banding due to segregation of minerals	Schist, granite, or volcanic rocks
Nonfoliated	Medium to coarse	Marble	Interlocking calcite or dolomite grains	Limestone, dolostone
Nonfoliated	Medium to coarse	Quartzite	Fused quartz grains, massive, very hard	Quartz sandstone
Nonfoliated	Fine	Anthracite	Shiny black organic rock that may exhibit conchoidal fracture	Bituminous coal

(Increasing Metamorphism)

Figure 33 Metamorphic rock identification key. Metamorphic rocks are divided into the two textual groups, foliated and nonfoliated. Foliated rocks are further subdivided based upon the size of the mineral grains. See Figure 5 in color image atlas.

Specimen Number	Foliated or Nonfoliated	Grain Size	Composition (if identifiable)	Rock Name

Figure 34 Metamorphic rock identification chart. See Figure 6 in color image atlas.

Notes and calculations.

Common Rocks

Date Due: _____

Name: _____

Date: _____

Class: _____

After you have finished this lab, complete the following questions. You may have to refer to the exercise for assistance or to locate specific answers. Be prepared to submit this summary/report to your instructor at the designated time.

1. Write a brief definition of each of the three rock types.

   Igneous rocks: _____
   _____
   _____

   Sedimentary rocks: _____
   _____
   _____

   Metamorphic rocks: _____
   _____
   _____

2. What unique factor about the arrangement of mineral crystals occurs in many metamorphic rocks?
   _____

3. Describe the procedure you would follow to determine the name of a specific igneous rock.
   _____
   _____
   _____

4. Describe the basic difference between detrital and chemical sedimentary rocks.
   _____
   _____

5. List the *texture* and mineral *composition* of each of the following rocks.

	TEXTURE	MINERAL COMPOSITION
Granite:	_____	_____
Marble:	_____	_____
Sandstone:	_____	_____

6. What are two possible environments for the origin of the sedimentary rock sandstone?
   _____
   _____
   _____

7. Of the three rock types, which one is most likely to contain fossils? Explain the reason for your choice.
   _____
   _____
   _____

8. What factor determines the size of the crystals in igneous rocks?
   _____

9. What is a good chemical test to determine the primary mineral in limestone?
   _____

10. What factor(s) determine(s) the size of crystals in metamorphic rocks?
    _____
    _____

11. If the sedimentary rock limestone is subjected to metamorphism, what metamorphic rock will likely form?

_____

12. With reference to the rock cycle, describe the processes and changes that an igneous rock will undergo as it is changed first to a sedimentary rock, which then becomes a metamorphic rock.

_____

_____

_____

13. Select two igneous, two sedimentary, and two metamorphic rocks that you identified, and write a brief description of each.

Rock type: _____

Rock name: _____

Description: _____

_____

_____

Rock type: _____

Rock name: _____

Description: _____

_____

_____

Rock type: _____

Rock name: _____

Description: _____

_____

_____

Rock type: _____

Rock name: _____

Description: _____

_____

_____

_____

Rock type: _____

Rock name: _____

Description: _____

_____

_____

Rock type: _____

Rock name: _____

Description: _____

_____

_____

14. Referring to Figure 35, list each rock's name and write a brief description of each.

A: _____

_____

_____

_____

B: _____

_____

_____

_____

C: _____

_____

_____

A.   B.   C.

Figure 35 Three rock specimens for use with question 14.

Geography 111: Physical Geography Lab
Lab Thirteen: Internal Processes

This lab is designed to help you better understand the internal processes which shape the Earth's surface. These internal processes include massive rearrangement of lithospheric plates (plate tectonics), volcanic activity and the deformation of Earth's surface through folding and faulting. As you observe the landscape around you, it is important to understand the processes which created and modified topographic features.

Materials:
Ruler

Objectives:
- Identify plate boundaries on a map or hypothetical map.
- Identify features associated with various plate boundaries.
- Draw a cross section of plate boundaries.
- Determine rate of speed of a lithospheric plate, by calculating distance and age of topographic feature.
- Create a profile from a topographic map.
- Calculate map scale.

Part 1: Plate Tectonics

Plate tectonics is the theory that the Earth's surface is made of giant lithospheric plates (comprised of the Earth's crust and the upper portion of the mantle) that float on top of the molten material found in the asthenosphere. These giant lithospheric plates move independent of one another and can converge, diverge or move past one another.

Assignment:

A.   Describe the characteristics (density, thickness, material) of the two types of crust.

   a. Ocean   _____

   b. Continental _____

B.   Illustrate the movement of the tectonic plate along each boundary type.

   a. Divergent

   b. Convergent

   c. Transform

Part 2: Tectonics Landforms

Each type of plate boundary produces a specific landform depending on the type of crust present at that boundary.

Assignment:

A. Complete the table below using the following landforms:

Landforms:

Mid-ocean Ridge

Rift Valley

Volcanic Mountain range

Volcanic Island Arc

Folded Mountains

Shield Volcano

Pressure Ridge and Sag Pond

Boundary Type	Lithospheric Crust	Landform
Divergent	Ocean-Ocean	
Divergent	Continental- Continental	
Convergent	Ocean – Continental	
Convergent	Ocean - Ocean	
Convergent	Continental -Continental	
Transform	N/A	
Hot Spot	N/A	

B. Apply your knowledge of plate tectonics and resulting tectonic landforms to the Tectonic Map of Hypothetical Ocean Basin found in the following <u>Plate Tectonics</u> Lab, <u>Problems- Part I</u>.

- Answer <u>Plate Tectonics- Problems- Part I-</u> Questions 1 – 7

Note: when completing the cross section "side view" in Question 7, use "side view" diagrams for reference. Here are some examples of side view diagrams which note plate direction (arrows) and landforms:

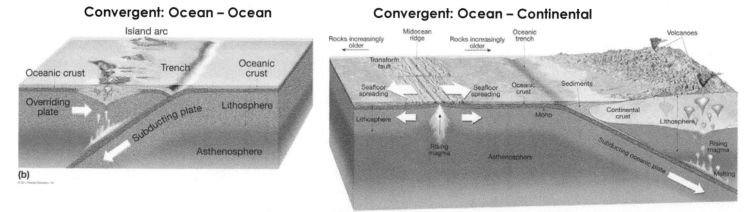

Convergent: Ocean – Ocean

Convergent: Ocean – Continental

(From Darrel Hess, <u>McKnight's Physical Geography: A Landscape Appreciation,</u> (Second California Edition))
"Courtesy of Pearson Education."

C. Using the information from the table in Section A above, identify the type of boundary that produced the following landforms:

Feature	Boundary	Lithospheric Crust	Landform
Iceland (Example)	*Divergent*	*Ocean*	*Mid-Ocean Ridge*
Andes			
East African Rift Valley			
Mid-Atlantic Ridge			
Red Sea			
Cascades			
Himalayas			
Aleutian Islands, Alaska			
Japan			

Part 3: Rate of Plate Movement

By comparing the distance and age of the rocks found in the Hawaiian Islands, you can estimate the rate of movement per year.

Rate of Movement = Distance from Hot Spot / Island Age

Assignment

A. Using the map of the Hawaiian Islands found in the following Plate Tectonics Lab, Figure 30-4, complete the following table:

Locations	Measured Distance on Map (inches)	Real-World Distance (inches) Use map scale (1:4,200,000) to convert	Island Age (in years) For example: 5,000,000	Rate of Movement (inches/year)
Kauai - Hawaii				
Oahu -Hawaii				
Kauai - Molokai				

B. Based on the average of your 3 answers in section A, what is the approximate rate of movement of the Pacific Plate in the Hawaiian Island region over the past 5.1 million years?

C. Using the average rate of movement, how far will the Pacific Plate move in 100 years? Show your work.

Part 4: Create a Topographic Profile

Using the sample topographic map below, construct a topographic profile from Point A to A'.

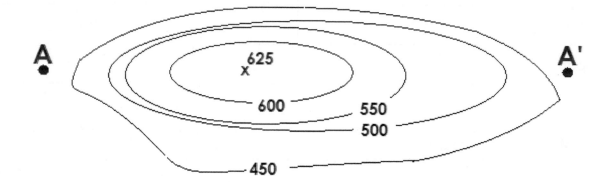

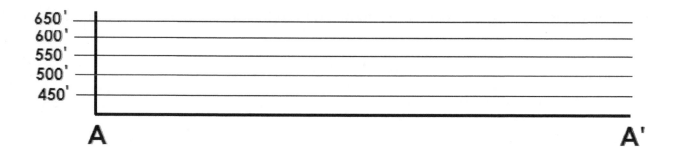

Lab 13a

PLATE TECTONICS

Objective:	To study the tectonic processes and topographic features associated with plate boundaries and hot spots.
Reference:	Hess, Darrel. *McKnight's Physical Geography;* 10th ed.; chapter, "The Internal Processes"; section, "Plate Tectonics."

PLATE TECTONICS

The model of **plate tectonics** is the starting point for understanding the distribution and formation of many collections of landforms around the world. Figure 1 is a map showing the principal plates and plate boundaries. These **lithospheric plates** are 65 to 100 kilometers (40 to 60 miles) thick and consist of the crust and upper mantle. The plates move over the layer of the mantle known as the **asthenosphere** at speeds averaging from 2.5 to 10 centimeters (1 to 4 inches) per year.

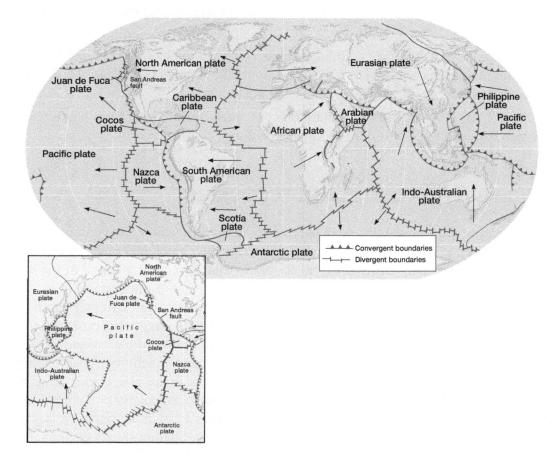

Figure 1: Major lithosphere plates. Barbed lines show collision; lines with offsets show spreading; single lines show transform boundaries; arrows indicate generalized direction of plate movement. (From Hess, *McKnight's Physical Geography*, 10th ed.)

PLATE BOUNDARIES

The three different kinds of plate boundaries are associated with different kinds of topographic features and tectonic activity.

Divergent Boundaries: At divergent boundaries (also called "spreading centers"), plates are moving apart. The most common kind of spreading center is the **midocean ridge** where new basaltic ocean floor is created (Figure 2). Spreading may also take place within a continent. In this case, blocks of crust may drop down as the land is pulled apart, producing a **continental rift valley**.

Convergent Boundaries: At convergent boundaries, where plates collide, three circumstances are possible:

1. If the edge of an oceanic plate collides with the edge of a continental plate a **subduction** zone is formed. The denser oceanic plate is subducted below the continent, producing an **oceanic trench**. As the oceanic lithosphere descends, water and other volatile materials are driven out of the ocean rocks, leading to the partial melting of the mantle. The **magma** that is generated rises, producing intrusions of **plutonic rock** such as granite and a chain of andesitic **volcanoes**, such as the Andes in South America or the Cascades in North America (Figure 2).

2. If the edge of an oceanic plate collides with the edge of another oceanic plate, subduction also takes place. An oceanic trench forms, along with a chain of andesitic volcanic islands known as an **island arc**, such as the Aleutian Islands in Alaska and the Mariana Islands of the western Pacific Ocean.

3. If the edge of a continent collides with the edge of another continent, the relatively buoyant continental material is not subducted. Instead, a mountain range is uplifted. The Himalayas are a dramatic example of this kind of plate boundary interaction.

Transform Boundaries: Plates slide past each other at transform boundaries, such as along the San Andreas fault system in California (Figure 3).

EVIDENCE SUPPORTING PLATE TECTONICS

Evidence supporting the theory of plate tectonics comes from global patterns of landforms and tectonic activity. In addition to the matching shape of the continental margins on both sides of the Atlantic Ocean (which spread apart from the Mid-Atlantic Ridge), the age of the ocean floor provides evidence of movement. The ocean floors are youngest at midocean ridges, where new lithosphere is being formed, and become progressively older away from a ridge in both directions. This was verified through ocean core samples, as well as **paleomagnetic** evidence (changes in Earth's magnetic field that have been recorded in the volcanic rocks of the ocean floor).

Plate boundaries are often the sites of significant volcanic activity. At spreading centers, magma is moving up to the surface, creating new lithosphere as the plates spread apart. Magma generated in subduction zones can produce a chain of continental volcanoes or a volcanic island arc.

The distribution of **earthquakes** also provides clues to plate activity. Most earthquakes around the world occur in association with plate boundaries. Shallow-focus earthquakes, within

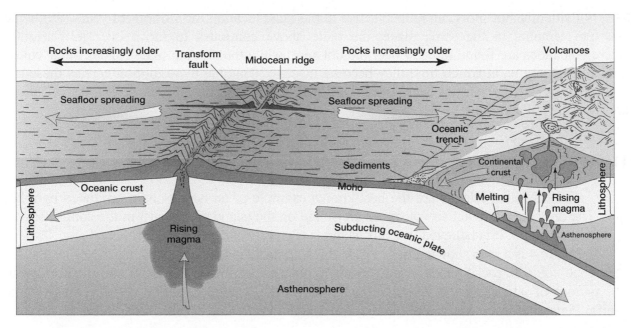

Figure 2: Plates move apart at spreading centers such as midocean ridges, collide at convergent boundaries such as subduction zones, and slide past each other along transform faults. (From McKnight and Hess, *Physical Geography*, 9th ed.)

about 70 kilometers (45 miles) of the surface, occur at all plate boundaries. However, in subduction zones, bands of progressively deeper earthquakes are observed, produced when an oceanic plate is thrust down into the asthenosphere.

HOT SPOTS

One of the important modifications of basic plate tectonic theory is the concept of the **hot spot**. These are locations where a fairly narrow plume of magma is rising from the asthenosphere to the surface, producing volcanoes. Many hot spots apparently develop from **mantle plumes** that originate deep within the mantle.

Hot spots may occur well away from plate boundaries, often in the middle of a plate. It is not yet completely understood why these hot spots occur where they do, but the existence of hot spots has been helpful in verifying plate motion.

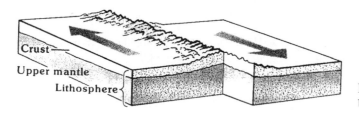

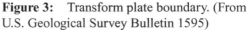

Figure 3: Transform plate boundary. (From U.S. Geological Survey Bulletin 1595)

Evidently, hot spots can remain active in the same location for millions of years. While the hot spot remains in the same place, the plate above continues to move over it. Currently active volcanoes are found directly over the hot spot, while the moving plate carries older volcanoes off the plume, at which time they become inactive. Ongoing plate motion carries these old volcanoes farther and farther away from the hot spot, resulting in a chain of extinct volcanoes known as a "hot spot trail."[1]

THE HAWAIIAN HOT SPOT

The Hawaiian Islands are the best-known example of an island chain produced by a hot spot. The only currently active volcanoes are found on the island of Hawai'i in the southeast part of the island chain. It is believed that this island is currently over the hot spot.

Figure 4 is a map showing the ages of volcanic rocks in the Hawaiian chain. Notice that the age of the volcanic rocks becomes progressively older as we follow the islands to the northwest. The pattern of islands in the Hawaiian chain shows the general direction of movement of the Pacific Plate, and from the ages of the rocks, we can infer the rate of plate movement.

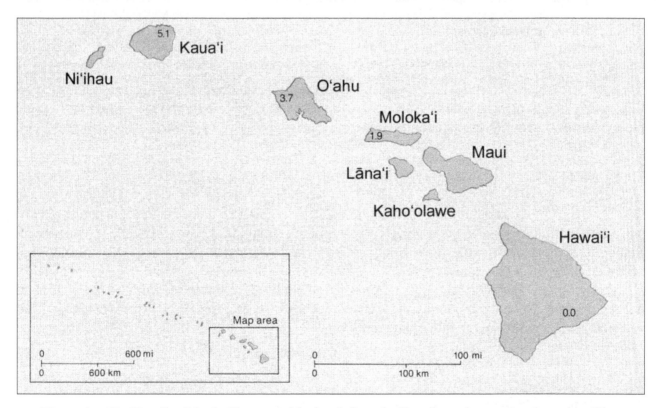

Figure 4: The Hawaiian Islands. The ages of the basalt from the Hawaiian volcanoes are shown in millions of years; map scale 1:4,200,000. (Adapted from McKnight, *Physical Geography*, 4th ed.)

[1]Recent geophysical evidence suggests that the locations of some mantle plumes may slowly change over time, making a complete explanation of some hot spots more complex than geologists once thought.

PROBLEMS – Part I Introduction

In the Part I problems for this exercise, you will study the tectonic map of a hypothetical ocean basin. The map shows the location of volcanoes, earthquakes, and the age of ocean floor rocks. From this map, you will determine the probable location of the plate boundaries and the locations of major topographic features in the region.

On the map, the edges of two continents are shown (in the upper right corner and the lower left corner). Six islands are also shown in the ocean basin.

The symbols used on the tectonic map are described below.

Earthquake Epicenter Location and Depth:

The locations of earthquake **epicenters** are shown with letters. The depth of an earthquake (the distance of the earthquake hypocenter or "focus" below the surface) is indicated with an "S" (shallow focus), "I" (intermediate focus), or "D" (deep focus):

S	= Shallow Earthquakes	0–70 kilometers (0–45 miles) deep
I	= Intermediate Earthquakes	70–200 kilometers (45–125 miles) deep
D	= Deep Earthquakes	200–500 kilometers (125–310 miles) deep

Active Volcano:
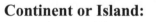

Continent or Island:
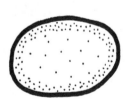

Age of Volcanic Ocean Floor Rocks:

The circled numbers represent the age of volcanic ocean floor rocks in millions of years.

For example, ⑳ indicates the location of 20-million-year-old rocks.

EXERCISE PROCEDURE:

The first step of the exercise is to draw in the approximate plate boundaries as indicated by the tectonic activity on the map.

Clues include:

(a)   The pattern of earthquakes. For example, subduction produces a pattern of deeper and deeper earthquakes as one plate plunges below the other.

(b)   The age pattern of volcanic ocean floor rocks suggests the location where new ocean floor is being created at a midocean ridge.

(c)   Volcanic activity may be associated with subduction, spreading centers, or hot spots.

Use the following symbols to indicate the extent of all plate boundaries. Both the map symbols, and a side view of the circumstance they represent, are shown below. Arrows indicate direction of plate movement.

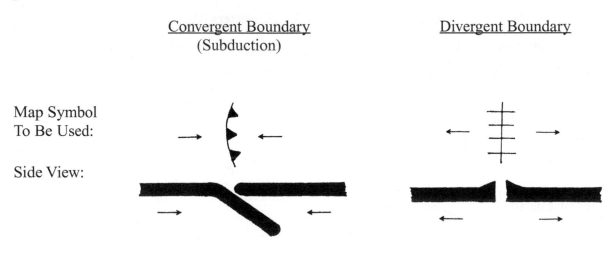

Convergent Boundary
(Subduction)

Divergent Boundary

Map Symbol To Be Used:

Side View:

Note:

- No transform boundaries are found on the map.

- Assume that only one of the volcanoes on the map is associated with a hot spot.

Name _____   Section _____

PROBLEMS—PART I

After drawing in the plate boundaries on the tectonic map below, answer the questions on the following page.

TECTONIC MAP OF HYPOTHETICAL OCEAN BASIN

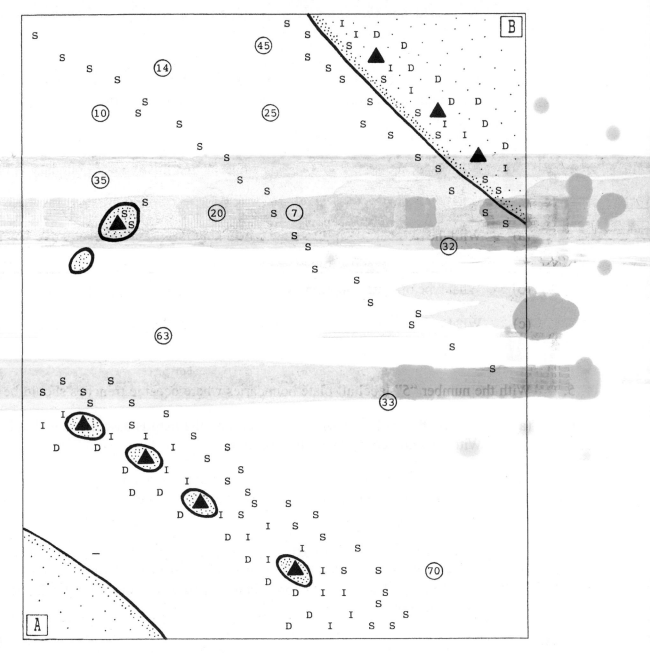

Scale: 1 cm = 300 km (1 inch = 500 miles)

Plate Tectonics

1. (a) How many different *plates* are clearly shown on the map? _____

    (b) How many of the plates on the map consist entirely of ocean floor
         (or ocean floor with islands)? _____

2. (a) With the number "2" indicate the most likely location on the map of a midocean
         ridge (such as the Mid-Atlantic Ridge).

    (b) What type of plate boundary is this? _____

    (c) What evidence *shown on the map* suggests that this type of boundary is present?

3. (a) With the number "3" indicate the most likely location on the map of a major vol-
         canic mountain range similar to the Andes in South America.

    (b) What type of plate boundary is this? _____

    (c) What evidence *shown on the map* suggests that this type of boundary is present?

4. (a) With the number "4" indicate the most likely location on the map of a volcanic is-
         land arc.

    (b) What type of plate boundary is this? _____

    (c) What evidence *shown on the map* suggests that this type of boundary is present?

5. With the number "5" label all plate boundaries where oceanic trenches should be found.

6. (a) Assume that only one of the volcanoes on the map is associated with a hot spot.
         With the number "6" label this volcano.

    (b) With a 2-centimeter (about one-inch) long arrow extending from this volcano, in-
         dicate the direction in which you would expect to find progressively older *extinct*
         volcanoes left by the hot spot.

7. In the space below, draw an approximate continuous cross section ("side view") of the
    ocean basin from Point "A" to Point "B" (from lower left to upper right). Use the previous
    "side view" drawings and Figure 2 for reference, and use arrows to indicate the relative
    direction of plate motion.

A
Lower Left

B
Upper Right

Name _____   Section _____

PROBLEMS—PART II

Using the map of the Hawaiian Islands and the ages of the basaltic lava (Figure 4), compute the approximate rate of movement of the Pacific Plate as it passes over the Hawaiian hot spot.

You will compare the age and distance between several different volcanoes on the islands. The ages of volcanic rocks on the islands are given in millions of years. Assume that the decimal point of an age marks the location of a volcano. For example, on the island of Hawai'i, "0.0" marks the location of the currently active volcano, Kīlauea.

In this exercise, you will compare Hawai'i (0.0 years—currently active volcanoes), Moloka'i (1.9 million years), O'ahu (3.7 million years), and Kaua'i (5.1 million years). For the purposes of this exercise, we will take the position of the Kīlauea volcano to represent the location of the Hawaiian hot spot (keep in mind that this is a simplistic assumption). We also assume that the Hawaiian hot spot is completely stationary over long periods of time.

1.   Complete the chart on the following page:

   (a)   First, determine the distance between each pair of locations listed on the chart. With a ruler, carefully measure the distance between locations on the map to the nearest millimeter if you use S.I. units and to the nearest 1/16 inch if you use English units. (If you use English units, convert fractions of inches to decimals to make other calculations easier.) This figure is the "Measured Distance on Map." Then multiply this measured distance on the map by 4,200,000 (the denominator of the fractional map scale) to determine the "Actual Distance" in millimeters (or inches).

   (b)   Next, determine the "Age Difference" in years between each pair of locations. (Be sure to include the correct number of zeros in your figure.)

   (c)   Finally, divide the "Actual Distance" between locations by the "Age Difference" to estimate the rate of plate movement in millimeters (or inches) per year.

Locations	Measured Distance on Map (in mm or inches)	Actual Distance (in mm or inches)	Age Difference (in years)	Rate of Plate Movement (mm or inches per year)
Kauaʻi to Hawaiʻi				
Oʻahu to Hawaiʻi				
Molokaʻi to Hawaiʻi				
Kauaʻi to Oʻahu				
Kauaʻi to Molokaʻi				

2.   Based on the average of your five answers in problem 1 above, what has been the approximate rate of movement of the Pacific Plate in the area of the Hawaiian Islands over the last 5.1 million years?

3.   Midway Island, to the northwest of Hawaiʻi, is also part of the Hawaiian chain and is believed to have been produced by the same hot spot. Midway is about 2430 kilometers (1510 miles) from the Kīlauea volcano on Hawaiʻi. Use the average rate of plate movement you calculated in problem 2 above to estimate the age of volcanic rocks you would expect to find on Midway Island.

4.   The actual age of the volcanic rock on Midway is about 27.7 million years. Suggest a reason why your answer for problem 3 above differs noticeably from this.

Lab 13b

FAULTING

Objective: To review the different kinds of faults and to study faulted landscapes.

Materials: Lens stereoscope.

Resources: Internet access (optional).

Reference: Hess, Darrel. *McKnight's Physical Geography;* 10th ed.; chapter, "The Internal Processes"; section, "Faulting."

TYPES OF FAULTS

Faulting occurs when stresses forcibly break apart and displace a rock structure. The displacement along a fault can be horizontal, vertical, or a combination of the two. Although there are many different kinds of faults, they all can be placed into four general categories.

Normal Faults: As shown in Figure 1, along a **normal fault** the movement is primarily vertical, exposing a steep fault plane. Normal faulting is the result of extension ("tension")—stresses working to stretch or pull apart the landscape (direction of stress shown with wide arrows).

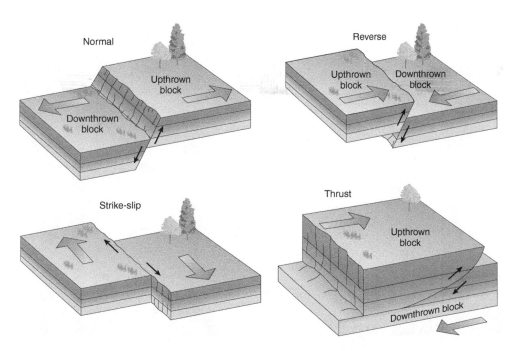

Figure 1: The principal types of faults. The large arrows show the direction of stress; the small arrows show the relative direction of displacement along the fault plane. (From McKnight and Hess, *Physical Geography*, 9th ed.)

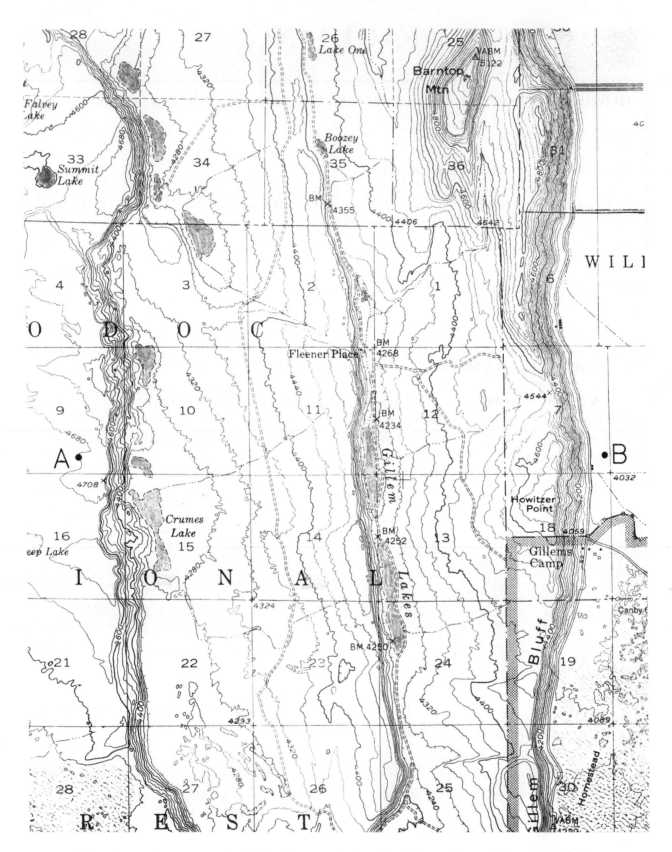

Figure 2: USGS "Mt. Dome, California," quadrangle (enlarged to scale 1:48,000; contour interval 40 feet; ↑N).

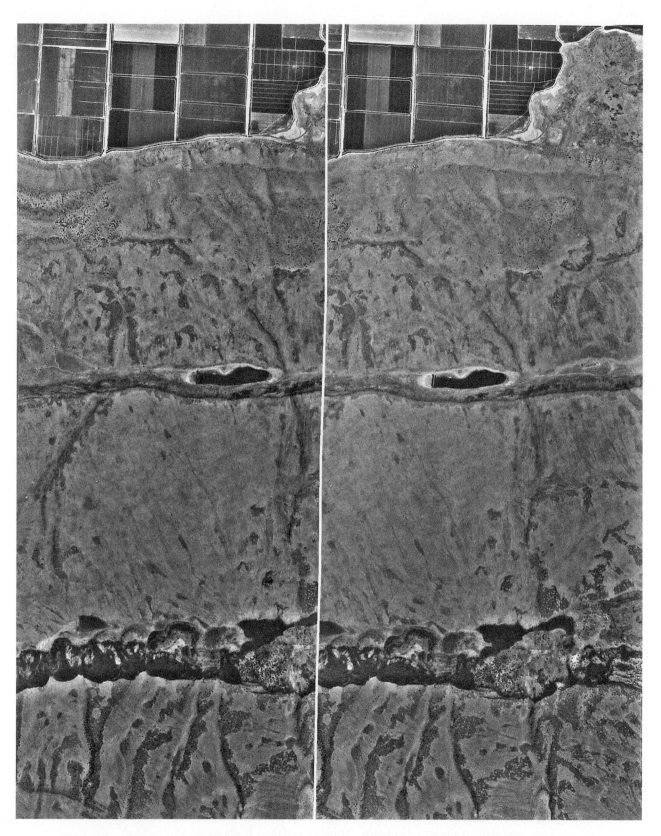

Figure 3: Stereogram of fault scarps near Mt. Dome, California. North is to left side of page (scale 1:40,000; USGS photographs, 1993; ← N).

Reverse and Thrust Faults: Movement along **reverse faults** (Figure 1) is also mainly vertical, but in this case compressional stresses have produced the fault displacement. **Thrust** (or "overthrust") faults also result from compression, but the upthrown block overrides the downthrown block at a low angle.

Strike-Slip Faults: The movement along a **strike-slip fault** (Figure 1) is primarily horizontal and is produced by shear stresses.

LANDFORMS PRODUCED BY FAULTING

There are many conspicuous landforms associated with faulting. For example, predominantly normal faulting throughout much of the Basin and Range province of the western United States has produced a series of fault-block mountains and down-dropped basins. Figures 2 and 3 show a faulted landscape in the Basin and Range province in northeastern California.

Tilted fault block mountains such as the Sierra Nevada (Figure 4) are produced by fault displacement along one side. When a block of land is downdropped between two roughly parallel faults, a **graben** is formed (Figure 5). When a basin is tilted down along just one side, it is sometimes referred to as a *half graben*. A mountain block between two parallel down-dropped blocks is known as a **horst**.

Figure 4: The Sierra Nevada is a tilted fault block mountain range. (From McKnight and Hess, *Physical Geography*, 9th ed.)

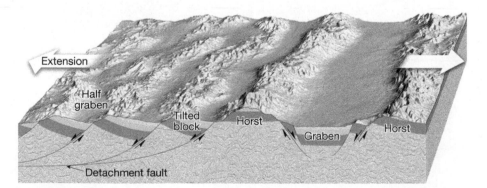

Figure 5: Horsts and grabens are bound by faults on both sides, while tilted blocks have been faulted along just one side, forming tilted fault-block mountains and *half grabens*. Extension may also result in *detachment faults*, where a steep normal fault ties in with a nearly horizontal fault below. (From Hess, *McKnight's Physical Geography*, 10th ed.)

Faulting

Name _____   Section _____

PROBLEMS—PART I

The following questions are based on the "Mt. Dome, California," quadrangle (Figure 2; enlarged to scale 1:48,000; contour interval 40 feet) and the stereogram of the same region (Figure 3; north is to the left side of the page). Three prominent fault scarps can be seen running north to south across the map, and will be referred to as the "western" fault, the "central" fault, and the "eastern" fault. These fault scarps are the result of normal faulting (41°49'39"N, 121°33'15"W).

1.   Determine the approximate amount of visible vertical displacement along each of the three fault scarps at their intersection with line AB (to determine the amount of visible displacement, measure the height [relief] of each fault scarp; it may be easiest to count the number of contour lines shown on each scarp to determine the elevation change):

Western Fault: _____ feet   Central Fault: _____ feet   Eastern Fault: _____ feet

2.   (a)   Is the height of the "central fault" uniform
           from north to south?   _____

      (b)   If not, describe the pattern of vertical displacement:

PROBLEMS—PART II—GOOGLE EARTH™

To answer the following questions, go to the Hess *Physical Geography Laboratory Manual* for *McKnight's Physical Geography*, 10th edition, Web site at **http://www.mygeoscienceplace.com**, then Exercise 33. Select "Exercise 33 Google Earth" to open a KMZ file in Google Earth™.

1.   Fly to Point 1 at the base of a fault scarp near Mount Dome in northeastern California (also shown in Figure 2 and Figure 3). Compare the height of the fault scarp here to that at Point 2. What happens to the height of the fault scarp as you move north from Point 1 to Point 2?

2.   Fly to Point 3, near the Gillem Lakes. Based on the surrounding topography, why have lakes formed here?

Name _____   Section _____

PROBLEMS—PART III

The following question is based on the "Mt. Dome, California," quadrangle (Figure 2; enlarged to scale 1:48,000; contour interval 40 feet). Three prominent fault scarps can be seen running north to south across the map, and will be referred to as the "western" fault, the "central" fault, and the "eastern" fault. These faults scarps are the result of normal faulting. Figure 3 is a stereogram of the same region (in Figure 3, north is to the left side of the page).

Using the graph below, construct a topographic profile from Point "A" to Point "B." Plot the index contours, as well as the crest and bottom of the fault scarps. The vertical exaggeration of the profile is approximately 6.7×.

Hint: Since the contour lines are very close together, it may be difficult to discern the elevation of the top and bottom of a scarp. To determine these elevations, find an index contour in the gently sloping area between two scarps, and then count the number of contour lines to the top or bottom of a scarp.

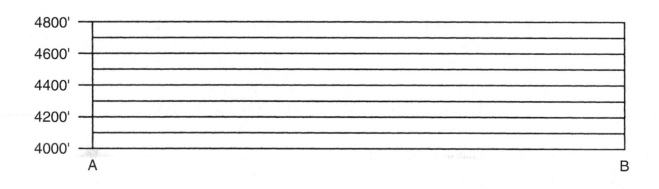

Geography 111: Physical Geography Lab
Lab Fourteen: External Processes

The purpose of this exercise is to help you familiarize yourself with the some of the external processes working to wear down the Earth's surface. Specifically we will be looking at Fluvial Processes whereby running water erodes the Earth's surface and transports the sediment elsewhere.

Materials:

red, blue, and green colored pencils   calculator

Objectives:

- Calculate gradient- elevation change / length.
- Identify drainage divide on a map.
- Identify streams on a topographic map.

- Identify direction of flow.
- Measure features on a topographic map.
- Identify features using contour lines.

Part 1: Stream Orders and Gradients

Land is raised my internal processes and leveled by gradational processes in order to reach equilibrium in elevation.

Gradation:	leveling and smoothing of Earth's surface by erosion and deposition primary agents are water, wind and ice
Drainage Basin:	geographic area contributing overland flow and ground water to a stream also called a watershed
Tributary:	a river that flows into another river
Stream Flow:	is a result of gravity- force pulls the water downslope and erodes streambed
Velocity:	speed of the river- the higher the velocity the more power it has to erode and transport material
Stream Orders:	a way of classifying streams within a drainage basin. The greater the stream order the larger the drainage basin

First Order Streams:	no tributaries
Second Order Streams:	two first order streams merge
Third Order Streams:	two second order streams merge

The stream order does not change unless two streams of the same order merge. For example, if a first order stream and a third order stream merge, downstream of this merge is still a third order stream.

Stream Gradient:	The slope of the stream. This is calculated by the following equation:

Gradient = Elevation Change / Length of River

Elevation Change (feet):	difference in elevation from the start of the stream to the end of the stream
Length (miles):	length of stream

Assignment:

A. Stream Order:
- Answer the following <u>Drainage Basins</u> lab- <u>Problems- Part I</u>- Questions 2 and 3

B. Stream Gradient:
Note: You will use the contour elevations to calculate the difference in elevation and you will use the map scale to convert the length of the stream into miles.

- Answer the following <u>Drainage Basins</u> lab- <u>Problems- Part I</u>- Question 4 and <u>Problems- Part II</u>– Questions 5- 7.

C. Drainage Basin:
Ridges: Topographic maps display ridges as curved lines pointing towards lower elevations.
Valleys: Topographic maps display valleys as "V"s pointing up towards higher elevations.

The map below shows Telegraph Canyon.
- Using a blue pencil, draw in the location of ephemeral streams.
- Using a red pencil, draw the drainage divide. Note: the entire drainage divide is not shown on this map. Locate the portion of the drainage divide found north of Telegraph Canyon and the portion found south of Telegraph Canyon.

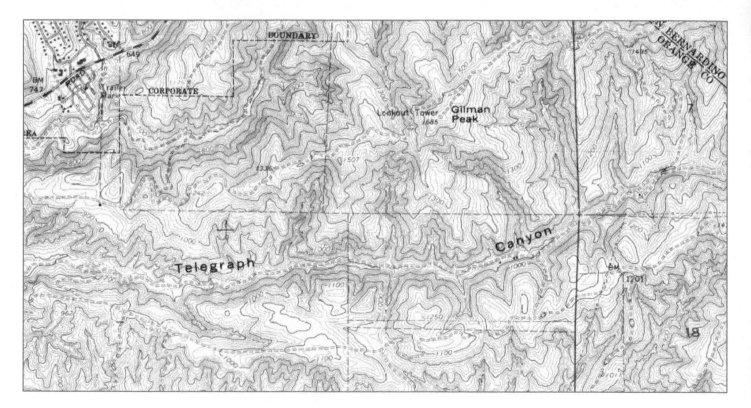

Source: USGS Yorba Linda Quadrangle 7.5' Series. Photorevised 1981.

Lab 14a

DRAINAGE BASINS

Objective:	To study stream drainage basins, stream order, and stream gradients.
Materials:	Lens stereoscope.
Resources:	Internet access (optional).
Reference:	Hess, Darrel. *McKnight's Physical Geography;* 10th ed.; chapter, "Fluvial Processes"; section, "Streams and Stream Systems."

STREAM SYSTEMS

Running water is the most important agent of erosion on the Earth's land surface. Most of this fluvial erosion is accomplished by the action of **streams**. One important consideration in the study of fluvial geomorphology is the way in which streams come together as a system.

Several different characteristics of stream systems can be recognized. Tiny streams flow together to form larger streams, and these streams in turn join to become still larger streams. We see that within any river system there is a hierarchy of streams, and within this hierarchy we can see differences in the gradient, the length, the area of land being drained, and the amount of water being carried by a stream.

DRAINAGE BASINS

A **drainage basin**, or **watershed**, is an area within which all water flows toward a single stream. Figure 1 is a diagram showing the drainage basins of three adjacent streams. The dashed line represents the **drainage divide** that delimits the drainage basin of the middle stream from the drainage basins of the streams on either side. Drainage divides are typically the high ground that separates streams flowing into one drainage basin from streams flowing into another.

As shown in Figure 1, a drainage divide may also include an area of **interfluve**—the part of a landscape where water moves downslope as unchanneled **overland flow**, rather than as the channeled **streamflow** found in **valleys**. Figure 3 is a stereogram of the Eds Creek drainage basin near Deer Peak, Montana. Map T-3 is a color topographic map of the same region.

STREAM ORDERS

One way of analyzing patterns of tributaries within a stream system is with the concept of **stream order**. A "first-order" stream is the smallest stream in a stream system and is defined as a stream without tributaries. Where two first-order streams join, a second-order stream is formed. Where two second-order streams join, a third-order stream is formed (Figure 2).

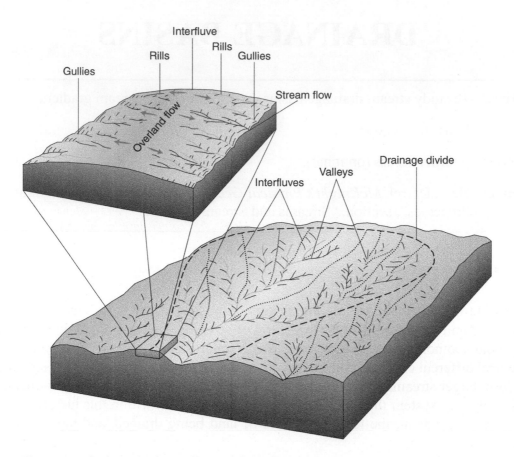

Figure 1: Drainage basins, valleys, and interfluves. Streams and valleys within a drainage basin are enclosed by a surrounding drainage divide. (From McKnight and Hess, *Physical Geography*, 9th ed.)

Notice that when a first-order and second-order stream meet, a third-order stream is not formed. Two second-order streams are required to form a third-order stream, two third-order streams to form a fourth-order stream, and so on.

In most well-established stream systems, there will be more first-order streams than all other orders combined, and each successively higher order will contain fewer and fewer streams. Also, as stream order increases, stream length and stream drainage areas tend to increase, while the gradient of streams tends to decrease.

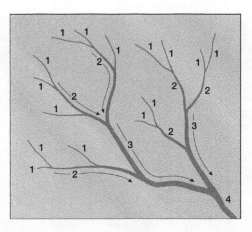

Figure 2: Stream orders. (From McKnight and Hess, *Physical Geography*, 9th ed.)

STREAM GRADIENT

The most common way to express the slope of a stream is by its **gradient**. If English measurement units are being used (as on the topographic maps in this exercise), the gradient of a stream is usually stated in feet of elevation change per mile. For example, if a stream drops 678 feet over a distance of 1.5 miles, the gradient is:

$$\text{Gradient} = \frac{\text{Elevation Change}}{\text{Number of Miles}} = \frac{678 \text{ feet}}{1.5 \text{ miles}} = 452 \text{ ft/mi}$$

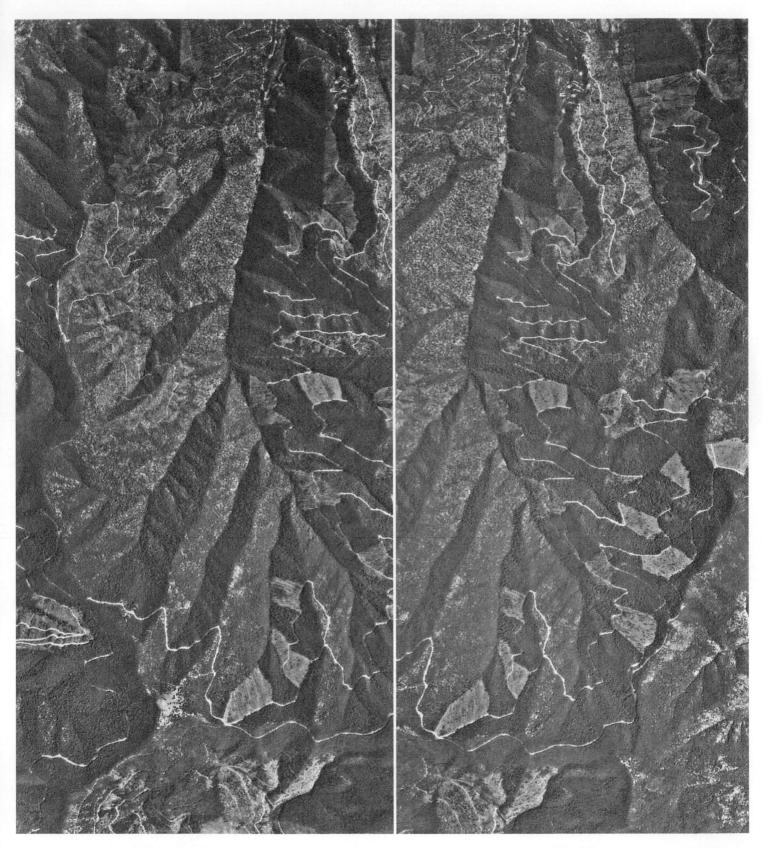

Figure 3: Stereogram of Eds Creek drainage basin near Deer Peak, Montana. North is to left side of page (scale 1:40,000; USGS photographs, 1995; ← N).

Drainage Basins

Name _____   Section _____

PROBLEMS—PART I

The following questions are based on Map T-3, the "Deer Peak, Montana," quadrangle (scale 1:24,000; contour interval 40 feet), and Figure 3, a stereogram of the same area showing the drainage basin of Eds Creek (46°54'26"N, 114°31'02"W).

1. The unimproved dirt road (shown as a double dashed black line) looping around past Deer Peak roughly follows which natural feature associated with the Eds Creek drainage basin?   _____

2. The stream pattern within the drainage basin of Eds Creek on Map T-3 is reproduced at right at a smaller scale. On this small map, trace the length of all first-order streams with blue lines, the length of all second-order streams with red lines, and the length of Eds Creek (as a third-order stream) with a green line. If you don't have colored pencils, number each segment, 1, 2, or 3.

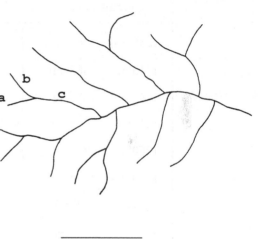

3. (a) How many first-order streams are shown?   _____

    (b) How many second-order streams are shown?   _____

4. Using Map T-3, determine the gradients of the two first-order streams labeled "a" and "b" on the map above, the second-order stream labeled "c" on the map above, as well as Eds Creek after it has become a third-order stream. Determine stream length to the nearest 0.1 mile (take your measurements from Map T-3, *not* the small map above). Use the graphic map scale.

Stream	Order	Elevation Drop (feet)	Length (miles) (to nearest 0.1 mi.)	Gradient (feet/mile)
a	1st			
b	1st			
c	2nd			
Eds Creek	3rd			

Name _____   Section _____

PROBLEMS—PART II

Answer the following questions after completing the problems in Part I.

5.   The table below gives the gradients of 12 more first-order streams and 4 more second-order streams in the Eds Creek drainage basin. Fill in the gradients of the streams calculated in Part I, problem 4 (streams "a" and "b" under first-order; stream "c" under second-order; Eds Creek under third-order):

1st-Order Stream Gradients		2nd-Order Stream Gradients	3rd-Order Stream Gradients
1680'/mi	1965'/mi	800'/mi	
1715'/mi	1485'/mi	680'/mi	
1225'/mi	1300'/mi	665'/mi	
1440'/mi	1335'/mi	800'/mi	
1200'/mi	1370'/mi		
1210'/mi	1355'/mi		
"a" _____ ft/mi		"c" _____ ft/mi	_____ ft/mi
"b" _____ ft/mi			(Eds Creek)

6.   Using the data from the table above, compute the following:

   (a)   Average gradient of first-order streams: _____ ft/mi

   (b)   Average gradient of second-order streams: _____ ft/mi

7.   What generally happens to the gradients of
   streams as the stream order increases?   _____

8.   Describe the general width and shape (cross section) of the valley floors of first-order streams in the Eds Creek drainage basin:

9.   How is the valley floor of Eds Creek different from the valley floors of the first-order streams? (Hint: Look at the difference in valley floor width.)

Name _____   Section _____

PROBLEMS—PART III

The following questions are based on Figure 4, a section of USGS "Dane Canyon, Arizona," quadrangle below, showing the southern edge of the Mogollon Mesa (34°24'33"N, 111°10'52"W), formed by a nearly flat-lying layer of resistant rock.

1. Compute the gradient of any first-order stream north of the mesa edge and the gradient of any first-order stream south of the mesa edge. On the map label the northern stream "a" and the southern stream "b."

Stream	Elevation Drop (ft)	Length (miles)	Gradient (ft/mi)
(a) North			
(b) South			

2. If gradient were the only factor controlling the erosive power of these streams, what should happen to the position of the mesa edge with time?

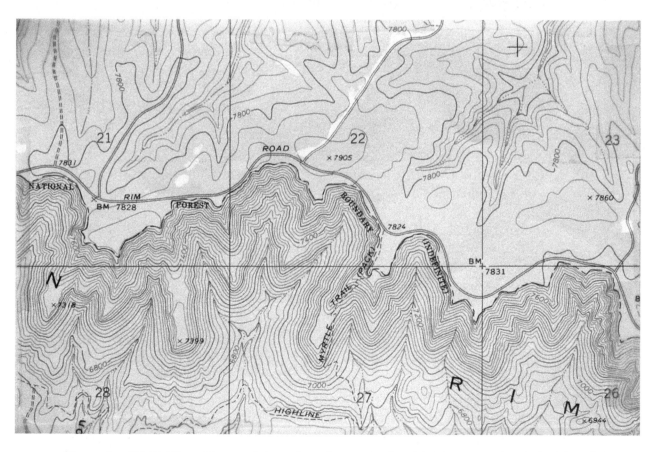

Figure 4:   USGS "Dane Canyon, Arizona," quadrangle (scale 1:24,000; contour interval 40 feet; ↑N).

Name _____   Section _____

PROBLEMS—PART IV—GOOGLE EARTH™

To answer the following questions, go to the Hess *Physical Geography Laboratory Manual* for *McKnight's Physical Geography*, 10th edition, Web site at **http://www.mygeoscienceplace.com**, then Exercise 36. Select "Exercise 36 Google Earth" to open a KMZ file in Google Earth™. In this exercise you'll compare the characteristics of streams in the Eds Creek drainage basin in Montana (also shown in Map T3 and Figure 3).

1. Determine the gradients of three segments of the Eds Creek drainage basin: a first-order stream between Points 1 and 2; a second-order stream between Points 2 and 3; and a third-order stream (Eds Creek) between Points 3 and 4. Use the ruler function to determine distances (to the nearest 0.01 miles) and the elevation change between points:

    (a) Fly to Point 2, then determine the gradient of the first-order stream (between Point 1 and Point 2):

    _____ ÷ _____ = _____ feet/mile gradient
    (Elevation change)   (Distance in miles)

    (b) Fly to Point 3, then determine the gradient of the second-order stream (between Point 2 and Point 3):

    _____ ÷ _____ = _____ feet/mile gradient
    (Elevation change)   (Distance in miles)

    (c) Fly to Point 4, then determine the gradient of the third-order stream (between Point 3 and Point 4):

    _____ ÷ _____ = _____ feet/mile gradient
    (Elevation change)   (Distance in miles)

2. What generally happens to stream gradient as you move downstream from the first-order stream?

3. Fly back to Point 2, and then to Point 4. How does the width of the valley floor change as you move downstream from the first-order stream to the third-order stream?

Lab 14b

FLOODPLAINS

Objective:	To study the formation and characteristics of floodplain landforms.
Materials:	Lens stereoscope.
Resources:	Internet access (optional).
Reference:	Hess, Darrel. *McKnight's Physical Geography;* 10th ed.; chapter. "Fluvial Processes"; section, "Floodplains."

MEANDERING STREAMS

In the upper reaches of a typical river system, or in other places where the gradient of a stream is steep, erosion (often downcutting) is the most prominent fluvial process. In contrast, in the lower reaches of a typical river system, or in other places where a stream is flowing down a gentle slope, a stream will begin to meander and depositional features become much more common.

Over time, a stream will meander back and forth across its flat alluvial valley floor, known as a **floodplain**. Figure 1 illustrates how a **meandering stream** shifts its course through the process of lateral erosion.

Erosion is concentrated on the outside bank of a meander since the water is moving fastest here as it flows into the turn. At the same time, deposition takes place on the inside bank, where the water is moving most slowly. Through this process of lateral erosion on the outside bank, and deposition on the inside bank, the position of the stream channel gradually shifts back and forth across the floodplain.

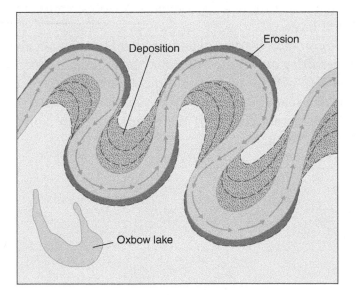

Figure 1: Lateral erosion and deposition of a meandering stream. (From McKnight and Hess, *Physical Geography*, 9th ed.; after Sheldon Judson, Marvin E. Kauffman, and L. Don Leet, *Physical Geology*, 7th ed., Englewood Cliffs, NJ: Prentice Hall, 1987, p. 264)

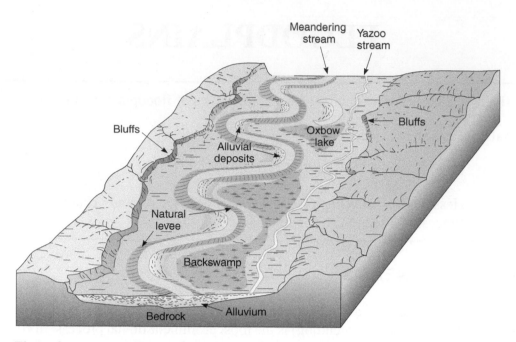

Figure 2: Common floodplain landforms. (From McKnight and Hess, *Physical Geography*, 9th ed.)

FLOODPLAIN LANDFORMS

The width of a major floodplain is often due, at least in part, to valley widening through lateral erosion, and floodplains are typically marked by low **bluffs** on both sides. However, most landforms found on a floodplain are largely the result of deposition. The floodplain itself is periodically inundated with flood waters. Along the course of the river, **natural levees** build up from the **alluvium** deposited along its banks during these floods (Figure 2).

Because of the nearly level terrain and natural levees that prevent water from draining back into the main river, poorly drained areas and swamps are typical of floodplains. Tributaries known as **yazoo streams** may run parallel to a main river for many kilometers. Yazoo streams are unable to enter because of the main river's natural levees.

When a stream is meandering tightly, it is common for one meander to cut into another, allowing the stream to take a shorter course. The resulting **cutoff meander** may be initially isolated as an **oxbow lake**. Eventually these cutoff meanders will fill up with sediment and dry out, first becoming a swamp, and then finally a dry **meander scar** (Figure 3).

Figure 4 is a stereogram showing the meandering course of the Souris River in North Dakota, and Map T-4 is a topographic map of the same region.

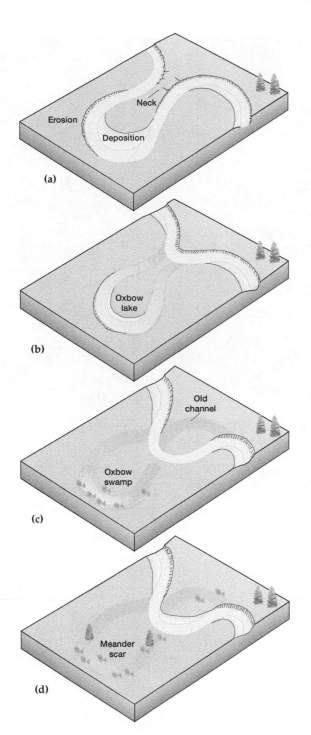

Figure 3: The formation of cutoff meanders on a floodplain. As the river cuts across the narrow neck of a meander, the cutoff river bend becomes an oxbow lake, which over time becomes an oxbow swamp, which in turn becomes a meander scar. (From McKnight and Hess, *Physical Geography,* 9th ed.)

MEANDERING RIVERS AS POLITICAL BOUNDARIES

Since meandering rivers often form political boundaries between states or counties, there is a need to fix these boundaries to avoid conflicts when the river shifts its course. For example, by the early 1900s, political boundaries had been permanently established along the Mississippi River. These boundaries remain fixed even if the river changes course. Today, boundaries often follow an old abandoned river channel rather than the present channel.

Figure 4: Stereogram of the Souris River near Voltaire, North Dakota (scale 1:40,000; USGS photographs, 1997; ↑N).

Name _____   Section _____

PROBLEMS—PART I

The following questions are based on Map T-4, a portion of the "Voltaire, North Dakota," quadrangle (scale 1:24,000; contour interval 5 feet) and Figure 4, a stereogram of the same region showing the Souris River (48°06'23"N, 100°48'05"W).

1.   (a)   In which direction is the Souris River flowing? From _____ to _____.

    (b)   How can you tell?

2.   (a)   What is the approximate width of the Souris River channel?   _____ feet

    (b)   What is the approximate width of the Souris River floodplain?   _____ feet

    (c)   What evidence suggests that the river is widening its valley through lateral erosion?

3.   Compare the present length of the meandering Souris River course shown on the map with the length of a river flowing down this valley if it were *not* meandering. (You can measure the distance with a piece of string, or your instructor can show you a more precise method.)

    (a)   Length of present meandering course: _____ miles

    (b)   Length of a straight course down the valley: _____ miles

4.   Natural levees can be seen along the Souris River in the center portion of the map (north of Westgaard Cemetery). Approximately how high are the levees?

                                                 _____ feet

Name _____   Section _____

PROBLEMS—PART II

The following questions are based on Map T-4, a portion of the "Voltaire, North Dakota," quadrangle (scale 1:24,000; contour interval 5 feet) and Figure 4, a stereogram of the same region showing the Souris River (48°06'23"N, 100°48'05"W).

1. (a) Explain the formation of the narrow, triangle-shaped lake just to the east of Westgaard Cemetery (in the NE $\frac{1}{4}$ of Section 3). You may use a sketch to illustrate your answer.

    (b) Describe the location of two more lakes, swamps, or topographic depressions along the Souris River that formed in a similar way. (You may refer to Public Land Survey township quarter sections to simplify your location description.)

2. (a) Describe a location where the formation of a new cutoff meander in the Souris River appears imminent.

    (b) Sketch the current river course:

    (c) Sketch the new river course after the cutoff:

Name _____   Section _____

PROBLEMS—PART III

The following questions are based on Map T-5, a portion of the "Jackson, Mississippi-Louisiana," topographic map (scale 1:250,000; contour interval 50 feet; dashed lines are supplementary contours at 25-foot intervals). This map shows the Mississippi River near the town of Vicksburg, Mississippi (32°49'56"N, 91°11'07"W). The eastern bluffs of the Mississippi River floodplain can be seen in the southeast corner of the map. The dashed black line along the Mississippi River shows the state boundary between Mississippi and Louisiana. Notice that the "boundary course" of the Mississippi River is quite different from the present course of the river. Some of the changes were natural, others were artificial. There is an extensive set of artificial levees along the course of the river (shown with closely spaced brown tick marks).

1. (a) Find "Willow Cut-off" and "Albemarle Lake" (an oxbow lake) in the center of the map. What natural features shown on the map suggest that a channel of the river once followed a course *between* the boundary course and the present course?

    (b) Name two other oxbow lakes shown on the map (either natural or artificially produced):

2. Compare the length (in miles) of the "boundary course" of the river with the main channel of the present course. (You can measure the distance with a piece of string, or your instructor may show you a more precise method.)

    (a) Length of present course: _____ miles

    (b) Length of "boundary course":   _____ miles

    (c) Amount of shortening: _____ miles

    (d) The present course length represents what percentage
         of the boundary course length? ("present" ÷ "boundary" × 100) _____ %

3. In general, how is the gradient of the present course
    different from the gradient of the boundary course?
    (In other words, is the present course steeper or less
    steep than the boundary course?)   _____

4. Compared to the "boundary course," why would the present course of the Mississippi River be an advantage to river traffic such as barges?

Name _____   Section _____

PROBLEMS—PART IV

The following questions are based on Map T-5, a portion of the "Jackson, Mississippi-Louisiana," topographic map (scale 1:250,000; contour interval 50 feet; dashed lines are supplementary contours at 25-foot intervals). For reference, the dashed contour line on "Paw Paw Island" in the southern part of the map shows an elevation of 75 feet.

1.   (a)   To the west of Hollybrook (south of Lake Providence along Highway 65), find the streams named "Otter Bayou" and "Swan Lake." What kind of floodplain landform explains the curved paths taken by these streams? (Hint: The landform is too low to be shown with this map's contour interval.)

      (b)   Which human-built feature nearby appears to have been influenced by the same kind of landform? _____

2.   (a)   Estimate the elevation of the town of Alsatia (west of the Mississippi River along Highway 65):   _____ feet

      (b)   What is the approximate elevation of the Mississippi River near Alsatia?   _____ feet

      (c)   Other than the levees, does there appear to be any land more than 25 feet higher than the river between Alsatia and the Mississippi River? (The dashed brown lines are 25-foot contours.)   _____

3.   The Yazoo River (from which the geographic term "yazoo stream" was taken) flows into the Mississippi River just south of this portion of the map. Name another yazoo stream (or "creek," "bayou," etc.) shown on the map that parallels the Mississippi for at least 10 miles:

PROBLEMS—PART IV—GOOGLE EARTH™

To answer the following questions, go to the Hess *Physical Geography Laboratory Manual* for *McKnight's Physical Geography,* 10th edition, Web site at **http://www.mygeoscienceplace.com**, then Exercise 37. Select "Exercise 37 Google Earth" to open a KMZ file in Google Earth™. The area shown is along the Mississippi River near Vicksburg, Mississippi (also shown in Map T-5).

1.   Fly to Point 1 and then to Point 2. What explains the curved striations in the fields here?

2.   Fly to Point 3. Explain the likely origin of this curved patch of vegetation on the floodplain floor:

APPENDIX
WEATHER MAP SYMBOLS

The charts and diagrams on the following pages show the symbols and codes used on standard weather maps.

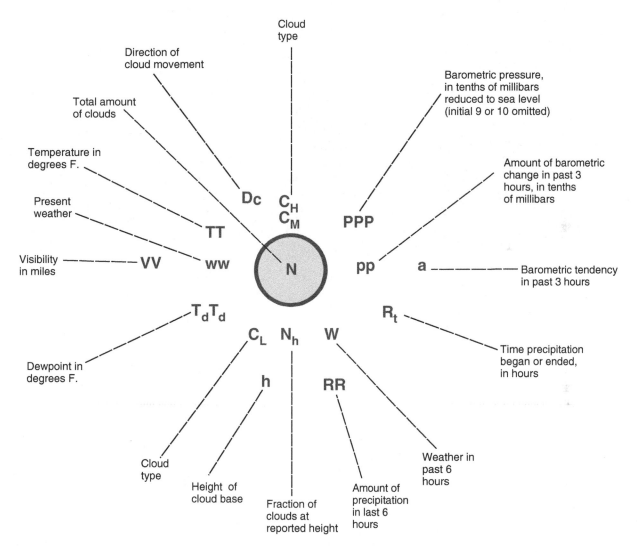

Figure 1: Standard weather station model showing placement of codes. (From McKnight and Hess, *Physical Geography*, 9th ed.)

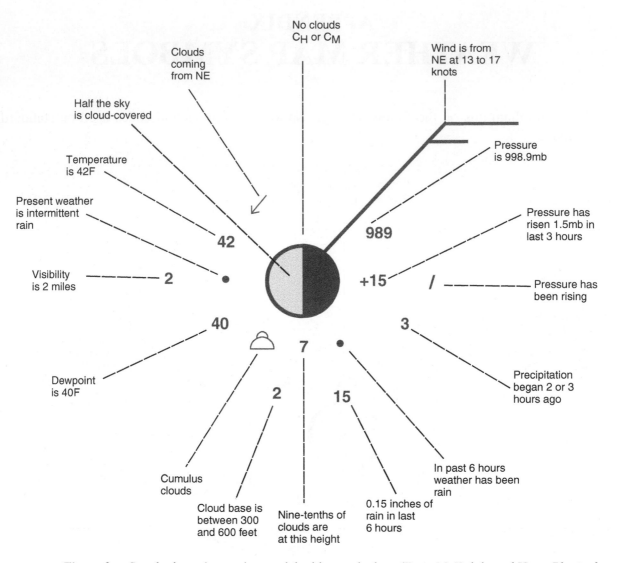

No clouds
C_H or C_M

Clouds
coming
from NE

Wind is from
NE at 13 to 17
knots

Half the sky
is cloud-covered

Pressure
is 998.9mb

Temperature
is 42F

Present weather
is intermittent
rain

Pressure has
risen 1.5mb in
last 3 hours

42

989

Visibility
is 2 miles

2

+15

/

Pressure has
been rising

40

3

Dewpoint
is 40F

7

15

Precipitation
began 2 or 3
hours ago

Cumulus
clouds

2

Cloud base is
between 300
and 600 feet

Nine-tenths of
clouds are
at this height

0.15 inches of
rain in last
6 hours

In past 6 hours
weather has been
rain

Figure 2: Standard weather station model with sample data. (From McKnight and Hess, *Physical Geography*, 9th ed.)

W W
Present weather

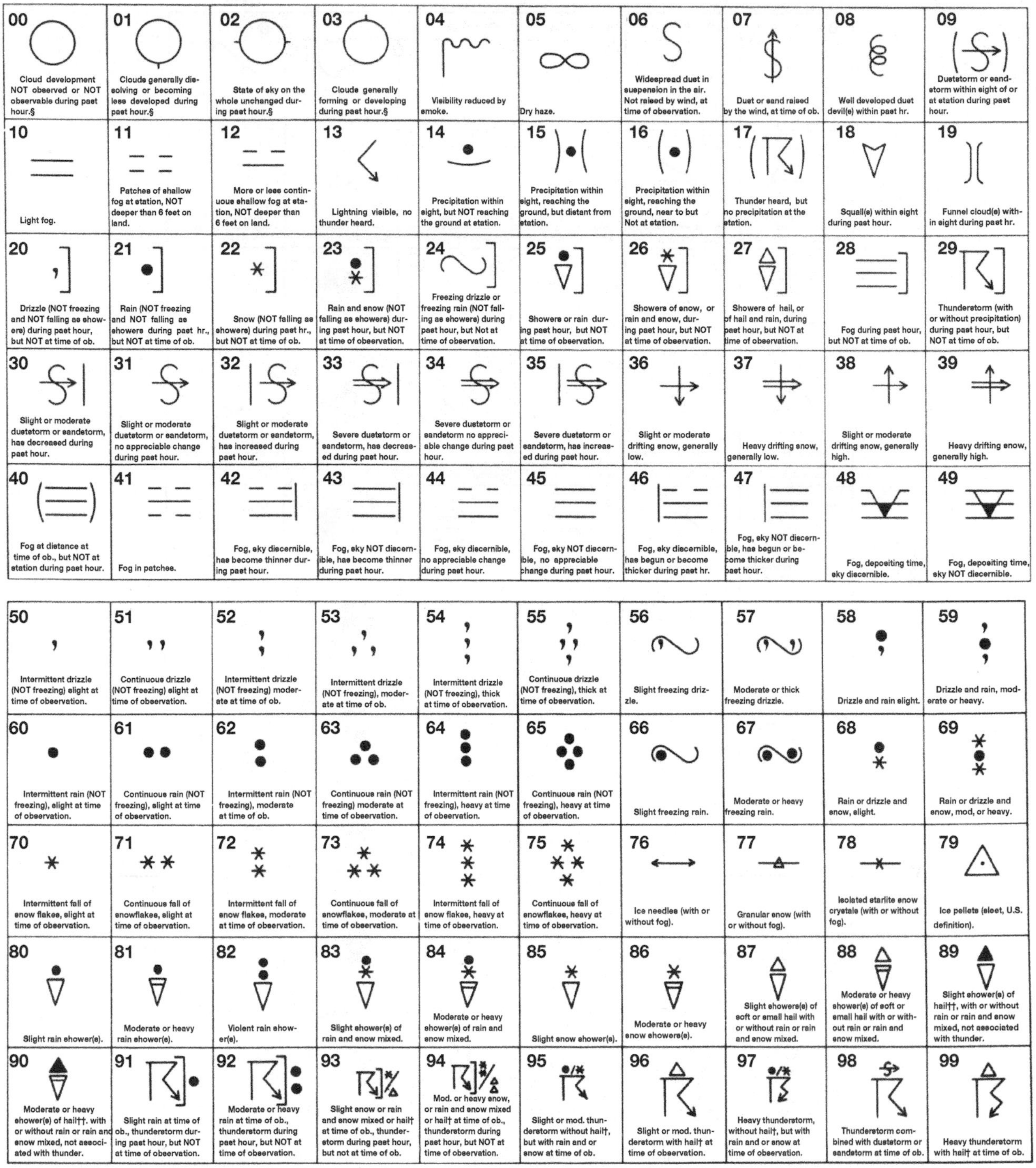

Figure 3: Standard weather station model symbols used to indicate "Present Weather" (ww). (From McKnight and Hess, *Physical Geography*, 9th ed.)

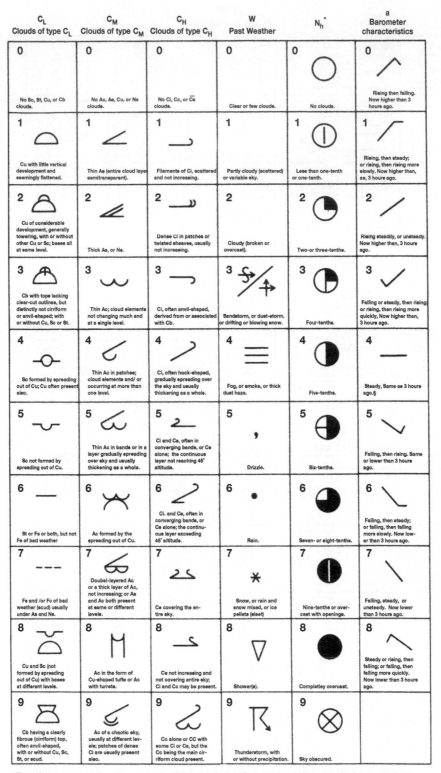

*Fraction representing how much of the total cloud cover is at the reported base height.

Figure 4: Standard weather station model symbols for "Low Clouds" (C_L); "Middle Clouds" (C_M); "High Clouds" (C_H); "Past Weather" (W); "Total Cloud Cover" (N_h); "Barometric Tendency" (a). (From McKnight and Hess, *Physical Geography*, 9th ed.)

h (height of cloud base)	Approximate Cloud Height	
	Feet	Meters
0	0 – 149	0 – 49
1	150 – 299	50 – 99
2	300 – 599	100 – 199
3	600 – 999	200 – 299
4	1000 – 1999	300 – 599
5	2000 – 3499	600 – 999
6	3500 – 4999	1000 – 1499
7	5000 – 4699	1500 – 1999
8	6500 – 7999	2000 – 2499
9	>8000 or no clouds	>2500 or no clouds

Figure 5: Standard weather station model codes for "Height of Cloud Base" (h). (From McKnight and Hess, *Physical Geography*, 9th ed.)

Symbol	Wind Speed (knots)
◎	Calm
	1–2
	3–7
	8–12
	13–17
	18–22
	23–27
	28–32
	33–37
	38–42
	43–47
	48–52
	53–57
	58–62
	63–67
	68–72
	73–77

Figure 7: Standard weather station model symbols for "Wind Speed." (From McKnight and Hess, *Physical Geography*, 9th ed.)

R_t Code	Time of Precipitation
0	No precipitation
1	Less than one hour ago
2	1 to 2 hours ago
3	2 to 3 hours ago
4	3 to 4 hours ago
5	4 to 5 hours ago
6	5 to 6 hours ago
7	6 to 12 hours ago
8	More than 12 hours ago
9	Unknown

Figure 6: Standard weather station model codes for "Time Precipitation Began or Ended" (R_t). (From McKnight and Hess, *Physical Geography*, 9th ed.)

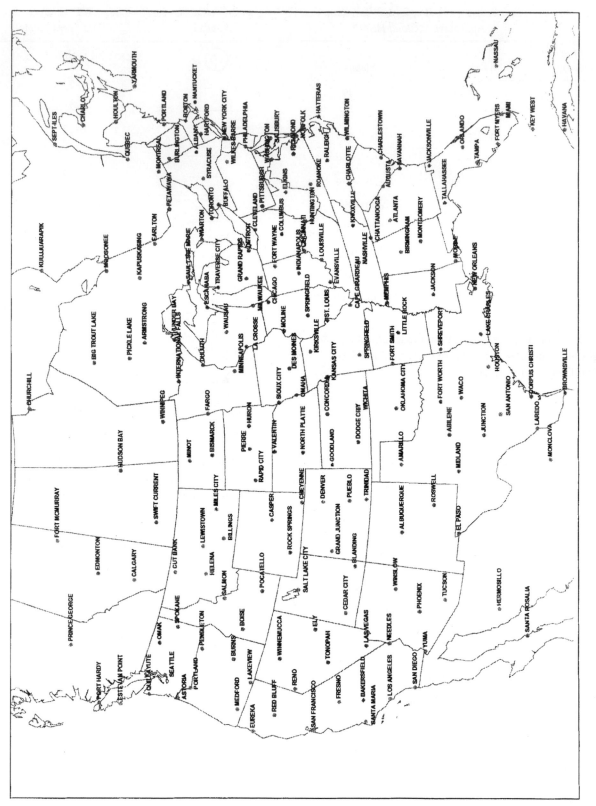

Figure 8: Daily Weather Map station names and locations. (National Weather Service)

TOPOGRAPHIC MAP SYMBOLS

Topographic Map Symbols

BATHYMETRIC FEATURES

Area exposed at mean low tide; sounding datum line***	
Channel***	
Sunken rock***	+

BOUNDARIES

National	
State or territorial	
County or equivalent	
Civil township or equivalent	
Incorporated city or equivalent	
Federally administered park, reservation, or monument (external)	
Federally administered park, reservation, or monument (internal)	
State forest, park, reservation, or monument and large county park	
Forest Service administrative area*	
Forest Service ranger district*	
National Forest System land status, Forest Service lands*	
National Forest System land status, non-Forest Service lands*	
Small park (county or city)	

BUILDINGS AND RELATED FEATURES

Building	
School; house of worship	
Athletic field	
Built-up area	
Forest headquarters*	
Ranger district office*	
Guard station or work center*	
Racetrack or raceway	
Airport, paved landing strip, runway, taxiway, or apron	
Unpaved landing strip	
Well (other than water), windmill or wind generator	
Tanks	
Covered reservoir	
Gaging station	
Located or landmark object (feature as labeled)	
Boat ramp or boat access*	
Roadside park or rest area	
Picnic area	
Campground	
Winter recreation area*	
Cemetery	Cem

COASTAL FEATURES

Foreshore flat	Mud
Coral or rock reef	Reef
Rock, bare or awash; dangerous to navigation	
Group of rocks, bare or awash	
Exposed wreck	
Depth curve; sounding	
Breakwater, pier, jetty, or wharf	
Seawall	
Oil or gas well; platform	

194

CONTOURS

Topographic

Index	6000
Approximate or indefinite	
Intermediate	
Approximate or indefinite	
Supplementary	
Depression	
Cut	
Fill	
Continental divide	

Bathymetric

Index***	
Intermediate***	
Index primary***	
Primary***	
Supplementary***	

CONTROL DATA AND MONUMENTS

Principal point**	3-20
U.S. mineral or location monument	USMM 438
River mileage marker	+ Mile 69

Boundary monument

Third-order or better elevation, with tablet	BM 9134 BM 277
Third-order or better elevation, recoverable mark, no tablet	5628
With number and elevation	67 4667

Horizontal control

Third-order or better, permanent mark	Neace Neace
With third-order or better elevation	BM 52 Pike BM393
With checked spot elevation	1012
Coincident with found section corner	Cactus Cactus
Unmonumented**	

Vertical control

Third-order or better elevation, with tablet	BM 5280
Third-order or better elevation, recoverable mark, no tablet	528
Bench mark coincident with found section corner	BM 5280
Spot elevation	7523

GLACIERS AND PERMANENT SNOWFIELDS

Contours and limits	
Formlines	
Glacial advance	
Glacial retreat	

LAND SURVEYS

Public land survey system

Range or Township line	
Location approximate	
Location doubtful	
Protracted	
Protracted (AK 1:63,360-scale)	
Range or Township labels	R1E T2N R3W T4S
Section line	
Location approximate	
Location doubtful	
Protracted	
Protracted (AK 1:63,360-scale)	
Section numbers	1 - 36 1 - 36
Found section corner	
Found closing corner	
Witness corner	WC
Meander corner	MC
Weak corner*	

Other land surveys

Range or Township line	
Section line	
Land grant, mining claim, donation land claim, or tract	
Land grant, homestead, mineral, or other special survey monument	
Fence or field lines	

MARINE SHORELINES

Shoreline	
Apparent (edge of vegetation)***	
Indefinite or unsurveyed	

MINES AND CAVES

Quarry or open pit mine	
Gravel, sand, clay, or borrow pit	
Mine tunnel or cave entrance	
Mine shaft	
Prospect	x
Tailings	Tailings
Mine dump	
Former disposal site or mine	

PROJECTION AND GRIDS

Neatline	39°15' 90°37'30''
Graticule tick	55'
Graticule intersection	
Datum shift tick	

State plane coordinate systems

Primary zone tick	640 000 FEET
Secondary zone tick	247 500 METERS
Tertiary zone tick	260 000 FEET
Quaternary zone tick	98 500 METERS
Quintary zone tick	320 000 FEET

Universal transverse mercator grid

UTM grid (full grid)	273
UTM grid ticks*	269

RAILROADS AND RELATED FEATURES

Standard guage railroad, single track	
Standard guage railroad, multiple track	
Narrow guage railroad, single track	
Narrow guage railroad, multiple track	
Railroad siding	
Railroad in highway	
Railroad in road	
Railroad in light duty road*	
Railroad underpass; overpass	
Railroad bridge; drawbridge	
Railroad tunnel	
Railroad yard	
Railroad turntable; roundhouse	

RIVERS, LAKES, AND CANALS

Perennial stream	
Perennial river	
Intermittent stream	
Intermittent river	
Disappearing stream	
Falls, small	
Falls, large	
Rapids, small	
Rapids, large	
Masonry dam	
Dam with lock	
Dam carrying load	
Perennial lake/pond	
Intermittent lake/pond	
Dry lake/pond	
Narrow wash	
Wide wash	Wash
Canal, flume, or aqueduct with lock	
Elevated aqueduct, flume, or conduit	
Aqueduct tunnel	
Water well, geyser, fumarole, or mud pot	
Spring or seep	

ROADS AND RELATED FEATURES

Please note: Roads on Provisional-edition maps are not classified as primary, secondary, or light duty. These roads are all classified as improved roads and are symbolized the same as light duty roads.

Primary highway	
Secondary highway	
Light duty road	
Light duty road, paved*	
Light duty road, gravel*	
Light duty road, dirt*	
Light duty road, unspecified*	
Unimproved road	
Unimproved road*	
4WD road	
4WD road*	
Trail	
Highway or road with median strip	
Highway or road under construction	Under Const
Highway or road underpass; overpass	
Highway or road bridge; drawbridge	
Highway or road tunnel	
Road block, berm, or barrier*	
Gate on road*	
Trailhead*	

SUBMERGED AREAS AND BOGS

Marsh or swamp	
Submerged marsh or swamp	
Wooded marsh or swamp	
Submerged wooded marsh or swamp	
Land subject to inundation	Max Pool 431

SURFACE FEATURES

Levee	Levee
Sand or mud	Sand
Disturbed surface	
Gravel beach or glacial moraine	Gravel
Tailings pond	Tailings Pond

TRANSMISSION LINES AND PIPELINES

Power transmission line; pole; tower	
Telephone line	Telephone
Aboveground pipeline	
Underground pipeline	Pipeline

VEGETATION

Woodland	
Shrubland	
Orchard	
Vineyard	
Mangrove	Mangrove

USGS-USDA Forest Service Single-Edition Quadrangle maps only.

In August 1993, the U.S. Geological Survey and the U.S. Department of Agriculture's Forest Service signed an Interagency Agreement to begin a single-edition joint mapping program. This agreement established the coordination for producing and maintaining single-edition primary series topographic maps for quadrangles containing National Forest System lands. The joint mapping program eliminates duplication of effort by the agencies and results in a more frequent revision cycle for quadrangles containing National Forests. Maps are revised on the basis of jointly developed standards and contain normal features mapped by the USGS, as well as additional features required for efficient management of National Forest System lands. Single-edition maps look slightly different but meet the content, accuracy, and quality criteria of other USGS products.

Provisional-Edition maps only.

Provisional-edition maps were established to expedite completion of the remaining large-scale topographic quadrangles of the conterminous United States. They contain essentially the same level of information as the standard series maps. This series can be easily recognized by the title "Provisional Edition" in the lower right-hand corner.

* Topographic Bathymetric maps only.

Topographic Map Information

For more information about topographic maps produced by the USGS, please call:
1-888-ASK-USGS or visit us at http://ask.usgs.gov

U.S. PUBLIC LAND SURVEY SYSTEM: TOPOGRAPHIC MAP

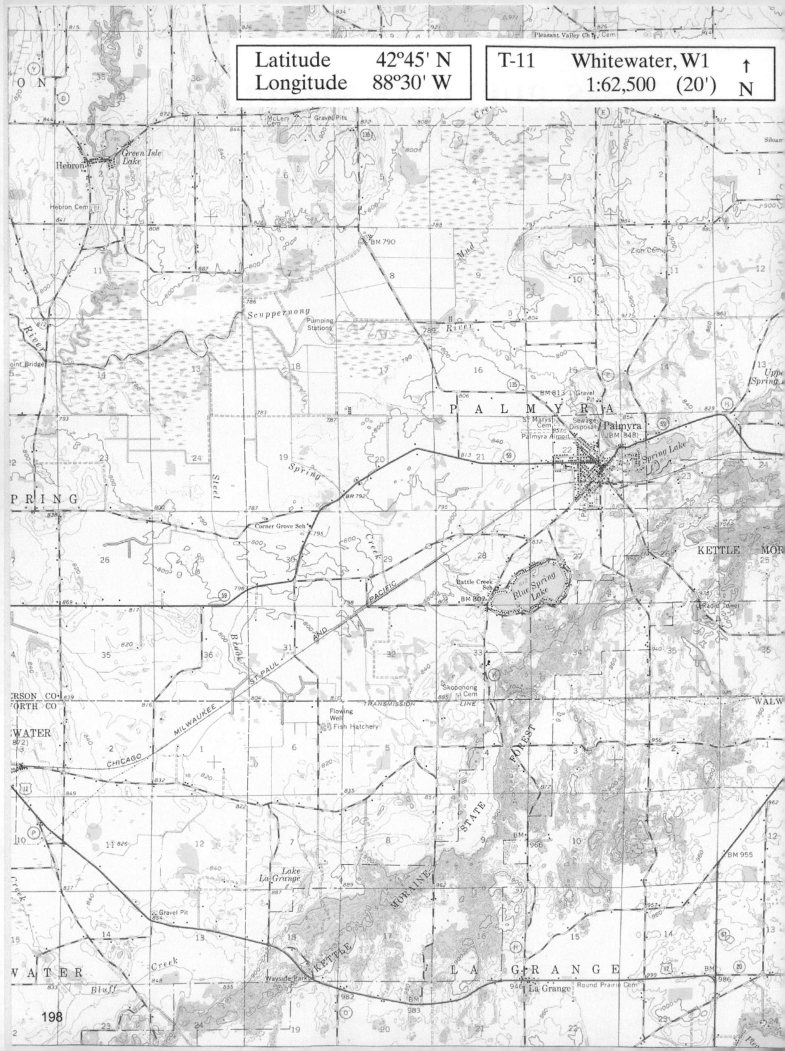

STEREO AERIAL PHOTOGRAPHS: TOPOGRAPHIC MAP

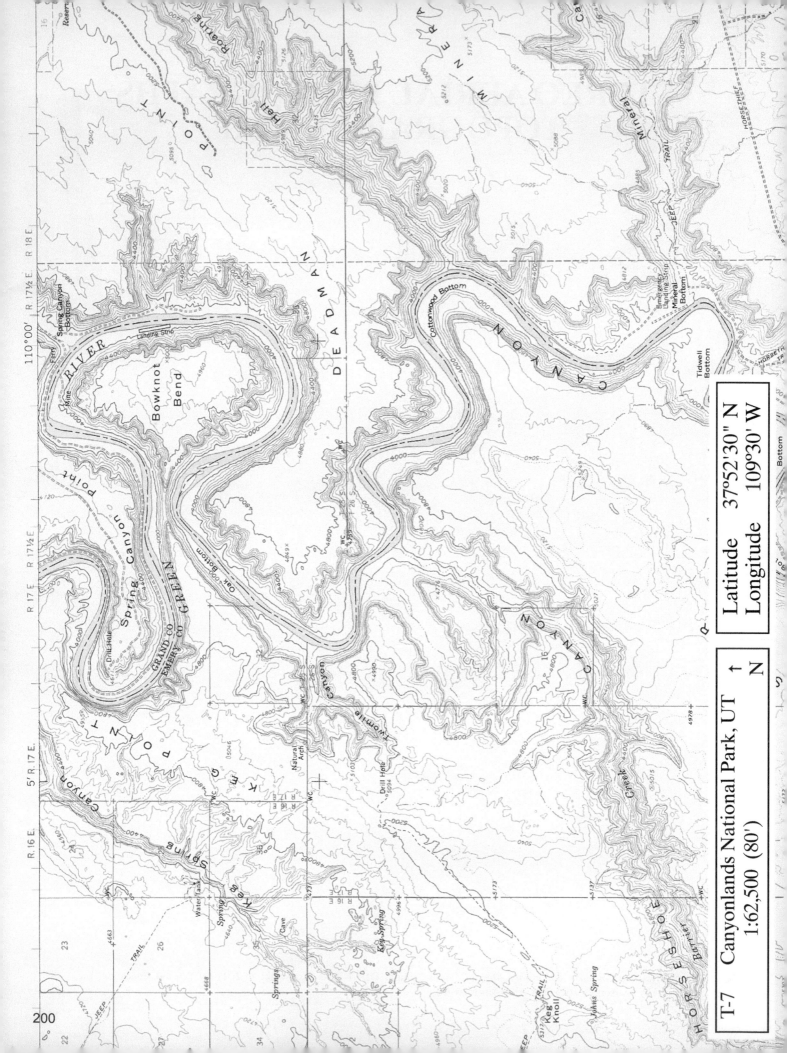

T-7   Canyonlands National Park, UT
1:62,500 (80')

| Latitude | 37°52'30" N |
| Longitude | 109°30' W |

N

200

VOLCANOES: TOPOGRAPHIC MAPS

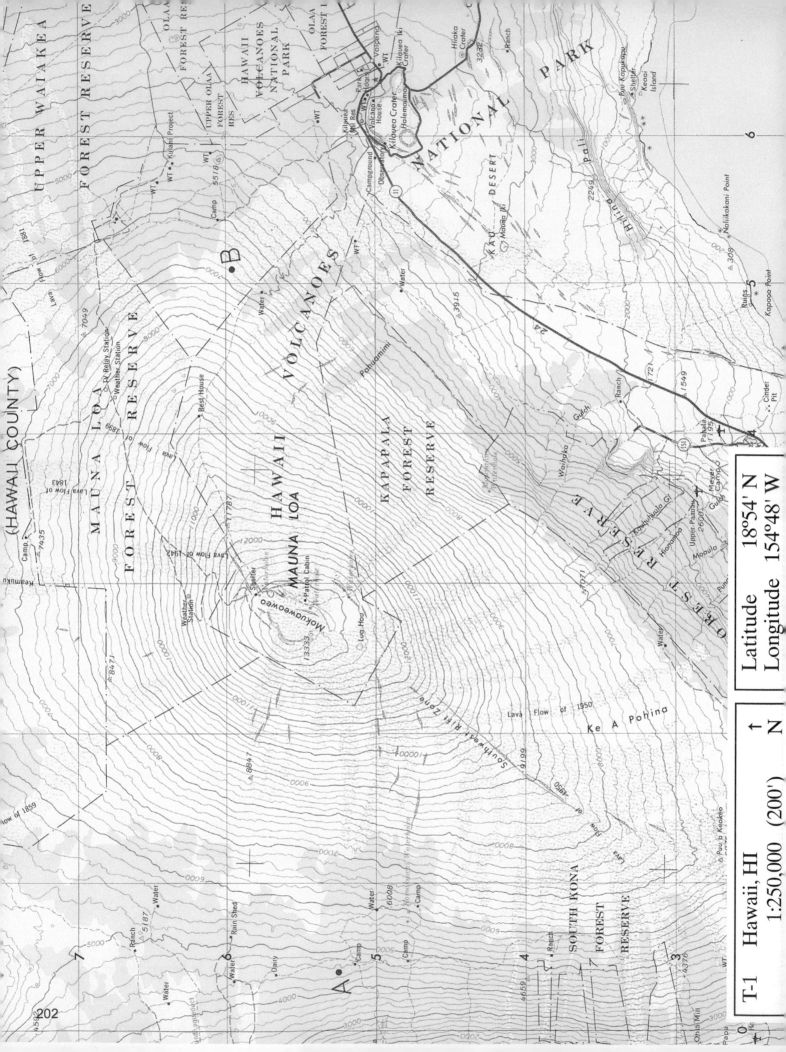

T-1   Hawaii, HI
1:250,000 (200')

Latitude   18°54' N
Longitude   154°48' W

N ↑

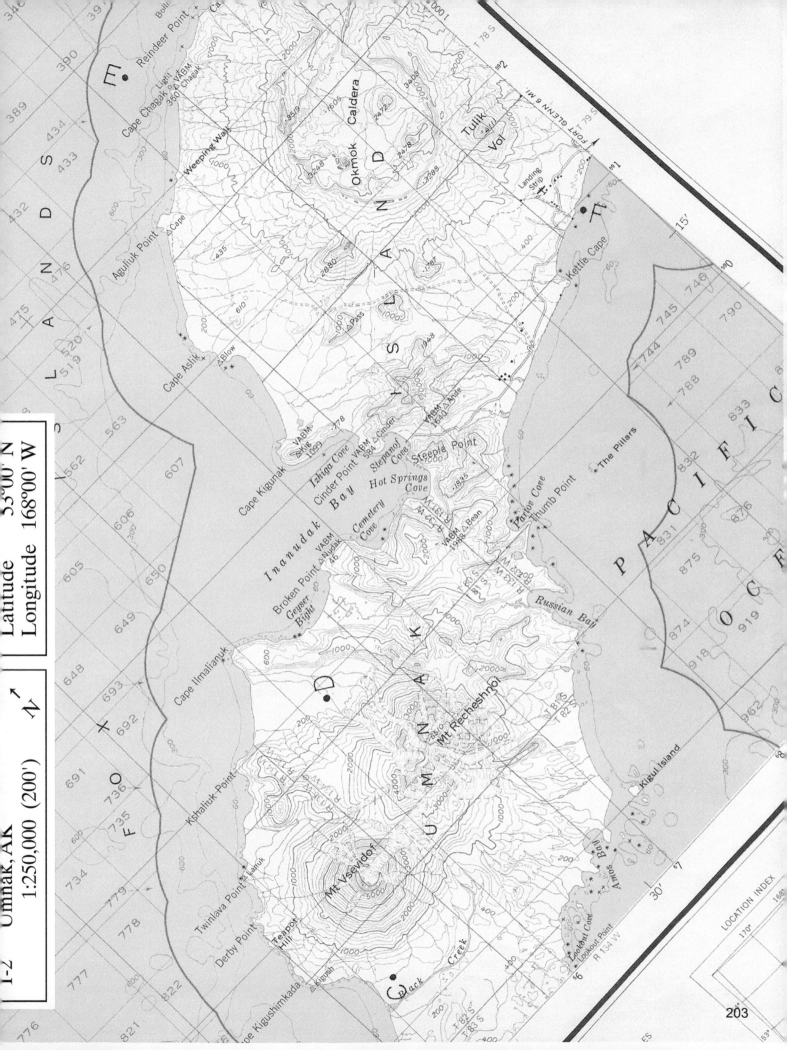

DRAINAGE BASINS:
TOPOGRAPHIC MAP

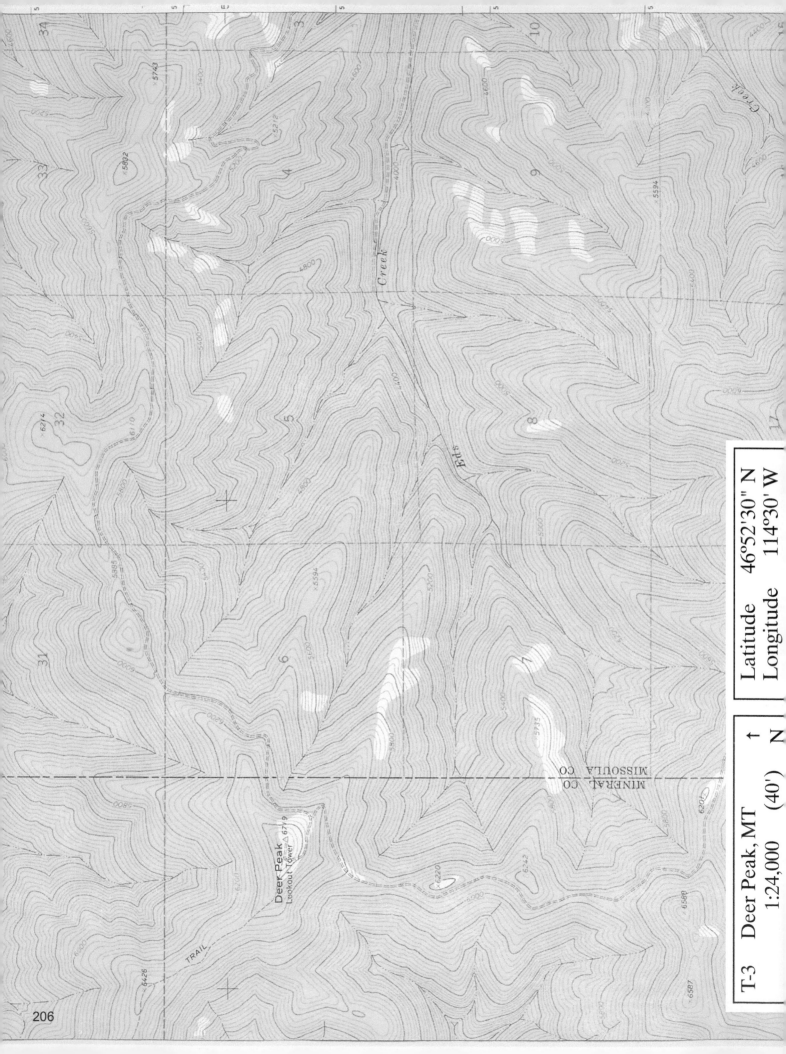

Latitude 46°52'30" N
Longitude 114°30' W

T-3 Deer Peak, MT
1:24,000 (40')

↑ N

FLOODPLAINS:
TOPOGRAPHIC MAPS

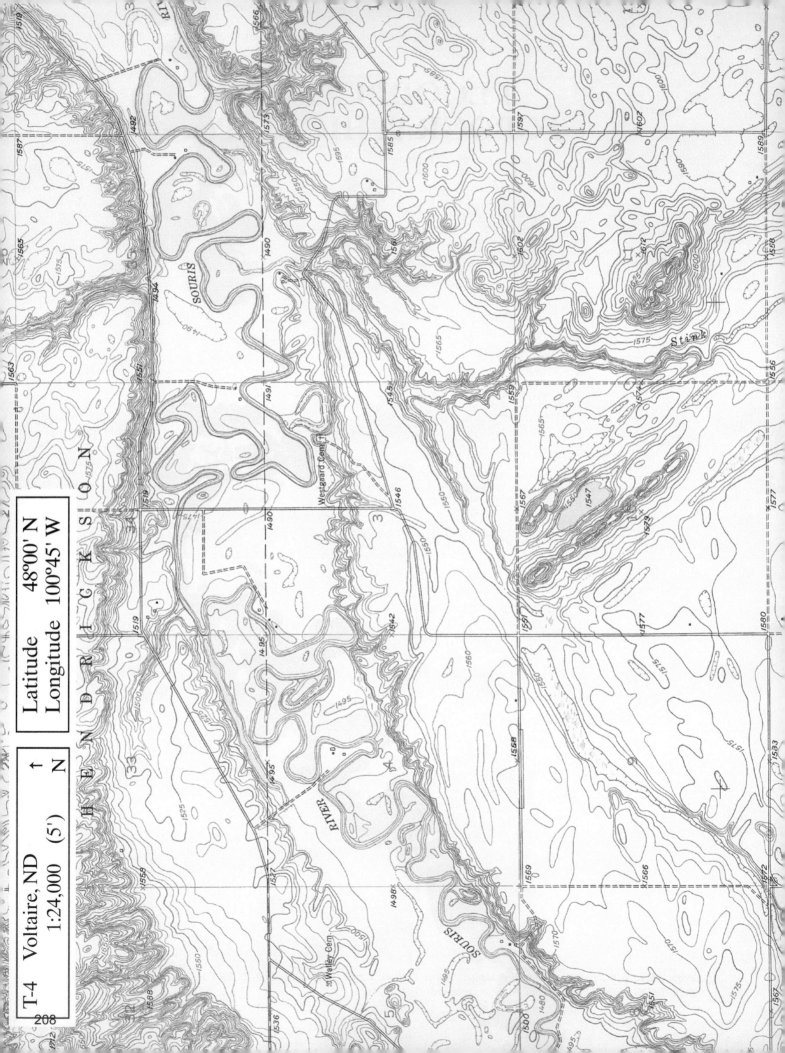

T-4 Voltaire, ND
1:24,000 (5')

Latitude 48°00' N
Longitude 100°45' W

N ↑
N

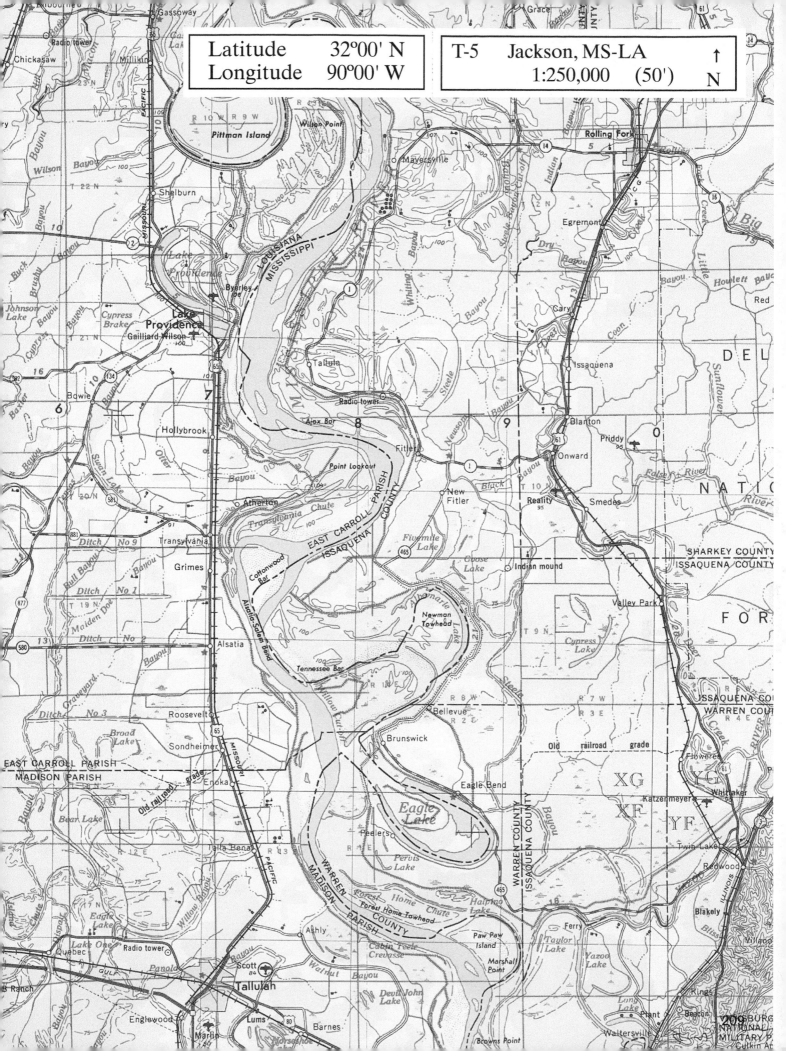

STREAM DRAINAGE PATTERNS: TOPOGRAPHIC MAPS

From *Physical Geography Laboratory Manual,* Tenth Edition, Darrel Hess. Copyright © 2011 by Pearson Education, Inc. Published by Pearson Prentice Hall. All rights reserved.

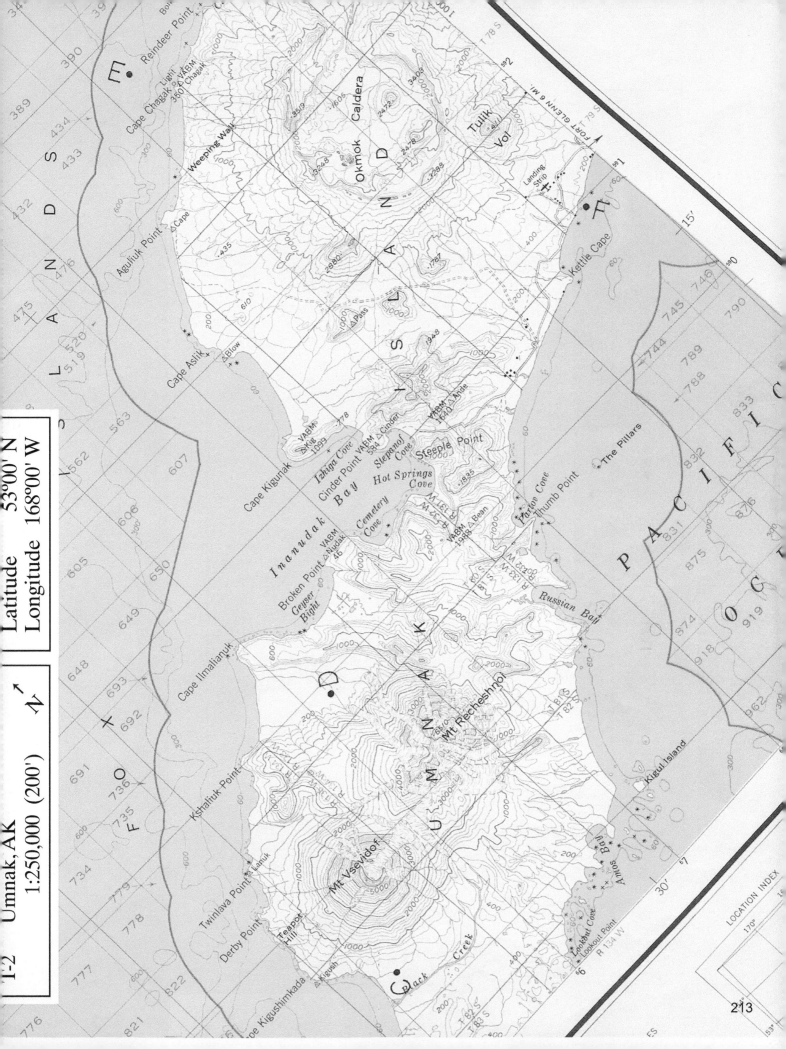

STREAM REJUVENATION: TOPOGRAPHIC MAPS

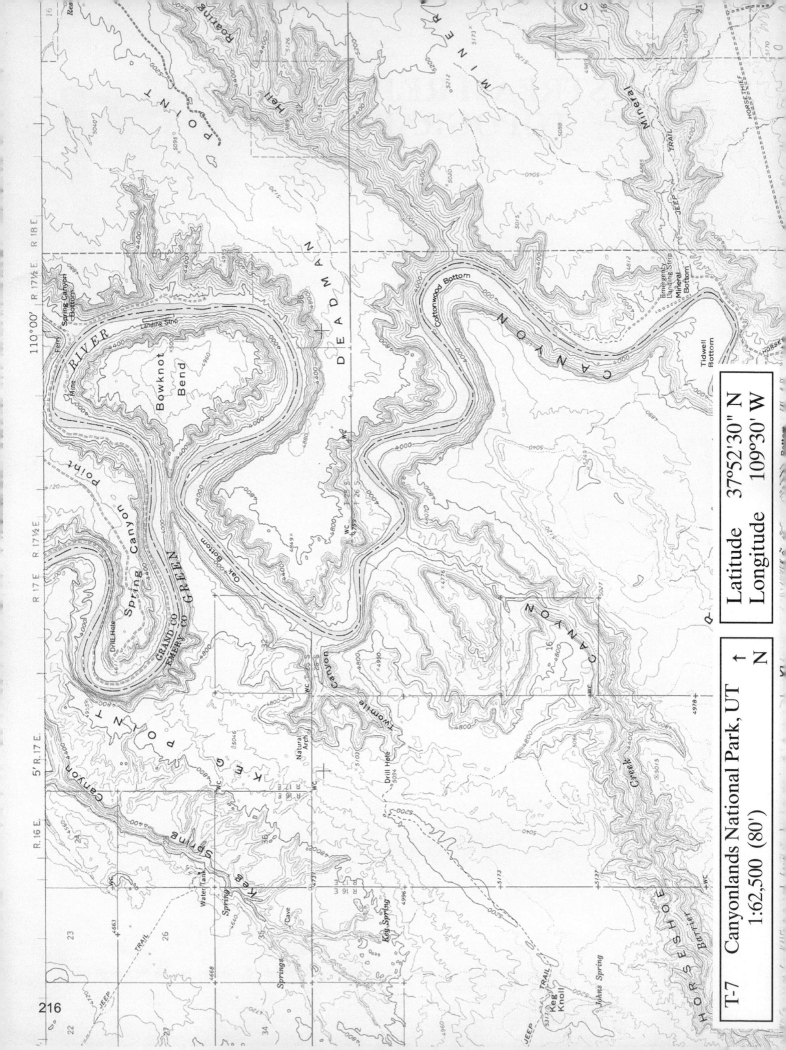

T-7 Canyonlands National Park, UT
1:62,500 (80')

Latitude 37°52'30" N
Longitude 109°30' W

N ↑

216

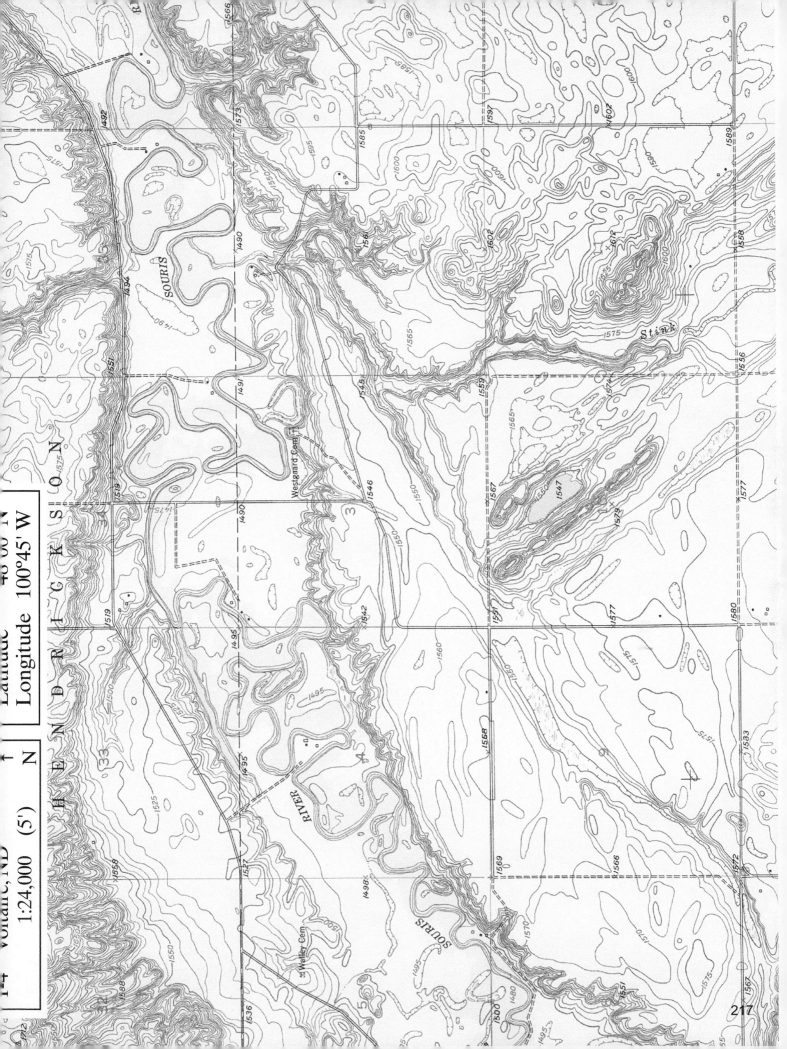

KARST TOPOGRAPHY: TOPOGRAPHIC MAPS

THE KNOBS

Cave

Campground

Opossum Hol

Campground

Golf
Course

Hundred Dome
Cave

Jessie James
Cave

Dome House
Cave

Gravel Slave Cave

Bald
Knob

Sewage Disposal
Pond

Oil
Well

Cem 575

Cem

Cem

577

578

585

31w

NASHVILLE

BM
615

65

AND

BM
603

LOUISVILLE

BM
585

Oil
Well

255

Gardner

Oil
Well

BM
618

Oil
Well

657

Oil Wells

BM
645

Oil
Well

BM637

Fairview
Ch

641

Oil Wells

Oil Wells

681

Mt V

EDMONSON CO
BARREN CO

BARREN CO
EDMONSON CO

MONSON CO

698

Oil
Well

T-9	Park City, KY	↑ N	Latitude	37°00' N
	1:24,000 (10')		Longitude	86°00' W

220

Apple Grove

1733

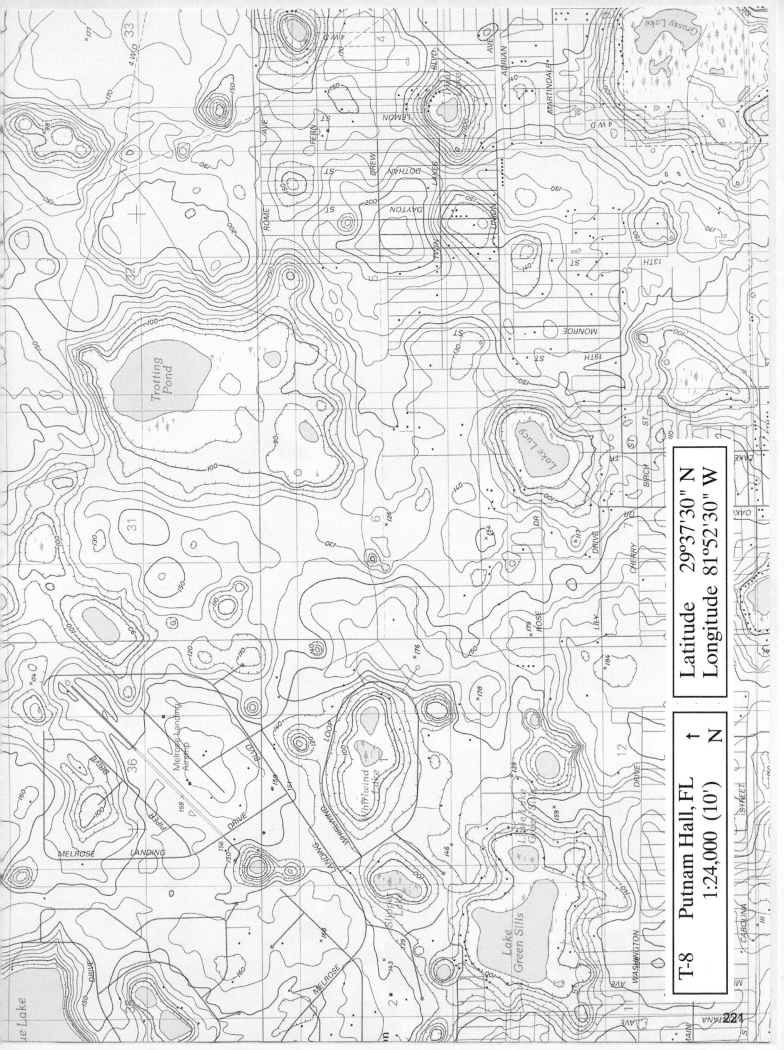

T-8	Putnam Hall, FL
	1:24,000 (10')

Latitude	29°37'30" N
Longitude	81°52'30" W

DESERT LANDFORMS: TOPOGRAPHIC MAP

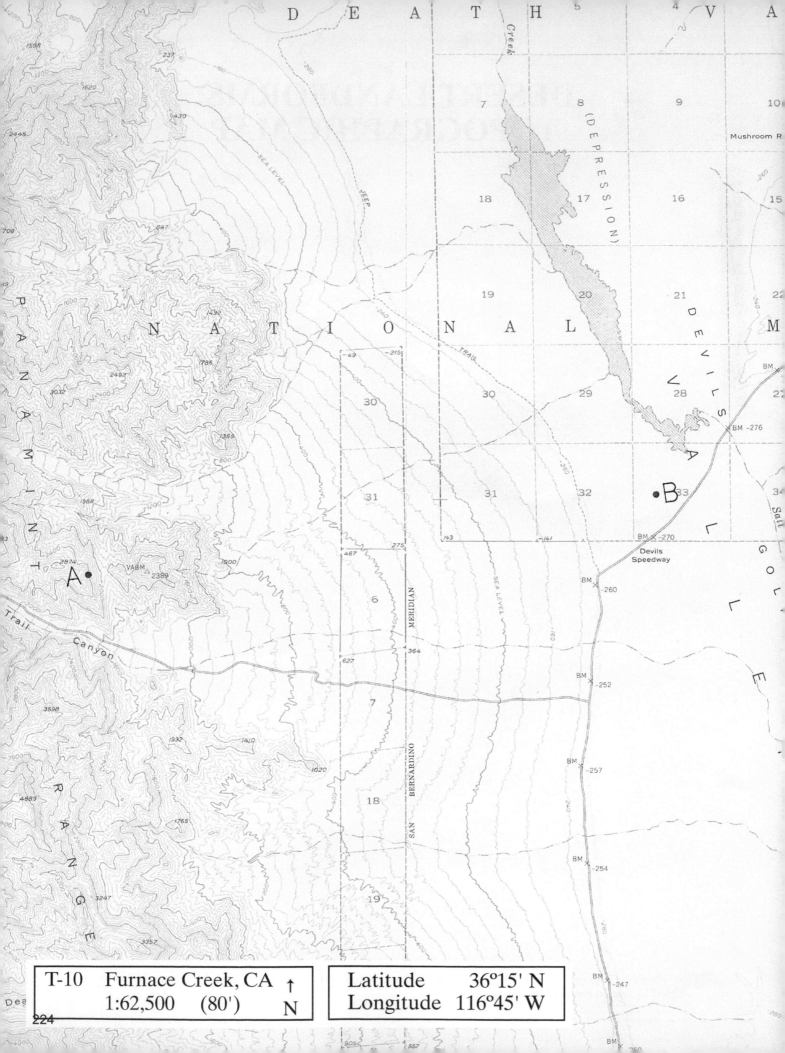

CONTINENTAL GLACIATION: TOPOGRAPHIC MAPS

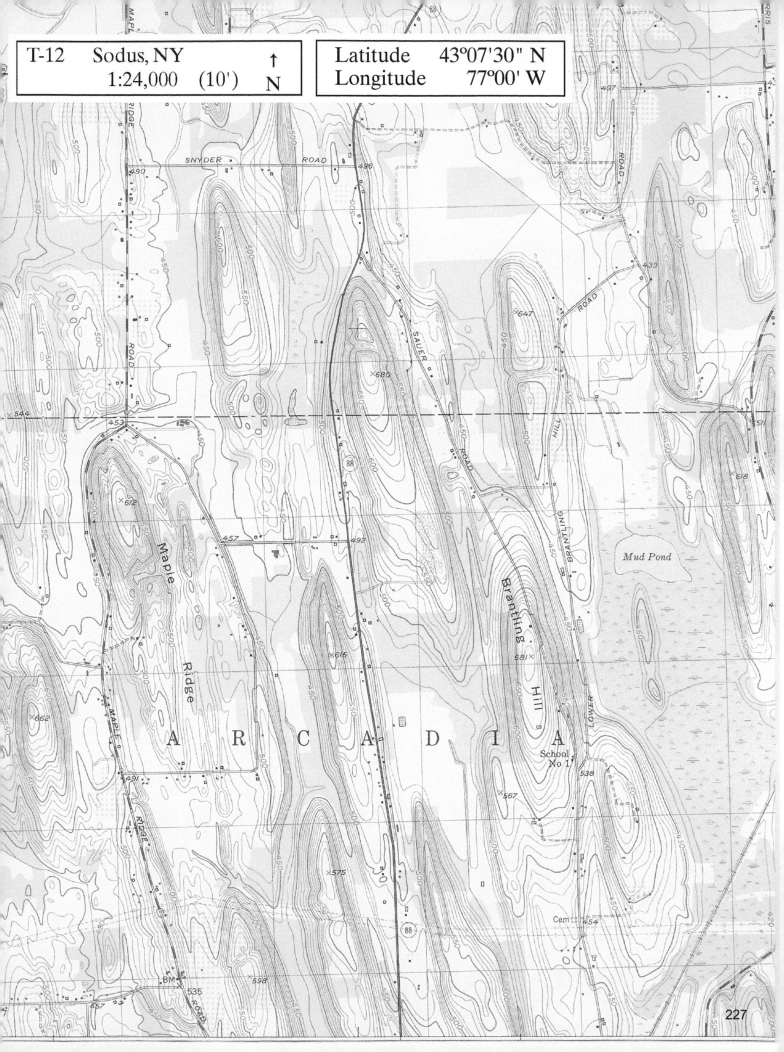

ALPINE GLACIATION: TOPOGRAPHIC MAPS

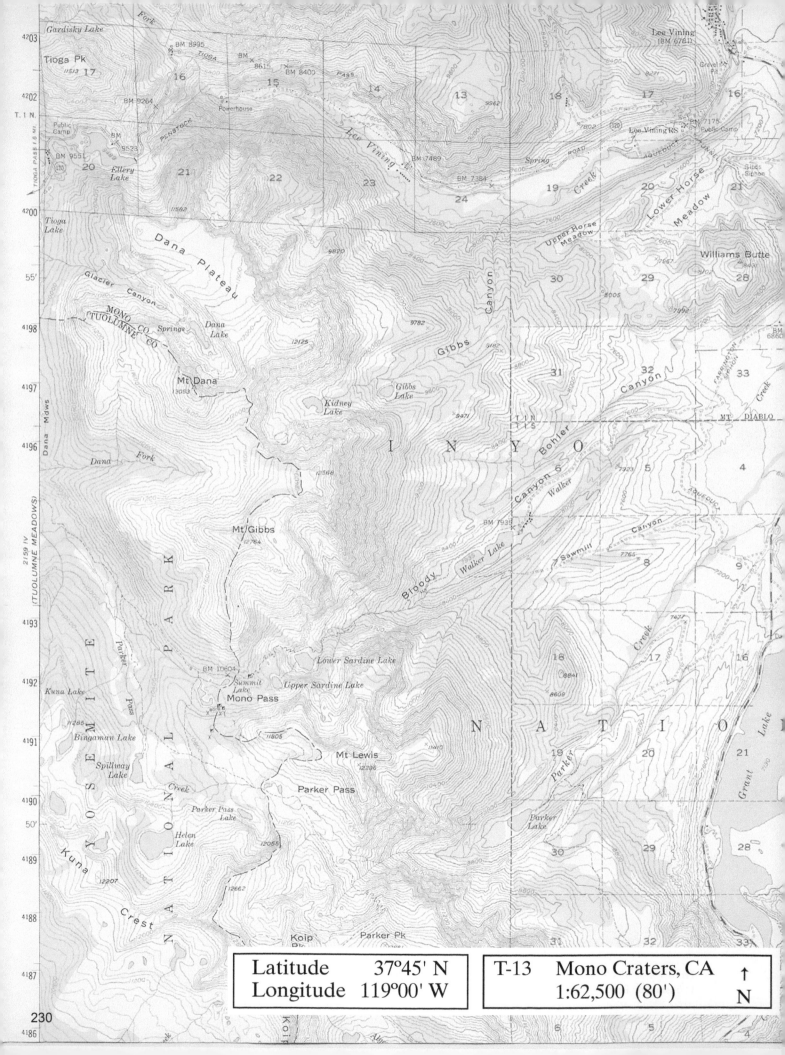

Latitude   37°45' N
Longitude 119°00' W

T-13   Mono Craters, CA
1:62,500 (80')

↑
N

NATIONAL FOREST

TRACY

ARM

TRACY ARM — FORDS TERROR

SOUTH SAW

WILDERNESS

COASTAL LANDFORMS: TOPOGRAPHIC MAPS

From *Physical Geography Laboratory Manual,* Tenth Edition, Darrel Hess. Copyright © 2011 by Pearson Education, Inc.
Published by Pearson Prentice Hall.

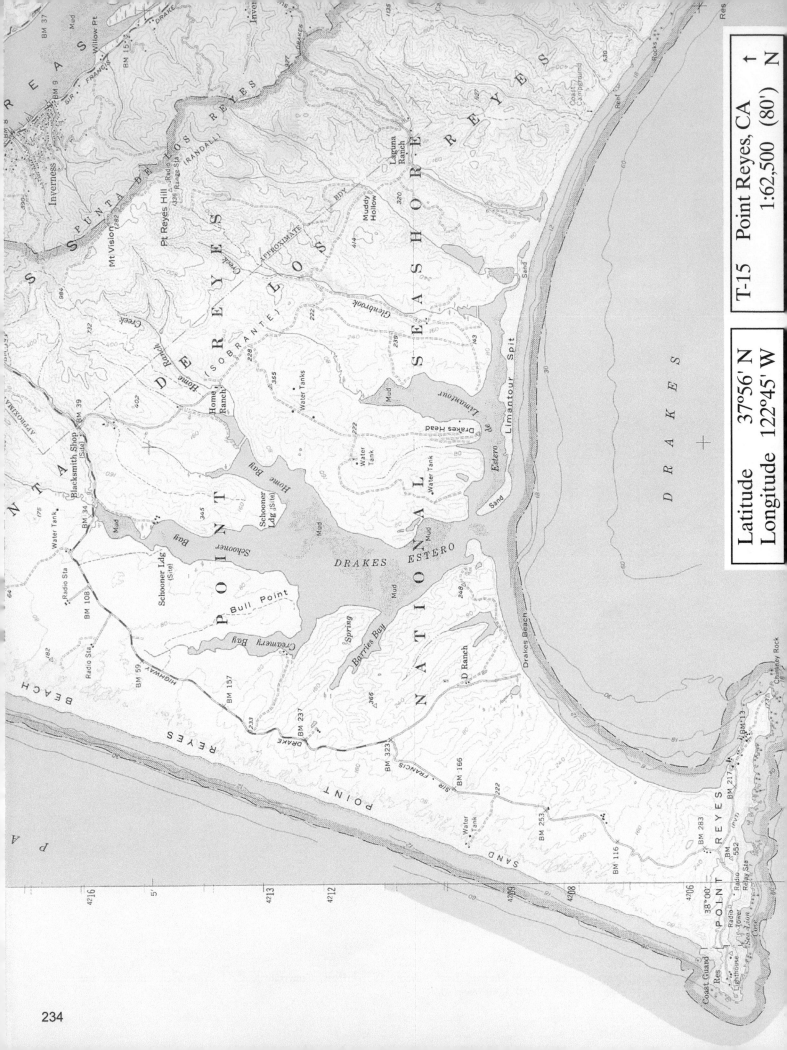

NUECES COUNTY
KLEBERG COUNTY

KINGSVILLE ROAD

Laureles Ranch

Chiltipin Creek

Tunas Creek

Ford

Windmill　42

KING RANCH　34

Windmill

Madero Lake

Jaboncillos Ranch

Alazan Mott

Comitas Lake

Sand Mud

Drum Point

Sand Mud

Windmill

CAYO DEL GRULLO

Oil

ALAZAN BAY

Sandy Hook

Oil

Riviera Oil Field

Riviera Beach

Kleberg Point

Starvation Point

LAGUNA SALADO

Pie de Gallo

Negrohead Point

KLEBERG COUNTY
KENEDY COUNTY

BAFFIN BAY

Black Bluff

Gas

Water

Windmill

Oil

ALTO DE LA CRUZ

Water
27

Shifting sand dunes

Shifting sand dunes

Shifting sand dunes

Shifting sand dunes

LAGUNA VISTA
Pita Island

ENCINAL PENINSULA

NUECES CO
KLEBERG CO

Fourmile Hill

Bird Island Oil Field

Channel

Sand Mud

North Bird Island

South Bird Island

BIG HILL

Windmill

Windmill

Parra Lake

Windmill

Windmill

PADRE ISLAND

LITTLE DAGGER HILL

GREEN HILL
Shifting sand dunes
DAGGER HILL

Compuerta

Point of Rocks

Alazan Bay Naval Range Station

Sand Mud

BIG BALL HILL

Boggy Slough

Griffins Point

Sand Mud

Penascal Rincon

INTRACOASTAL WATERWAY

Rocky Slough

Channel

Yarborough Pass

Gaging station

MIDDLE GROUND

mud

Potrero de las Caballos

Cuba I

LAGUNA MADRE

Potrero Grande

Sand Mud

Potrero Cortado

sand

mud sand

sand

sand

sand

sand

mud

mud sand

sand

sand

mud

Potrero de las Canelas

Potrero Farias

Potrero Lopeno

sand

Sand Mud

mud

235

Index

Page references followed by "f" indicate illustrated figures or photographs; followed by "t" indicates a table.